EXPLANATION POINTS

EXPLANATION POINTS

Publishing in Rhetoric and Composition

EDITED BY
**JOHN R. GALLAGHER AND
DÀNIELLE NICOLE DEVOSS**

UTAH STATE UNIVERSITY PRESS
Logan

© 2019 by University Press of Colorado

Published by Utah State University Press
An imprint of University Press of Colorado
245 Century Circle, Suite 202
Louisville, Colorado 80027

 The University Press of Colorado is a proud member of
the Association of University Presses.

The University Press of Colorado is a cooperative publishing enterprise supported, in part, by Adams State University, Colorado State University, Fort Lewis College, Metropolitan State University of Denver, University of Colorado, University of Northern Colorado, Univeristy of Wyoming, Utah State University, and Western Colorado University.

∞ This paper meets the requirements of the ANSI/NISO Z39.48–1992 (Permanence of Paper).

ISBN: 978-1-60732-882-7 (paperback)
ISBN: 978-1-60732-883-4 (ebook)
DOI: https://doi.org/10.7330/9781607328834

Library of Congress Cataloging-in-Publication Data

Names: Gallagher, John R., 1983– editor. | DeVoss, Dànielle Nicole, editor.
Title: Explanation points : publishing in rhetoric and composition / edited by John R. Gallagher, Danielle DeVoss.
Description: Logan : Utah State University Press, 2019. | Includes bibliographical references and index.
Identifiers: LCCN 2019019171 | ISBN 9781607328827 (paperback) | ISBN 9781607328834 (ebook)
Subjects: LCSH: Authorship. | Academic writing. | Scholarly publishing.
Classification: LCC PN146 .E97 2019 | DDC 808.02—dc23
LC record available at https://lccn.loc.gov/2019019171

Cover illustration © tsinik/Shutterstock.com

*We dedicate this book to John's father, John Edward Gallagher.
He wanted to publish a book about career advice, something that
instigated our conversations about publication advice in composition
and rhetoric. He is a good father.*

CONTENTS

SECTION 4: GETTING (MORE AND DIFFERENT TYPES
OF) FEEDBACK: NAVIGATING REVIEWERS AND
UNDERSTANDING EDITORIAL RESPONSES

EXPLANATION POINTS

INTRODUCTION

John R. Gallagher and Dànielle Nicole DeVoss

An Origin Tale. The story of this collection is a serendipitous one: the two of us found ourselves hanging out after a session at the 2016 Rhetoric Society of America (RSA) conference in Atlanta. Dànielle overheard John thanking Laurie Gries for helpful editorial feedback on a piece he submitted to *Enculturation*. Laurie had advised John to think about where readers could get bored—her advice was "I'm afraid readers will skim the ending. Can you guard against that?" John, thanking her, exclaimed, "It was great advice delivered at the perfect moment!" John wished aloud that there were a book of editorial advice in rhet/comp, one with short chapters containing the best advice from scholars, editors, and researchers. Dànielle, overhearing his comment, said, "That would be a great book collection! We're going to write that book!" John and Dànielle chatted for a few minutes, fantasizing about what such a book might be and do.

Later that day, Dànielle mentioned the idea to another conference attendee, who eagerly offered her business card, saying, "I want to write for that book, and I want to *read* that book!" (See Sarah Kornfield's chapter in this collection.)

We went our separate ways at the conference, only to cross-email each other a few hours later (literally at the same time), and then to meet in the lobby of the hotel for an impromptu late-night work session to crank out what became the call for chapters for the collection.

Impetus. One of our core goals for this book—an impetus that emerged that day at RSA and that has served to anchor this project—is to collect, curate, and archive some of the best advice on writing and publishing that our field has to offer. This is the advice that we pass along to our students and to each other; it's the advice that we find ourselves giving time and again as we mentor graduate students; it's the go-to advice that we remind ourselves of as we're seeking inspiration on a new project, or as we work to wrap up a particularly challenging writing task. It's the advice we overhear a colleague sharing with another that we scoop up

DOI: 10.7330/9781607328834.c000

and pass along ourselves. It's the advice we see in abbreviated version shared online in tweets and bursts and updates—forgotten, otherwise, due to the speed of social media. It's the best of the best.

This advice is, at its heart, representative of an exceptionally generous field—of a group of scholars who, rather than compete with one another, lift each other up and recognize the enormity of the tasks we tackle as we research and write and publish in rhetoric and writing studies: for the field, to the field, and, at times, beyond the field. We would argue that rhet/comp is a uniquely democratic field, especially in the current political climate. Much of our work is oriented toward change we can make—whether those changes be small, potent gestures that occur in the classroom, or large, loud movements that ripple outward from within our national organizations. We are also, generally, a field of individuals and collaborators who work together to *move* the field forward (rather than compete with one another in ways that can stifle the evolution of our disciplinary thoughts and practices). We hope that this book serves as part and parcel of what we do and who we are as a field—that this book curates, constellates, and presents this generosity and the ways in which we do good by each other, in ways always attentive to student learning, research processes, institutional complexities, and the other variables that shape our research, writing, and publishing lives.

This advice is also, at its heart, very reminiscent of all things writing. That is, it's complicated. It's recursive. Sometimes it's offered in a fairly linear way; other times it's constellated toward different orientations. We don't present "the writing process" here as a set or fixed thing; thus we don't present the advice collected here as any sort of linear or fixed trajectory.

Kairos. We're delighted that this book is being published a little more than twenty years after the publication of Gary Olsen and Todd Taylor's edited collection, *Publishing in Rhetoric and Composition*, itself an incredibly important resource for our field. Our hope with this collection is to extend, reorient, and update Olsen and Taylor's work: *Explanation Points* seeks to integrate the narrative and first-person experiences into the pragmatism of publishing advice in rhet/comp.

In many ways, the publication landscape has changed since 1997. Born-digital pieces and webtexts are now commonplace (although, admittedly, all humanists continue to wrestle with issues of access, the expanse of different digital tools, and the protection of file preservation and sustainability). The social media landscape has exploded, and serves well to connect us beyond annual conferences. Although publication venues continue to emerge across media, publishing houses continue to condense and shrink. The field itself is dramatically more diverse and we have included authors from a variety of backgrounds and career stages; *Explanation Points* includes multiple voices: graduate students, senior faculty, non-tenure-track faculty, tenure-track faculty, and mid-career faculty are all represented in this collection. We have included the advice of professors emeriti at research-intensive institutions, and the advice of faculty at community colleges and other teaching-intensive institutions. The field is also now *fields*, with a variety of foci: digital rhetoric, social media analysis, circulation studies, as well as necessary developments in archiving and curation theory, computational rhetorics, and more, and these perspectives emerge not as the focus for chapters but as the larger landscape from which authors share their advice.

In many ways, however, our writerly landscape has not changed. Advice collected here encourages writers to read and to listen, and to identify the *kairotic* moment (and even *chronos*-based moments) at which to enter a scholarly conversation. Advice focuses on getting started, on brainstorming, and on managing projects. Advice relates to sharing drafts, collaborating, and rethinking or revising—all practices that transcend any one writing task or publication venue. Advice relates to navigating reviewer feedback and understanding publication production processes. Advice relates to the after words (literally), or transitioning from one major project to the next. All of the advice in this collection is as relevant and as applicable today as it would have been five, ten, twenty, or even fifty years ago.

Overview. We hope that this book reads like a conversation. We hope you find yourself in the pages, *hearing* the voices of these scholars as they share their advice with you. Although we've created a structure with which to hold and present the chapters, we believe that, together, this collection offers holistic advice—readers will have to take these pieces and fit them together. That's part of implementing good advice.

Section 1, "Getting Started," presents advice for inventing, brainstorming, and managing projects. This section presents suggestions for taking a good idea and getting it down on the page (or saved to the hard drive or the cloud), making time to conceptualize publication projects, and for storyboarding ideas or managing content. Readers will immediately notice that this section is longest, with multiple pieces echoing similar themes. This decision is rhetorical and intentional; we believe that getting started can take an inordinate amount of time and necessitates both persistence with an idea and a range of different strategies for moving forward. For this reason, we have included multiple approaches that tackle similar issues: creating community, trusting oneself, and content management are just three themes echoed across several voices from various institutions.

Section 2, "Getting Feedback," includes advice on how to best share drafts, collaborate, and (re)develop ideas. This section presents advice for making the most of workshopping opportunities, approaching others to collaborate, and seeing the forest *and* the trees. We often encourage collaborative work in writing classrooms, and more and more, our larger humanities units recognize that collaboration perhaps *is* the default orientation for producing work in a digital, networked world (a world that no longer orbits, perhaps, around the single-authored monograph). However, we rarely discuss *practices* of collaboration, which several authors address in this section. Chapters also address the strategic (re)deployment of ideas—how to nurture an idea to a conference presentation and beyond into a manuscript, and managing a publication pipeline.

Section 3, "Finding a Foothold," presents recommendations for identifying audiences and targeting publication venues. Finding a foothold includes reading and reviewing, writing to and for particular audiences, and considering different venues. As graduate students, we are trained to read journals and oriented toward those that carry the most disciplinary heft, but we perhaps aren't mentored as closely or carefully about how to orient to different venues *as* authors. Chapters in this section offer advice on finding fit, connecting with readers, navigating author guidelines, and considering a range of publication-related issues (e.g., communication with editors, copyright and fair use, crafting code, and shaping webtexts).

Section 4, "Getting (More and Different Types of) Feedback," provides advice relating to the review process and good ideas for dealing with (inevitable) failure, navigating reviewer comments, and undertaking revise and resubmit processes. A topic that we discussed and wrestled with, as editors of the collection, is the fact that a key aspect of disciplinary service is serving as manuscript reviewers and/or joining editorial boards. However, the entire review process remains generally murky to many of us. We may be taught practices of peer review across our lives as students, but we are rarely oriented toward the complexities of reading, absorbing, digesting, and acting on reviewer and editor feedback on our work. Nor are many of us formally trained to serve as reviewers or editors. Chapters in this section thus include advice from editors representing journals and book series about navigating this task as editors and communicating with authors about their work. This section also includes advice from authors who have received the range of responses most common to the publication trajectory: reject or revise and resubmit.

The final section of the collection, "Moving On," includes advice related to post-publication—or advice most applicable after completing a lengthy, time-consuming writing project. The advice in this section suggests ways to be a publicity vehicle for your work, to pivot to the next project, and to take a breather before moving on. Multiple pieces here stress the labor and situated activity that occur *after* publication.

Publishing is hard work. Writing is hard work. As we so often wind up arguing in our institutions, writing *can't* be taught, learned, and mastered in one class—or in one book collection. It's a life-long practice; it's a career-long (and beyond, as some of our emeriti authors note) practice. And writing, as we all well know, is messy work. Conducting research, moving classroom practices to pedagogical stances presented in manuscripts, nurturing good ideas, navigating large-scale research projects, engaging in the emotional labor related to making ourselves vulnerable by sharing our work, and the myriad other complexities of generating ideas on the page or the screen can't be entirely represented in one collection (even one with seventy-seven chapters). What we hope to offer here, across these chapters and in these sections, are small, *potent* pieces of advice. Take them. Try them out. Try them on. Share them with others. Build from them.

All Together Now. We present the following to summarize and snapshot the advice offered in this collection and to entice you, we hope, to spend time with these scholars and their suggestions:

AMIDON: Know how intellectual property impacts your writing and leverage fair use.

ANSON: Storyboard projects, and storyboard across projects.

BARRÓN: Listen to stories, read stories, and learn to tell stories.

BARTON: Protect an hour a day for research.

BAUMANN: Consider good timing.

BERNHARDT: Look outside academia for opportunity.

BLAIR: Know your audience.

BLAKESLEY: Listen for a while and catch the tenor of the argument—then write what you know and care about.

BLOOM: Find a dissertation topic you can fall in love with.

BOST: Voice, positionality, and community are three principles useful for evaluating advice.

BROWN: Pester editors politely.

BUCK: Choose readers who will serve as coach and critic.

BURNETT: Don't just revise—manage the process of revising and resubmitting.

CARTER: Publishing is only the beginning.

COMER: Find the right publication for your work.

COOLS: Separate yourself from your writing.

COOPER: Make sure your work gives your readers a payoff.

COTICH: Speak to others as you would like them to speak to you.

CUSHMAN: Learn to keep learning.

CUTRUFELLO: Prioritize reviewer comments when revising and resubmitting.

DOBRIN: Understand the importance of self-promotion in an age of academic analytics.

DUFFY: Locate first, invent second.

ELLIOT: Use quantitative approaches and frameworks to tell stories with evidence.

ENOCH: Work through a request to revise and resubmit in steps.

EYMAN: Webtexts should integrate text, design, and code as rhetorically powerful parts of a piece.

FARIS: Develop content management strategies to keep your project organized.

FISHMAN: Engage the WHIMSY Protocol.

FLOWER: Move your writing from writer-based to reader-based through collaborative planning.

GALLAGHER AND DEVOSS: Create a pipeline to publish on a continual basis.

GONZALES: Create and nurture networks for your writing projects.

GRABILL: Don't do anything you can't write about.

GRIES: Identify the scholarly contribution you want to make, and have a ten-year plan.

HALBRITTER AND LINDQUIST: Rock on.

HARRIS: Think of your dissertation not as a draft of your first book, but as materials for it.

HAWK: Listen to what's being said—at conferences, in journals, and in books.

HENSLEY OWENS: Publishing a book isn't really the end of anything.

HESSE: Remember this isn't the last thing you'll ever write.

HICKS: Read like a writer; write for your reader.

HORNER: Don't take the advice of manuscript reviewers, *use* it.

INOUE: Find a resistant reader, then practice compassionate, rhetorical listening.

JENSEN: Adopt approaches to reduce the intimidation of the submission process.

JOHNSON-EILOLA AND SELBER: Think of editorial relationships as partnerships or collaborative endeavors to facilitate both conceptual and concrete feedback.

KIRSCH: Sit down and write, get up and move.

KORNFIELD: Revise and resubmit ASAP.

KUMARI: Start with what you know.

LAVECCHIA, MORRIS, AND MICCICHE: Think like a copyeditor.

LECOURT: Reconsider old arguments as possibilities for new publications.

L'EPLATTENIER AND MASTRANGELO: Work so that editors think fondly of you.

LETTNER-RUST: Rejection tells you what your next step is.

LINDQUIST AND HALBRITTER: Recognize the productive complications of collaborations.

LOCKHART, GLASCOTT, LEWIS, MIDDLETON, PARRISH, AND WARNICK: Understand editors' perspectives and advice.

LUNSFORD: Imagine you are entering a conversation among equals, all of you devoted to pushing the boundaries of knowledge.

MANTHEY: Establish a pipeline, and then make and maintain connections and collaborations to maintain it.

MCCORKLE: Assemble a crew.

MCKEE: Everyone starting out has felt to some degree and at various times nervous and doubtful; grab hold of your right—your imperative—to join public and scholarly conversations.

MEDINA: Chip away at projects by making the most out of slivers of time.

MINA: Know that an editor's approach to providing feedback matters as much as the feedback itself.

MULLIN: Be sure to consider personal characteristics along with scholarly credentials when choosing collaborators.

PALMERI: Your dissertation is just the text written so far.

PALMQUIST: Consider open-access publishers and the affordances of making your work more available.

PARKS: The best writing emerges out of a collaborative conversation.

PERRYMAN-CLARK: Be strategic, especially if your baby is new and so is your role as tenure-track WPA.

POE: Engage in editorial work to create an enduring conversation in the field.

RHODES: Queer your research (and shout in the Burkean parlor, then toilet-paper the yard).

RICE: Publications don't end; they lead to future projects.

RIDOLFO: Make the best use of the time you have (case in point: voice memos while commuting).

ROSE: Be brave and be bold.

SHIPKA: Keep a daily work log.

SILVER: Believe in your idea while reframing your rhetorical exigence.

SKINNELL: Embrace rejection as a heuristic for conducting self-assessment.

SMITH: Go to the writing center or form a writing group.

STEDMAN AND DANFORTH: Seek out smart people and then collaborate with them.

SULLIVAN: Writing *is* revising.

TEBEAU: Know that the best ideas have their roots in the familiar, where you can uncover new connections and ways of seeing.

TOTH AND JENSEN: If you are working to transform the field, plan a campaign, not just a publication.

TRIMBUR: Originality is overrated.

YANCEY: Trust the process.

SECTION 1

Getting Started

Inventing, Brainstorming, and Managing

1

LOVE, BEAUTY, AND TRUTH
On Finding a Dissertation Topic

Lynn Z. Bloom

I've just returned from a storybook wedding: a beautiful bride in a long white dress married Prince Charming on an autumn afternoon ablaze with colored leaves, the couple embraced in love articulated by grandparents, parents, siblings, friends, and of course each other, wedded also to an egalitarian future of true love forever. Because they've lived together for a while, they understand many of the dimensions of this partnership, but not all—for who can know everything at the outset of a work continually in progress? Yet they are optimistically committed to the work—and play—that will make the rough places smooth and this dream come true.

Love. There are significant parallels between this romantic account—which may sound like a fairy tale but I believe, based on my own marriage of fifty-eight years, that fairy tales can come true—and writing a dissertation. For finding a dissertation topic—alluring, enticing, worth the effort of penetrating its mysteries and understanding its nuances—is like finding the right person to marry. You have agency in your choice, and you will want to pick the one you love the most. From among many possibilities, you've selected the one that most appeals to you, one in which you're pleased to make a huge investment.

If you're not happy about your topic, delighted with its potential, able to turn it around and around in the light to admire its many facets, then stop right here and scour the terrain until you find another that lights your fire. The beauty you find in the topic will lead you to love it, and your enthusiasm will inspire your committee. Is it new? Exciting? Is it generative in intellectual possibilities, in potential for publication and further research? Do you want to commit to a relationship with it?

Love will keep you wedded to this project for the long haul until you finish, driven by passion for the topic itself and for the enterprise—the exploration, ingenuity, and work involved. As in a marriage, you will need to love your project beyond measure because there will be times

DOI: 10.7330/9781607328834.c001

of frustration and irritation, when the research is not working out as smoothly as you'd anticipated, when you'd like to throw it out the window and walk away. Unlike marriage, which expects a lifetime commitment, a research project requires a realistic timetable. Although you can get a ballpark sense of the time involved from your experience in writing a typical twenty-page term paper, a dissertation will require more time than merely multiplying the time spent on each chapter. Each part has to fit into the whole, and building both the infrastructure (such as refining and explaining the methodology, or providing a comprehensive bibliography) and the superstructure (integrating all the separate parts) takes additional time.

We tend to underestimate the time a long project will take. Especially if the topic is cutting-edge, and when new sources—written, material, more ethereal—pop up daily, if not hourly, online, in the culture, among people with a stake in the project—as subjects, committee members, colleagues, specialists, statisticians. Fidelity to your topic can help to keep you from the primrose path of wayward romance; every new thread in the research web takes time and, however enticing, following tangential strands can lead you astray.

Beauty. In your dissertation you are not aiming for perfection but for elegant beauty—always capable of improvement but good enough to remain attractive and to get the job done. "We must labor to be beautiful," said Yeats, whose aesthetic in "Adam's Curse" also underlies the work of the doctoral student. Conscientious advisors will help their students to see the beauty in doable projects that can be completed in a predictably finite time. In helping my doctoral students to get through and get out expeditiously, I advise them to plan their research time starting with the ending date.

When do you want to finish? Then, how long will it take to do the research? To write each chapter? To revise the total? To have the work reviewed, and possibly revised again? I encourage them: estimate the amount of time the project will take. Double it. You may by now be in the ballpark; if not, add 25 percent more. You will find beauty by observing that ending date, which is likely to be determined by funding; when will your TAship or research support run out? Every delay will be costly in terms of job market timing and income forgone. If necessary, pare down the scope of your research to keep within the time frame. Stick to the main point, the principal supporting evidence or analysis. You can explore the interesting byways later on.

Short books of 70,000–80,000 words—under 200 pages—represent university presses' current ideal of beauty. A svelte configuration for your own research, five main chapters, max, plus an introduction and a conclusion will keep that work on the runway. Every chapter you don't write is a chapter you don't have to research or revise, joining the lineup of beautiful potential topics for later investigation. Beauty is always a work in progress.

Truth. Mark Twain understood "You can't pray a lie." When Huck Finn realizes that the hunt for the fugitive slave is proceeding as he and Jim are "a-floating along" the Mississippi, "talking and singing and laughing," he thinks he should turn Jim in: "I was trying to make my mouth *say* I would do the right thing," but "deep down in me I knowed it was a lie," "the words wouldn't come," "my heart warn't right." He examines the evidence, "But somehow I couldn't seem to strike no places to harden me against him, but only the other kind." He decides, "All right, then, I'll *go* to hell," inadvertently making the morally right decision, one that he understands deep in his heart. So he is able to "take up wickedness again," beginning by going "to work and stealing Jim out of slavery again"—a source of pleasure, power, and ingenuity.

Dissertation writers, too, need to be honest with themselves. Once upon a time—this is a cautionary tale—a good friend was trying to write her dissertation amid the responsibilities and distractions of running a household with a husband in medical residency, three rambunctious little children, teaching composition, and a gourmet cook's perfectionism that made even peanut butter and jelly sandwiches look as if they'd leapt off the pages of a cookbook. She wanted to write about Swift, her foremost literary love, but in those pre-internet days when library searches took weeks and months to nail down the minutiae, she needed a way to get through and get out before the end of the century, then forty years away. To research an eighteenth-century topic would take at least two years and unaffordable trips to England.

So she sought what she always called "a quick and dirty" dissertation topic, one she didn't love. She figured that the less she had invested in it the more easily she'd stick to the topic's straight and narrow and the sooner she'd finish. She settled for what she considered a ho-hum topic, serviceable but not, in her eyes, beautiful—an analysis of James Branch Cabell's fictional county of Poictesme, her advisor's passion but not her own. Despite some pressure from the advisor to ventriloquize his ideas, she never finished. She could not pray that lie. She couldn't bring herself to give enough time to Cabell's never-never land while spending her best efforts on the real world she loved the most—family, teaching, and cooking. Finally she simply stopped writing.

In fact she had another choice. She could have selected a smaller slice of the subject she loved for her dissertation and nibbled away at other portions of the larger Swiftian topic after she finished. Her first words on the topic—staking out the territory, capturing the beauty and truth she loved—didn't have to be her last. Nor do yours.

Research, like the rest of life, moves on; there will be a lifetime to fall in love with new topics, irresistibly beautiful, and to pursue them in the quest for truth.

2

SIT DOWN AND WRITE, GET UP AND MOVE

Gesa E. Kirsch

When you sit by a pond or a slowly winding stream, the city's impatient tempo drains away, and from the corners of the mind, thoughts come out and sun themselves.

—Lorus Milne and Margery Milne

Pairing these two activities—sitting down to write, getting up to move—has been very productive for me, no matter the writing task or stage of a project at hand.

Sit Down and Write. When I start a new writing project, whether it is a conference paper, essay, article, book chapter, grant proposal, or research report, I give myself permission to write quickly, without stopping, editing, or censoring the thoughts that emerge, just as I often ask my students to begin with freewriting when they explore a new topic. I draw inspiration from writers like Julia Cameron, Peter Elbow, Natalie Goldberg, and Donald Murray, who encourage us to "show up at the page" with pen and paper, allowing ourselves be surprised by what appears in front of us.

When I sit down to write, I jot down phrases, list ideas, misspell words, ramble a bit, jump around, omit transitions, write fragments, break all the rules. I write even when I know that I still have a lot of reading to do, when I do not know what colleagues have said on a subject, when I still have much to learn. I like to get initial thoughts and ideas onto the page to see what excites me about a topic, why I care about the subject matter, what questions emerge, what speculative answers I might offer, why I think the research at hand is worth investigating. Giving myself permission to write early, before an exhaustive literature review, gives me freedom to explore, find my passion, change directions, rethink my position, and later on, to engage more deeply with the authors I will read on the subject matter.

DOI: 10.7330/9781607328834.c002

My word choice above was deliberate; I still like to start with *pen and paper* for exploratory drafts, allowing me to write anywhere, anytime, at the spur of the moment. The simplicity of these two items offers a distraction-free approach; I can avoid format and font choices, autocorrect features, illuminated screens and, most centrally, the temptation to connect to the internet. There is now compelling research that shows that handwriting is a different cognitive process than typing; the former appears to challenge the mind to synthesize, organize, and prioritize in ways that keyboarding does not (for a summary of this research, see Hotz 2016; May 2014). Moreover, I like to set boundaries for technology, limiting interruptions; therefore, I *mute all my devices* at all times—no beeping, chiming, chirping, or vibrating. When I sit down to write, I protect my time and space, keeping distractions to a minimum.

For a second iteration of my writing, I usually do move to the computer, often energized by freewriting, notes by my side, ready to elaborate, develop a point, articulate an idea, refine questions. All the while, I still aim to observe with interest, not judgment, the writing that unfolds (keeping the internal critic and editor at bay).

Lately, I have been setting a timer for forty-five minutes, enough time to allow me to generate quite a bit of text, hone in on a revision, or tackle an editing or proofreading task. That amount of time goes by quickly but can be quite productive, I find. If I sit still for more than an hour or two, I have discovered, I tend to lose momentum, focus, and energy; hence my need to move.

Get Up and Move. Once my timer rings, I get up and move. If it's late in the morning, I'll head out for a short run, take a brisk walk (around campus or my neighborhood), or attend the occasional yoga class. Any of these activities can do wonders: it gets my blood flowing and lungs pumping, brings oxygen to my body, gives me new energy, and lifts my mood. Some of my runs/walks are social, others solo, allowing me to clear my head and observe my environment—the shoreline along the Charles River, the traffic roaring in the distance, the blue sky overhead, fellow runners and walkers enjoying the outdoors. Or, on a rainy day like this morning, I walk with umbrella in hand, feeling the mist on my skin, listening to cars splashing water from puddles, observing other walkers, bundled up tightly, leaning into the wind, the umbrella a shield for all that may come their way. At other times of the year, I listen to the snow crunching underfoot, observe the muted winter tones—gray, white, and black—of a New England cityscape, or squint my eyes against the sun hanging low on the horizon, even at noon time, on a winter's day. As the epigraph by Lorus and Margery Milne suggests, spending time outside can greatly contribute to creativity, insight, and inspiration.[1]

I love getting out of doors, but when time pressures don't permit a small excursion, I still get up, walk a bit, stretch, climb the stairs, or attend to a task that gets me out of my chair for fifteen minutes to a half hour. After a brief break, I'll set the timer again, refreshed and clear-headed, ready for another writing session. Suddenly I know exactly what I need to do next, how to organize my thoughts, how to proceed.

And so it goes: two short focused writing sessions with some movement in between are all that's necessary to keep me motivated and productive. It does not take all day, not even half a day; all it takes is blocking out some time in my calendar, writing regularly for some amount of time most every day. I have learned that I do my best writing in the mornings, but I remain flexible, writing whenever I can claim forty or fifty minutes. As long as I schedule writing sessions several days a week, my projects move along; I am close enough to the writing, the research questions, and the ideas to know where I have left off and what to do next. I can maintain momentum, excited to return to my work in progress.

Coda: Often and Early. I distinctly remember my surprise when, more than two decades ago, a well-published, highly successful woman professor told me during an interview that she reserved weekends for things other than academic work (I published this interview as part of a larger study, *Women Writing the Academy* [Kirsch 1994]). Inspired by this fine advice, I learned early in my career to reserve weekends "for other things." Hence, I have come to recognize the importance of writing regularly, at least several times a week. It's kept my life balanced and productive, the academic work only one aspect of my rich lived experience. Robert Boice, the well-known psychologist and professor who studied the writing habits of academic faculty members, offers this sound advice: "Writing, in usual practice, need be nothing more than a modest daily priority, one that ranks well below more important priorities like social life and exercising. Unrealistic priorities and goals, like most New Year's resolutions, typically fail and torment" (1994: 239).[2]

NOTES

1. In their recent book *Wired to Create*, Scott Kaufman and Carolyn Gregoire review many well-known writers, authors, and philosophers who wrote about the importance of walking for their thoughts, and they offer new research that documents the ways in which movement contributes to creativity (2015: 40–41).
2. For a concise summary of Boice's advice, see the Academic Coaching & Writing 2017.

REFERENCES

Academic Coaching & Writing LLC. 2017. "How to Structure Your Writing Time, Using the Boice Method," January 4. http://www.academiccoachingandwriting.org.

Boice, Robert. 1994. *How Writers Journey to Comfort and Fluency*. New York: Praeger.

Hotz, Robert Lee. 2016. "Can Handwriting Make You Smarter?" *Wall Street Journal*, April 4.

Kaufman, Scott Barry, and Carolyn Gregoire. 2015. *Wired to Create: Unraveling the Mysteries of the Creative Mind*. New York: Perigee, Random House.

Kirsch, Gesa E. 1994. *Women Writing the Academy: Audience, Authority, and Transformation*. Carbondale: Southern Illinois University Press.

Lorus, Milne J., and Margery J. Milne. 1945. *A Multitude of Living Things*. New York: Dodd, Mead, and Company.

May, Cindi. 2014. "A Learning Secret: Don't Take Notes with a Laptop." *Scientific American*, June 3. https://www.scientificamerican.com/article/a-learning-secret-don-t-take-notes-with-a-laptop/.

3
DOUBLE DIPPING

Andrea Abernethy Lunsford

It was 1976. I was a graduate student at Ohio State in the midst of dissertation research and writing when I got a request from a publisher to review the manuscript of a book called *Errors and Expectations*. I kept reading the note over and over again: surely it wasn't meant for me. Mina Shaughnessy was a hero to me (and lots of others); I had read everything of hers I could get my hands on and been influenced in my dissertation research by what she had to say about students she dubbed "basic writers." Review her manuscript? Yikes!

Eventually I pulled myself together and agreed to write a review. Then I read the manuscript, taking mountains of notes and being carried away by her argument: that students whose prose appeared "hopeless" (in her colleagues' words) were in fact working within the language system as they understood it. Teachers needed to listen to students, to hear the logic they were adhering to, to understand literally where they were coming from in their writing before jumping to the conclusion that they were hopeless, illiterate, "not college material." What a breath of fresh air in the atmosphere created by the "Johnny [and Jane] Can't Write" furor of the mid-1970s!

I remember sitting on my sofa with the manuscript, inspired by its message and in awe of its author, and feeling writer's block or something very much like it. I kept trying to begin . . . and then trying again. And again. Nothing seemed to work; my brain felt frozen. Then I took drastic measures. I gave myself an ultimatum: "Get with it, girl," I said to myself. "This is a task you can do, and you are not going to get up from this sofa until you have written two pages. I don't care how long it takes—no time for a glass of tea. No bathroom breaks." I sat there for quite a while, musing and daydreaming, but then I began imagining myself talking to Shaughnessy about what she had written, asking her questions and even hazarding answers to some of them, passing the conversational ball back and forth. And finally I began to write. Imagining a conversation

DOI: 10.7330/9781607328834.c003

turned out to be the way for me to engage with the manuscript and with Shaughnessy herself, not as a professional compared to me, a wet-behind-the-ears graduate student, not as someone whose work awed me, but as someone I just wanted to talk to, engage with, learn from and with. So I wrote the review and sent it off—no great shakes, but I felt satisfied, not to mention relieved.

That metaphor of the conversation, *of talk*, has stayed with me through the ensuing forty years. When I begin a writing project, I immerse myself in the topic I'm writing about and in the work of those who have thought hard about it, imagining that I am part of a conversation among equals, among those of goodwill who want to push the boundaries of our knowledge further. This model has worked much better for me than the "kill the ancestors" approach I grew up with in the academy, where young scholars felt the need (or were urged, sometimes required) to take on the work of some earlier figure to show how misguided or wrongheaded or shortsighted it was and how their own work would fill the gap or correct the picture. I preferred the pleasure of conversation to the anxiety of influence then, and I still do.

I learned another lesson from this experience, one referred to in the title of this brief essay. Because I worked so hard on that review, read so much by and about Shaughnessy and about the larger context surrounding "basic writers," I decided that I should try to put all this effort to work in a new direction. That was my first attempt at "double dipping," as I wrote a brief essay on Shaughnessy's work and then turned that into a conference presentation. As I moved beyond graduate school into my first job at the University of British Columbia, I was learning lessons in building a curriculum vitae as well as in joining academic conversations.

Over the years I've had plenty of colleagues who practiced "double dipping," but they tended to begin with a conference paper and then build on it to produce a manuscript and then publish it as a journal article. I'm sure that's still an effective way to proceed, because it provides a chance to put ideas out there and get response from conference goers before developing a full-blown essay. But it didn't work well for me. Once I'd given the conference paper, I felt the urge to move on to the next project. (Patience is not one of my virtues.) So I always tried to write a scholarly essay first—and then condense it into a conference presentation, though because of the lag time in getting a response and reviews from journals, I'm often able to give the conference paper and get feedback that will help me when I get the response (often revise and resubmit) from the journal I've submitted the essay to.

One of my earliest essays on basic writing was accepted by *College Composition and Communication,* the journal I had targeted for it. That targeting was strategic: I did my homework by reading through the last two years' issues, taking notes on themes and threads running through as well as on topics that seemed absent or ignored. I also made notes on how my research on basic writers fit in—how it conversed and resonated with previously published essays. And I practically memorized the submission guidelines to make sure I followed them scrupulously. At the end of this process, I could imagine the arc of the essay I wanted to write, how it would begin and end, and how it would respond to and engage the work of others. For me, this "prewriting" is an especially exciting time; I am always energized by this learning experience and by the conversation that takes root in my mind.

Everyone surely has his or her own writing rituals and processes. For my part, I like to write in an absolutely calm and quiet space, and for long stretches, pausing every hour or so to read my work out loud and to revise as I go. And as I write, I feel like those I'm in conversation with are sitting on my shoulder, nudging me forward, cautioning, always engaging me. Perhaps because I've thought so long (and written so frequently) about audience, those I'm writing to are always with me, from beginning to end, in my imagination. Once I have a draft (even what Peter Elbow refers to as a "zero draft"), then I ask a few trusted colleagues to take a look and to talk with me about the draft. And because I am a passionate advocate of collaborative writing, I often have a coauthor who is a built-in responder, and we go back and forth with drafts, often eight or ten times, before settling on what goes out to a journal.

This collaborative process raises another issue for beginning scholars: how much weight will be given to coauthored pieces? Lisa Ede and I (and plenty of others) have been fighting this battle for thirty years now, insisting that collaborative work "counts" as much as single-authored work, and in the last few years, I think the tide is turning, even in the humanities, where the single-author model has been the gold standard. The rise of new technology and multimedia discourses have made it more clear than ever that people need to work together to produce first-rate work! Still, if you are a new assistant professor, especially in an English department, you should ask for clarification on this issue, and insist on getting a straight answer. My hope is that the answer will be welcoming and encouraging of collaboration, because that will mean that you can ask bigger research questions, take on more complex projects—ones our time calls for. But if you find that your department does not value collaborative work, publish some single-authored pieces first and then begin collaborating when you have tenure.

As you work toward tenure or some other form of job security, however, remember that "double dipping" can help you. Once an essay is ready to send out for publication review, it's fairly simple to take the major points in the essay and prepare presentation slides to use in discussing the issue at a conference. If your presentation proposal is accepted, you'll have one item to include on your vitae; if the essay is accepted, that's a second item. (It's a good idea to give them slightly different titles to tailor them to the journal audience as opposed to a live conference audience.)

One final piece of advice is one I have sometimes—but not always—been able to follow myself. Whenever possible, try to view whatever research or writing project you are working on as a piece of the patchwork quilt that will make up the body of work you are building. That is, try to think "big picture" as much as you possibly can. When Lisa Ede and I first began working on collaboration and collaborative writing, we were also both working on issues related to feminism and rhetoric. But we didn't immediately think "big picture" and hence did not connect these two strands of our research until some years later. That seems shortsighted and naive now, in hindsight, but we just didn't connect the dots right away. When we did, that broadened vision helped us to link these aspects of our work to create new and more complex projects. Maybe that's a kind of triple dipping!

The best advice of all is to trust yourself, to know that you have fine ideas to contribute, that you have important work to do, work that will make a difference in the lives of your students and your field of study. If you have to sit yourself down on a sofa or at a desk and give yourself ultimatums to get started, as I did all those years ago, then do it!

4

THE IMPORTANCE OF STORIES

Nancy G. Barrón

Writing starts with listening to stories, reading others' stories, learning to tell stories, and writing down stories after telling them many times. Writing well is the accumulation of many revised stories that show the unique perspective of the writer.

Situating Stories. *Salte de aqui y no regresas hasta que tienes razón.* This was a common response to what I thought was a very clearly stated argument. Loosely translated, it means "Go away and don't come back until you make sense." As a child, I heard this many times from my father, who wasn't persuaded by my argument for a family trip, ice cream, or an increased allowance. I had to listen to his stories about his father, about his need to work, and about the broken faucet that needed to be fixed. I needed a story that would make sense to him, that would convince him that a brief trip to the beach could be part of a weekend that would otherwise be spent fixing the house.

In my family, to participate in a conversation takes much practice. First, there is a decision to make on what story to tell, or what story to retell that may prompt someone else to provide a story that is new or newly retold. My parents often discussed in the car which stories they would tell as we headed to a family member's home. They prepared to participate in the conversation by making sure the story was appropriate, and that they could remember it well enough to make it worthy of being told. Second, it is important to know how a story needs to be told. Humor is usually appreciated, though drama sometimes helps with drawing in the audience. Why be merely factual, describing bumper-to-bumper traffic on the way to a family visit, when you can present a vivid scene that includes angry drivers, a broken-down car, loud music, and shouting? Third, the story needs to suit the audience. Stories were told differently depending on if they were told to adults only and or if they were told while children were present. Being aware of who was listening

DOI: 10.7330/9781607328834.c004

to what you had to say was an essential component in how my parents adjusted the stories they told to their families and their friends.

When I started telling my own stories, I learned that sometimes the language spoken determined the presentation or style of the story. My father's mother had a reputation for telling a story in Spanish very theatrically. She embodied different characters, changed her voice, used her arms and facial expressions to provide unspoken context. Our neighbor Ruby always sang her stories. Her Oklahoma accent provided emotional context when her introverted nature didn't allow for too much arm movement. It seemed that she was always asking questions and somehow the drama was envisioned. I learned to begin stories with dramatic questions and then answer them in a complex story that drew from many storytellers. I learned from my father and my mother how to begin a story and how to prompt someone else to participate. They taught me that I needed to make sure that I chose a story that others could join in. A monologue, they told me, is fine, but it is no longer storytelling. Including others into a story takes work and skill. It means that I need to ask who might have a perspective that will enhance a detail, or who can provide support that is missing from my telling? How, in other words, I can find and use my sources well.

Academic writing has much in common with storytelling. Storytellers learn from other storytellers. Academics learn from other academics. Stories are redrafted and adjusted to the message and the audience. Academic texts, similarly, are revised and rewritten. In many ways, writing in the academy can be an extension of storytelling, of screenwriting, of speechmaking. Academic writing can start because of a discussion held at a café or during a hike. The best part of writing is that you have the opportunity to retell, to refine what you said. By telling our story several times, we learn how to reorganize the larger parts and where to include more details. Once the larger story is ready to go, then it's a lot easier to write.

We live by stories and narratives that we hear. We readjust our thinking based on new stories that we hear. And we tell our own stories, sometimes brief and sometimes lengthy, based on what we know from the past and from what we are making sense of currently. Stories that include participation from those who enhance the overall purpose are most useful when the story's content requires support.

Accepting that writing is not just writing but that good writing is purposeful can lead to a practice of examining what is needed for the document to be credible and understood. Who can participate? Which authors? Who has the experience to enhance your point? Which authors? What did they say? Include it in your story. What do you need to know more about so that you aren't listing information but presenting new insights?

What Stories Help Us See. Written arguments are not distinct points in history. They are the accumulation of what we heard, read, and discussed with colleagues, students, or friends. Writing that matters uses our own experiences to address the needs of a specific community and asks the community to engage in discussions, actions, or continued rethinking of established ideas.

If we see our written arguments as narratives and stories that others can follow, we provide our audience with opportunities to learn more about a specific area of interest, and to then use this new knowledge to participate in new ways of meaning-making. For example, we can provide a vivid image similar to a movie scene to help our audience understand a specific point. This allows readers to bring in their own images and their own experiences to supplement what is provided in a text.

Seeing writing as storytelling, with our own perspectives included, avoids writing that imitates other people's writing in the field. We have been trained to include the field's contributions in our research. We do so with literature reviews or by displaying parenthetical lists of the field's top forty authors. Paying attention to the stories of others is important, but sometimes we forget that the story we want to tell needs to become our story and not the story of others.

Telling stories many times helps us become stronger writers. It helps us learn what is important for one audience and not important for another. It helps us clarify points, and it helps us identify a method of communication, a style that suits the message and also the audience. My suggestions for starting a writing project, whether you are an aspiring or prolific writer, are:

- Learn to listen to stories, and learn to understand that the same story can be told many different ways.
- Learn to read the storyteller/author, to understand why she decided to focus on a specific aspect of a story even though you know that there are many more ways to tell the story. (You can translate this into reading a scholarly article.)
- Learn to tell your own stories and write them down. Use the same story/topic and tell your story differently based on the message you are trying to get across and the audience that you want to influence with your story. Know when to refer to other stories, and know when your own story needs to stand out.

5

OVERCOMING THE CLINANDRIUM CONUNDRUM

Carrie Strand Tebeau

Prove yourself. It's a challenge that bubbles up in academia all the time, the moments when you're offered a stage or a page and it's time to say something smart. I found myself struggling with this challenge in my first semester of graduate school during an essay-writing seminar taught by Thomas Lynch, a writer I'd met on the pages of his books well before I met him in person. Sitting beside him at the seminar table, I felt a little starstruck and eager to please. On the first day he had a seemingly simple assignment for us: come to class next time with one truly excellent word to share with the class. But how do you prove yourself with one word? I wanted to show off my writing prowess, my command of sonics, my clever selection of signifier. I wanted to dazzle. I had no idea what word to choose. I finally resorted to pulling my fat *American Heritage Dictionary* off the shelf and reading it, starting at the very beginning. I scanned through all the As, all the Bs, and half the Cs before settling on the winner: *clinandrium.* It's an irrefutably beautiful word; as you pronounce it your tongue twirls in balletic fashion through your mouth, flicking off the back of your teeth before rippling through the front and settling in at the bottom of your jaw in a deep hum. Its meaning is equally graceful: it's the hollow where the anther rests in an orchid.

Everyone in the seminar shared complex words, their sounds surviving from ancient languages, their meanings winnowed down to precision on their long ride from antiquity into our present-day dictionaries, where we'd eagerly discovered them for class, hoping to sound smart. That is, everyone except for a student named Julia. Julia's word was *salt.* As soon as she said it, I knew I'd lost the tacit best-word competition.

Salt is a word you can taste; you know it deeply, intimately. Salt is a thing you have understood since childhood; a seasoning that transcends both history and cultural boundaries. There is a shaker of it in nearly every kitchen in the world. Early on, people learned how to preserve

DOI: 10.7330/9781607328834.c005

their food with it. We need it in our bodies to generate metabolic functions. It is one of the five basic types of taste. Our oceans are tinged with
it; it's the reason our planet is covered in water yet we fear running out
of water to drink. The Bible punishes with salt, turning Lot's wife into
a pillar of it. Pliny the Elder references fleur de sel in *Natural History*. It
was once a form of currency, and is how the word *salary* was born. Salt
is a word that stuffs your whole mouth with its singular satisfying sound.

What *salt* has over *clinandrium* is our deep history with its meaning. It
has a significance that is at once utterly simple and yet deeply layered.
We all have a connection to salt, and our shared understanding creates
a web of possibility for how we might link ideas and create new ways of
thinking about something ancient. It gives us the opportunity to consider something that is fundamentally a part of being human. When
Julia said *salt* I realized how much I was guilty of overthinking, and even
though I'd found a lovely word, it wasn't as resonant as I'd wanted it
to be. Reading the dictionary is not the best route to discovering the
gems of language—we find them in speech and in experience, in our
ears and on the pages of good books. Being relatively undiscovered is
not the secret of a good word. Of course there are pleasures in finding
something new, but it's easy to fall into the trap of thinking that only
something new and complex will suffice when it's time to prove yourself.

I am reminded of *clinandrium* all the time in my academic life. The
first time I submitted a proposal to a call for papers and it was accepted,
I felt a little horrified—I'd actually have to take 500 words worth of an
idea and make it extended and concrete. I teach composition at a community college, a path I'd found after earning my poetry MFA, and the
journal that accepted my work was a national publication, one mostly
filled with the wisdom of rhet/comp PhD-holding professors from four-
year universities. Instead of feeling proud of myself for having secured
a publication opportunity, I felt a surge of insecurity. How could I prove
myself worthy of the acceptance? How could I make my voice sound like
something that belonged beside the intelligent words of everyone else in
the journal? It was the same thing I'd felt at the beginning of my graduate school seminar—a moment when I had an opportunity to impress,
and I wanted to do it well. *You must perform*, I told myself, which was true
but also unreasonable. Performance suggests artifice, which can mimic
truth while not actually being truth. But as I began writing my paper I
wasn't thinking about this; I felt consumed with a charge to succeed.

There is a specific table I like to use for academic writing. It's in the
public library on the second floor, where it's quiet enough to imagine
you can hear the books whispering out their words. The table faces a

window through which you can see nothing but the profusion of oak leaves on the tree outside of it. The wide window frame is old carved wood, and when I write there I feel connected to a long history of words and the other people who have collected them in this exact spot. I brought my laptop to this table; my plan was to chip away at a draft for several hours until the ideas began to flow more easily. They did not flow more easily. My computer was a jungle of open tabs, each one containing an article I wanted to reference in my work. I kept flitting between them, trying to make their ideas line up with my own. I wrote paragraph after paragraph of polysyllabic words. I quoted other paragraphs of polysyllabic words. I kept checking the word count at the bottom of my screen, which moved with such incremental slowness I felt certain I would be writing this paper for another three years.

When half a day finally, mercifully elapsed, I read back over my work. It was a clinandrium—it did, after all, contain the accepted idea from my proposal, and in that sense, it was new and interesting, a thing worth saying. But I saw that I had also obfuscated my intent to write well. I had prized an academic voice over the content of my ideas in my effort to sound smart. This is not to say that good writing is not allowed access to difficult vocabulary, but rather that pretentious wording can sometimes stand in as a proxy for solid argumentation. I had barely expressed anything, despite prattling on for three thousand words. Furthermore, I had woven together so many ideas from other work that my own argument stood on the sidelines of the essay—it was the equivalent of reading the dictionary and reporting back with a new word I'd found, rather than relying on something I understood deeply. What my work needed was a giant dash of salt.

I returned to the library table later in the week and reread what I'd written. I copied and pasted the most solid section of it into a new document; I now had four sentences from which to work. But this time, I was prepared to write honestly. I picked up my pen and made little rhythmic sketches in the corner of my notebook until I started drawing triangles over and over, and realized that I could organize my key thoughts into a three-pronged heuristic. Once I carved away everything that I had borrowed or strived for, I was able to write with clarity and precision.

It is a slow lesson, and I continue to learn it, but when you find yourself stretching far outside of what you already understand in pursuit of dazzle, it's seldom there. The best ideas have their roots in the familiar, where you can uncover new connections and ways of seeing. Starting a paper by searching for ideas you've never had before is a surefire way to come up with a clinandrium—a draft that, even if intrinsically interesting, lacks solid footing. It's better instead to begin by turning over the ideas that always populate your head. If you have been invited to write, then you are good enough to write, whether you teach at a two-year college or a prestigious university. What you say will be compelling, particularly if you allow it to be honest, familiar, and an essential reach into what we need to understand as part of being human.

6

YOU *CAN* DO THAT IN RHETORIC AND COMPOSITION

Byron Hawk

When I first pitched the idea for my dissertation on vitalism to my director, Victor Vitanza, his response was something along the lines of "You can't do that in rhetoric and composition, you'll be crucified." Those might not have been his exact words, but they are the words that continue to resonate in my head. Importantly though, rather than hearing "*You can't do that*," I heard "You can't do that *in rhetoric and composition.*" The message seemed clear to me that the key to doing research is to do it in relation to a field. So rather than abandon the project, I set out to invent a rhetorical situation in rhetoric and composition that made the material I wanted to engage a reasonable thing to do in light of the field's conversations. This one message is the advice I regularly give my own students: they can, potentially at least, write about anything that interests, motivates, or compels them, but they can't do it in a vacuum. Scholarly research is about both discovering and inventing the conversations you are responding to as you are engaged in them and making sure that through the process you produce new ideas, connections, practices, and exigencies that potentially set the stage for others to invent the discipline in return.

Follow Disciplinary Conversations. You can't take a position in relation to a field without first being attentive to its larger conversations. Gary Olson (1997) argues that scholarship is a series of ongoing conversations that engage issues in the field through conferences, articles, and books that don't always reach consensus. Rather than build toward consensual truth, the conversations are generative: they produce discourse, ideas, and rhetorical and pedagogical practices. Olson's advice for a first move, if you want to join these conversations, is to listen to what is being said, both in the field writ large but also in the particular journal or journals you will be publishing in. The conversations will have major

DOI: 10.7330/9781607328834.c006

and minor perspectives, can be hotly debated, and are usually practiced indirectly through writing rather than direct exchange or even citation in some cases. Some issues will have already been settled or exhausted and don't need to be rehashed. Others may need to be resurrected or reinvigorated, but only listening to the conversations will provide a sense of which issue is which.

Gesture toward Knowledge of These Conversations in Your Writing. You should typically lay out versions of these conversations in writing to establish an exigency for your own work. Richard McNabb (2001) studied a corpus of submissions to *Rhetoric Review* and found that the majority of rejected manuscripts failed to situate their claims in the field. The key rhetorical gesture, McNabb found, is to shift interpretive authority out of nonepistemic individual, practical activity (classrooms, workplaces, department meetings, conferences) and onto a constructed epistemic disciplinary matrix (subjects, works, ideas, and methods). Nonepistemic gestures typically show no recognition of current disciplinary problems or conversations. Instead, they locate the problem in the author's personal experience, defer disciplinary context through more general details, or describe the field's knowledge in an acontextualized literature review. Epistemic gestures, on the other hand, draw immediate attention to the disciplinary conversations that provide an exigence for the author's research. You should negotiate your claims in the context of the field's current knowledge, established authors, and accepted methods to show that new knowledge is being produced in the discipline.

Foreground the Cost of the Disciplinary Problems You Identify. You should always be clear and direct about what is at stake in the disciplinary problems that ground your contribution. Often proposals or articles will point to a "gap" in the disciplinary conversations to show that something hasn't been addressed. But this, in and of itself, isn't enough to constitute a disciplinary problem. Joseph Williams (2011) argues that introductions should include a destabilizing condition that generates costs or consequences for the field. A gap in knowledge or flaw in understanding only constitutes a problem if not developing a response incurs a cost to the field or its practices—readers need to see the problem as a significant one that has an impact on them, the field, or their students. Williams derives a useful heuristic for article introductions: Stasis, Problem with Condition + Cost, and Solution or Response. Stasis is some established position in the field that is then disrupted by a problem. The problem should include both an articulation of the conditions that create it and the costs that come from ignoring it. The solution can be laid out in detail or suggested as a response to the problem and left to the rest of the article for further elaboration. This rhetorical move holds back from fully giving the argument away and creates some tension or suspense for the reader, who will want to read on if the costs are seen as disciplinarily significant.

Truth be told, the problem isn't with newer members of the discipline. The problem is that in graduate school these rhetorical moves typically aren't taught directly. Graduate students are mostly left to figure them out on their own, or if they are lucky through the mentoring efforts of their dissertation directors. In "Discipline and Publish," Collin Brooke (2012) sees in McNabb's account a problem that carries a cost. Our graduate level writing instruction is more akin to current-traditional rhetoric than process pedagogies, and our graduate courses are organized more around topics and canons than disciplinary conversations. These practices set our graduate students up for difficulties if not failures. Brooke's solution is to address these problems more directly and explicitly by teaching conversations rather than canons, and foregoing the seminar paper for more direct rhetorical instruction in academic writing. Disciplinary knowledge isn't something that stands alone outside of its productions, but is intimately a function of disciplinary conversations and the collective practices that produce them and give them salience. In retrospect, I can read all of this advice back into my conversation with my mentor. But I've tried to follow Brooke's advice and move these conversations from the office to the classroom.

REFERENCES

Brooke, Collin. 2012. "Discipline and Publish: Reading and Writing the Scholarly Network." In *Ecology, Writing Theory, and New Media*, edited by. Sidney Dobrin, 92–105. New York: Routledge.

McNabb, Richard. 2001. "Making the Gesture: Graduate Student Submissions and the Expectation of Journal Referees." *Composition Studies* 29 (1): 9–26.

Olson, Gary. 1997. "Publishing Scholarship in Rhetoric and Composition: Joining the Conversation." In *Publishing in Rhetoric and Composition*, edited by Gary Olson and Todd Taylor, 19–33. Albany: SUNY Press.

Williams, Joseph. 2011. *Problems into problems: A Rhetoric of Motivation*. Fort Collins, CO: WAC Clearinghouse.

7

WHAT'S INTERESTING?
Originality and Its Discontents

John Trimbur

The best advice I ever received about writing journal articles came from Kenneth A. Bruffee. He told fifteen of us who were fellows in 1980 at Ken's Brooklyn College Institute on Training Peer Tutors that the key to publication in composition (or in any field, for that matter) was to say something "interesting." The point, he assured our group of eager but semi-clueless academic fledglings, was that we didn't need to have groundbreaking, paradigm-shifting ideas to get an article or conference paper accepted. The aim of writing, Ken said, was to interest readers, to occupy their attention.

Now I am quite aware this advice must sound totally self-evident, a version of what we take for granted today as the Burkean parlor or what Bruffee himself would later call "joining the conversation" to explain his social constructionist approach to teaching writing. But looking back on that moment in 1980, there was also something less straightforward and more complicated in Ken's advice. That is, I now think Ken was trying to save us from ourselves and our literary educations, from how the notion of genius and its emphasis on originality and individual creativity—in the hundred years from the Romantics to Ezra Pound's high modernist injunction to "make it new"—left us feeling we needed some startling intellectual breakthrough to have a publishable idea. In the language of early 1980s composition, Ken wanted to redefine what "brainstorming" might usefully mean to us, for us to see it not as an individual frontal assault to free the personal insights locked in our socially conditioned minds but instead as the communal practice of rhetorical invention—as artful participation in the public life that enabled us to have interesting thoughts in the first place and to converse with others through the displaced talk of writing.

In any case, for me, Bruffee's advice was revelatory. Like many of the fellows in the institute, I was running a writing center at the time

DOI: 10.7330/9781607328834.c007

but had almost no background in rhetoric and composition and little understanding of how academia actually worked. I had been trying, for example, to get conference proposals accepted that were inspired by the Black Mountain and Beat-inspired poetry scene in Buffalo I knew from graduate school days, papers on the relation of Charles Olson's projective verse or Jack Kerouac's spontaneous bop prosody to composition instruction, or how automatic writing in surrealism or Yeats's trance writing prefigured Peter Elbow's freewriting. In other words, I was getting nowhere around 1980, at the height of the process movement, tagmemics, Rogerian rhetoric, and composing research. My ideas must have sounded like white noise to people in the field.

What Ken helped me understand is that I was trying too hard to be original. It's not that I wasn't listening to the conversation in composition; the problem was that I wasn't listening in the right way. In my insecurity, I was trying to enter the conversation by grand gestures, by impressing readers rather than engaging with them. It's not so simple as "knowing your audience" in the textbook sense. It's a matter of knowing how to intersect readers' consciousness and to hold its attention for a moment, over the duration of an article or conference paper, by creating a space for others to consider some recognizable issue or problem, something with a sense of urgency that was already on their minds, even if they hadn't quite realized it. So the upshot was that the term *interesting*, which in other instances can amount to an empty signifier or a dismissive shrug, came to represent for me a way to understand the limits of originality and the necessary presence of others at the scene of writing.

But it also posed the problem of *how could I know* with any degree of certainty whether a particular idea that I might come up with would actually be "interesting" to others? I began to worry. How could my writing possibly prompt the flash of recognition on readers' part that I knew was needed? In effect, I was discovering the other side of the ideology of originality, namely, the equally debilitating feeling that anything I thought was so obvious that everyone else must already be thinking it. In giving up on the modernist quest for novelty, I started to believe I had nothing left to say. If the old ideologies of originality were bankrupt and everything was socially constructed, all I could do was rehash what was already known. This melancholic sense of belatedness, I soon learned from composition's turn to theory in the 1980s, was a big part of the postmodern condition.

In retrospect it's pretty clear that this felt sense of arriving too late and having nothing to add to the conversation, just like the earlier problem of originality, came from my overemphasis on the author function.

I was getting stuck at the point of production and not taking sufficient account of how writing circulates and takes on worldly force. What got me unstuck was the realization that all writing (and not just avant-garde literature) is experimental, a query that tests the uses and limits of the writer's intentions by setting them into motion. There were no guarantees, I came to see. I couldn't work everything out ahead of time in my head. But that's exactly what makes writing an experiment: that it's inseparable from its circulation, the threat of rejection or misunderstanding, and the ever-present possibility that moments of articulation can occur when the writing sent into the world fashions intellectual ties, affective bonds, and political alliances with others.

Here are a few ways I've found helpful in carrying out such an experimental approach to writing:

- Don't write to the field as a whole. Pick an individual or group of people who has shared interests. (Throughout the 1980s, I often wrote directly to Ken Bruffee and the other fellows in the institute, branching out by the end of the decade to write to Patricia Bizzell, whose interests I found myself aligned with.)

- Find or create venues to try out ideas. You can do this through conference papers on panels with like-minded colleagues, work with other compositionists in your area to set up local and informal self-organized seminars, or workshop your projects in an in-person or online writing group of five or six colleagues (see also Smith's chapter in this volume).

- Finally, think of submitting a manuscript to a journal as a probe of the interests of others in the field. Journals, of course, aren't reading services to get peer feedback, but it is useful to take readers' and editors' reviews as not just summary judgments on the fate of the manuscript but also as information about what others find interesting.

8

START WITH WHAT YOU KNOW

Ashanka Kumari

In the wizarding world of Harry Potter, Hogwarts students are tasked with taking OWLs, or Ordinary Wizarding Level examinations. In my muggle (nonmagical person) education, specifically in elementary, middle, and high school, I completed K/W/L charts instead. These charts consisted of three columns, each labeled with one of the three letters K, W, and L that were meant to help us engage with and reflect on field trips, books, and class lessons, among other educational activities.

For example, here's how I might have filled out a K/W/L chart as I got ready to attend a trip to a museum of natural history. Prior to the trip, we were asked to fill out the K and the W: what do we **K**now and **W**ant to learn? *I know this museum has dinosaurs in it. I know I want to see a stegosaurus. I know they have small brains . . . I want to learn what else this museum has to offer. Does it have art? I want to learn about whales too—does this museum have a whale exhibit?*

Following the activity, we were asked to complete the L: what did we **L**earn? *I learned that there are duck-billed dinosaurs that have webbed feet. I learned that this museum does have a whale exhibit and that whales fall under the category of cetaceans . . .*

As a newly minted PhD in rhetoric and composition; associate editor of *Kairos: A Journal of Rhetoric, Technology, and Pedagogy*; copy editor for *Enculturation: A Journal of Rhetoric, Writing, and Culture*; and former editor of *Cardinal Compositions* and the *Crimson White* newspaper, among other publications, I have begun to professionalize as an editor and publisher in the field. And this recurring K/W/L heuristic has returned again and again in my writing process when I approach publishing projects. Always start with what you know. This is how I start getting words on paper.

In the remainder of this piece, I will work through this heuristic using an example from my own experience publishing an article in the *Journal of Popular Culture*. Today, this article lives as an argument that focuses on

DOI: 10.7330/9781607328834.c008

how Beyoncé and Lady Gaga, two self-proclaimed feminist performers, rhetorically use multiple naming practices to rewrite their own identities and, in doing so, offer new creative possibilities for performance. As we know, writing so often evolves, and this article was no exception.

What I Know. The article began as a seminar paper project in a Rhetoric of Women Writers course during the second semester of my master's program. What I knew then was that I wanted to write a piece about naming, identity, and female pop musician naming practices specifically. I also knew I was enamored with bell hooks's discussion of her naming practices as a writer, from an interview we watched in class. I *also* knew that I was particularly interested in the intersections between bell hooks's naming practices and those of female pop artists like Beyoncé, Madonna, and Lady Gaga.

What I Wanted to Learn. From here, and with the support of my seminar professor and feedback from classmates on my idea, I went beyond what I knew to what I *didn't* know to create research questions surrounding what I wanted to learn more about to write. For instance, are multiple naming practices a convention only among *female* pop artists? Who else uses pseudonyms or alternate identities outside of authors and pop artists? What goals do these figures have for changing or taking on different names and personas?

I also wanted to know how to take this seminar paper beyond . . . well, a seminar paper. This project felt bigger than any I had yet pursued in graduate school, and also, as I was preparing to apply to doctoral programs, I knew I would need a solid writing sample. I wanted to know how to get my work in a recognizable venue outside of my classroom.

To move toward potential answers to my questions, I explored. I wandered through library stacks as I had museums as a child. I looked at and read not only the books that came up in search engine results, but also the ones next to them. I researched conferences that would be interested in my topic and submitted a proposal. I returned to what I knew—how to research library databases, read rhetorically and strategically, and ask questions—to get at what I wanted to learn.

What I Learned. I learned a lot. About Beyoncé and Lady Gaga. About Judith Butler and Michel Foucault. And about the publishing process.

First, and perhaps most significant, publishing is *hard* work. This particular project took three years from potential prospect to published pages; it went across literally dozens of drafts, eyes, computers, ears, pens, comments, and presentations before I pressed the submit button. This process takes a lot of time and patience. While you might write one type of paper for a graduate seminar, the paper you submit for publication is an alternative variation. In other words, writing for publication means taking what you have now learned from the work of the seminar paper and reworking it for a new, potentially broader, field-based audience. In my case, I took the seminar paper that once focused on the intersections among bell hooks's, Beyoncé's, and Lady Gaga's naming practices and reworked it to fit a pop culture audience, which eventually meant taking out my bell hooks sections and expanding the other two.

With that said, it's important to get multiple perspectives on your ideas both before and during the writing process. Most academic journals have a "blind" peer-review process, which means that readers don't know your name or necessarily the background of your work—they quite literally judge you for your writing. Regardless, journal editors come from all different scholarly backgrounds, so you have no idea how any one person might perceive your work. The best way to practice this is to get at least a handful of different people to read your work *prior to* submitting it to a journal. This helps you both to work through potential gaps in your research you might not realize and to gain a sense of how your work might be interpreted. For instance, in the process of having different people read my drafts, I learned that not many readers knew about Beyoncé's many alter egos and personas because few had written about them in the past.

Finally, I learned that using K/W/L and starting with what I knew first as my interests—issues of naming, identity, Beyoncé, and Lady Gaga—led to both one of my favorite projects I've ever worked on and to publication in a major journal. And that's pretty magical.

9

BELIEVE IN YOURSELF AND IN YOUR ABILITY TO JOIN PUBLIC AND SCHOLARLY CONVERSATIONS

Heidi A. McKee

Believe in yourself and in your right—and imperative—to join public and scholarly conversations; believe in the importance of those conversations; and seek the mentors who believe in you.

Thinking about and then actually preparing conference presentations and publications for academic and public audiences can feel scary. Doubts are common, particularly for those diving in for the first time: what right do I have to speak? I don't know enough, my thinking on the topic is still developing, I don't feel confident, I don't know what to say or even how to say it, and so on. You may find this hard to believe when you look at the CVs, read the published articles, and attend conference presentations of experienced professionals, but everyone starting out has felt to some degree and at various times nervous and doubtful.

So how do you find the courage and wherewithal to take that first plunge as well as the perseverance to keep learning and growing, even, at times, in the face of rejection? Quite simply, you need to believe in yourself.

What you do in rhetoric and writing studies is important. The teaching, research, and thinking that you are doing, the participants' stories you hear (contemporary and from the archives), the pedagogical approaches you develop, the theoretical insights you discover, the ideas, programs, and people for which you advocate are significant. Just as studies have shown that the teams with the most diversity and the most voices participating come to the best decisions, so too does our broad field of rhetoric and writing and our many subfields and the broader public society benefit from your participation in scholarly conversations.

But saying believe in yourself and then actually feeling and acting on that belief can be daunting. If you wait until you never have a doubt or worry—if you wait until that article manuscript or book chapter is

DOI: 10.7330/9781607328834.c009

perfect—you will, quite simply, never join those conversations. No presentation or publication is ever perfect or ever enough. There is *always* more that could have been said or researched.

Embracing that recognition is freeing, enabling you to say, in a sense: here's what I'm looking at, here's where my thinking is at this point on this topic, here are some holes that I know are there and where I personally and we as a field need further research, but let me share what I've found so far. That being said, you do need to do your homework and situate your thinking and research in the field and you do want to tailor your communications to the venue and genre in which you seek to communicate—you don't want to plunge in blind—but you will never know all there is to know on a subject.

To support you in your work, be sure to seek out and find people who believe in you—in both personal and professional circumstances. You need people in your life who simultaneously say you can do this while also challenging you to change and grow. You may find these people within your immediate program, but you also can find them in broader communities, which is why it is so helpful—necessary even—to attend regional and national conferences, to join workshops and special interest groups, and to lurk and participate in listserv and social media forums in your areas of interest. Through connecting with and interacting with others, through following and studying the conversations you seek to join, you will simultaneously learn the conversations of your field and subfields and build your confidence in your ability to enter those conversations.

Publishing my first article was a process that began, though I didn't know it at the time, in my first semester of doctoral study. In my first semester at the University of Massachusetts–Amherst, I was daunted by the idea of being an academic. Teaching I understood and felt confident in, but research and publishing? That was a different story. To me, the whole world of publishing seemed, well, otherworldly. How could I, just a schoolteacher from Wyoming with, at that point, only one fully completed graduate seminar directly in rhetoric and writing studies, ever know enough to join such conversations?

Importantly in that first year, in all of the graduate courses I took, the professors—Anne Herrington, Charlie Moran, and Jean Nienkamp—spent class time not just talking about the scholarship we were reading but also analyzing how the scholarship was written and delivered. For our semester seminar papers we were always asked to research and then pick a specific journal and audience to which we were writing. This opportunity to write to a "real-world" audience within the much less daunting and scary space of a seminar was hugely helpful because, as we all know when teaching our students but sometimes forget in our own academic writing, it's hard to write well if you don't know to whom you're writing and in what context.

My first article arose too out of a fortuitous scaffolding of my thinking and research. I now follow this scaffolding process with more intention for all of my projects, but at the time I sort of fell into it. In my first semester of a contemporary rhetoric seminar, I wrote about the rhetorics of online communication across difference, focusing on a textual analysis of the posts students wrote in an online discussion forum. The next semester in a research methods class I interviewed the most frequent participants in that discussion, students at different institutions and from diverse racial and ethnic backgrounds. At this point I was just researching questions of interest with no focused intention on publishing.

Then that summer of 2001 I attended CIWIC, a workshop series hosted by Michigan Tech. One evening at one of the workshop gatherings, I talked with Cindy Selfe about my research into online discussions and the important insights students shared with me. She said, "That sounds great; you should submit a manuscript to *Computers and Composition*" (the journal she coedited with Gail Hawisher). I said that I'd received great feedback from UMass faculty on my seminar paper, but I wasn't sure if what I was working on was really article material. Cindy, in her generous way that serves as a model for us all, invited me to send her the manuscript. She called it a *manuscript* while I still thought of it as a *seminar paper*, but that very change of wording was empowering in and of itself. So I sent her my manuscript, and she read it, providing two single-spaced pages of feedback and encouragement.

Upon receiving that feedback, I dived into the manuscript and revised it. I knew I still didn't know enough and I had a lot of doubts about my ability to actually produce an article, but what fueled me to keep trying was the support of my faculty mentors and my firm belief in the importance of sharing the voices and perspectives of the students whom I interviewed. I *never* had doubts about the value of their words and perspectives. So I sent the manuscript off to *Computers and Composition*. Several months later I received a request to "revise and resubmit." Building from the reviewers' useful and, at times, challenging feedback and from feedback from colleagues at conferences where I presented on the topic, I revised the essay yet again, sent it in, and it was accepted (McKee 2002).

I learned so much in the process of writing that article—not just about the issues discussed and about methods and methodologies for conducting qualitative research—but also about the publishing process. I realized that the publishing process is not about you're in or you're not, you've got it or you don't, but rather about an ongoing opportunity to learn and grow and to join conversations. I learned how larger-scale projects such as a journal articles develop over time and often build from many scaffolded interactions. I now actively seek out that scaffolding so as to engage in a rich, interactive development process.

I also am so grateful to the faculty mentors who believed in me and who helped me foster belief in myself. Their invitations to share, to present, to write were and are tremendously important. In addition to providing in-class and out-of-class mentorship for students, I frequently coauthor and co-present with graduate and undergraduate students because I believe I have so much to learn from them. We all have so much to learn from each other, and after all that's what scholarly publications and presentations are about: learning from each other.

Please know if you are new to the field or uncertain of your place in the field how much your perspective matters and is and will be valued. In all of your work—teaching, research, administration, community partnerships, and so on—aim to share what you're doing with others, through conference presentations and through publication. Believe in the quality and importance of the work you are doing and believe in your right and ability to participate in community conversations. And, as you go forward in your careers, always aim to help others develop, foster, and sustain belief in themselves.

REFERENCE

McKee, Heidi. 2002. "'Your Views Showed True Ignorance!!' (Mis)Communication in an Online Interracial Discussion Forum." *Computers and Composition* 19:411–34.

10
REFINE YOUR RHETORICAL EXIGENCE

Naomi Silver

There is a vitality, a life force, an energy, a quickening that is translat-
ed through you into action, and because there is only one of you in all
of time, this expression is unique. And if you block it, it will never exist
through any other medium and it will be lost. The world will not have
it. It is not your business to determine how good it is nor how valuable
nor how it compares with other expressions. It is your business to keep it
yours clearly and directly, to keep the channel open.

—Martha Graham

If you're at all like me, when you're beginning a new project—especially
a project that may be interdisciplinary, intermedial, multimodal, mul-
tigenre, and therefore potentially risky within conventional academic
frameworks—you will be regularly beset by self-sabotaging, paralyzing
questions: Who will read this? Why does it matter? Isn't it too idiosyncratic, too personal? Do I even know enough to compose it? Am I really
just an intellectual dilettante?

However, with just a little tweaking, these initially disempowering
questions can be revised and reframed as concrete, purpose-focusing
prompts to help you refine your rhetorical exigence:

- ~~Who will read this?~~ → Who is my audience? Does this work perhaps
  invoke new audiences that first need to be imagined and given shape?
  How can I best name them and invite them into the composition?
- ~~Why does it matter?~~ → What is my purpose? What commitments are
  spurring me to do this work, and to do it in this particular way? What
  would be lost by not doing it in this way?
- ~~Isn't it too idiosyncratic, too personal?~~ → What are my genres? What
  are my key terms? In what voice am I composing? How can I align my
  work with existing genres in order to make it more recognizable to
  diverse readers?
- ~~Do I even know enough to compose it?~~ → Who am I in conversation
  with? What research do I need to do to enter these conversations?
  How can I draw links to existing bodies of work?

DOI: 10.7330/9781607328834.c010

- ~~Am I really just an intellectual dilettante?~~ → What is my context? What connections can I create? With whom do I need to consult or collaborate to approach this work ethically and nonappropriatively?

These revised questions are fresh in my mind today as I push myself through the early stages of a new project.

I recently started working on a multimodal and multimedia project that aims to bring together modern dance composition and performance practices with embodied theories in writing studies. This project grew out of my desire to respond to the killing of Michael Brown and other Black men and boys at the hands of American police officers, and to participate in the protest rhetorics that quickly developed to resist and intervene in those events. This desire crystallized for me in the days following the release of the Ferguson grand jury testimony that failed to convict the police officer who shot Michael Brown. For this trial, sixty-two witnesses were interviewed over three months, some of them multiple times, yet in the end, the grand jury did not believe it had sufficient clarity on the events of that afternoon—and particularly the physical actions of Michael Brown himself—to convict Darren Wilson of any wrongdoing. This failure denotes a problem not only of meaning in words, but of meaning in bodies—of how we read and understand the movements of bodies, our own and other people's, and how we compose and dispose our bodies to move. In response, I felt highly motivated to compose not a position paper, an academic argument, or a manifesto in words, but a screendance composed in mobile bodies and moving images, and enacting and annotating the conflicting movements described by the witnesses. These modes (and this medium) seemed to me to constitute the best means of getting at the questions, problems, and arguments the events raised for me.

But I quickly ran into roadblocks. Namely: I hadn't choreographed a dance in a couple of decades; I work in a writing program and writing center, not a dance program; I'd never planned and shot a film; and I had only minimal experience editing digital video. Those are issues of medium and form. There is also the broader issue of message: I'm a white woman who wants to make a dance about the death of a young Black man. Given the complex range of responses by Black viewers to some depictions of Michael Brown's death by white artists, I needed to determine if I have the right to tell any part of this story, and if so, how I can tell it in a way that creates connections and listens rather than appearing to claim ownership and risk alienating audiences I wish to engage.

Based on these thoughts and experiences, once you find your rhetorical exigency, resituating and resolving the questions above, there are some further ways to turn believing into doing.

Seek the expertise you need. For me that meant, first, auditing a screendance class co-taught at my university by a filmmaker and a choreographer to learn more about the form and get hands-on experience filming dance and editing digital video. It also meant taking some local dance classes at my university and in my community, and seeking out a more intensive dance-making experience via a summer institute offered by the company Dance Exchange in Washington, DC. Because Dance Exchange is committed to community engagement and social justice work, connecting with this organization helped me with my next step in the process as well.

Find collaborators who can ask you hard questions and help you do the work appropriately/nonappropriatively. Through Dance Exchange, I had the opportunity to interview choreographers engaged in social justice issues about their processes and their commitments. I also had the opportunity to preview my project to a community explicitly engaged in questions of ethics and ownership in art-making, and which included several African American dance-makers and artists who were generous with their questions and feedback (both critical and supportive) regarding my project. One important thing I learned from these conversations is that I cannot make this dance alone. So I have been making connections with choreographers in my own community whose work aligns with my project idea, and I'm conversing with potential collaborators to begin the actual work of composing a dance, and then a screendance.

Present early versions of the work. Although you may not feel ready, take small steps in sharing your composition and seeking feedback. Composing is learning, of course, and the opportunities I've had to present small pieces of the work in conferences and workshops have helped me to crystallize my ideas and test them out in a low-stakes way—even if it was nerve-wracking at the time.

Be patient. Pulling a new project together always takes time, but especially when it requires gaining new expertise and making new connections. The idea for this project dates back to December 2014, and it is still very much in process. This time has been crucial to lay the groundwork and do due diligence, and without it the project would not be able to exist, much less move forward.

Believing in your unconventional idea takes commitment and sweat equity. It is a process full of emotional and conceptual discomfort and possible risk. It means asking hard questions, but posing them productively and generatively/generously. Failing to believe in your idea is certainly worse: the attempt to justify it, to rein it into more clearly accepted forms leads us to risk losing sight of the genuine interest, the driving question, the urgent problem that gave rise to the idea in the first place.

11

BE A CONTENT STRATEGIST

Michael J. Faris

Develop content management strategies to keep your project organized. Content management practices are *distributed memory* practices, help-ing you to retrieve files, spend less time jogging your memory about a project, and collaborate more effectively with others. Depending on the project, an academic writer can be managing hundreds, if not thousands, of digital files. We revise drafts frequently, often resulting in multiple versions of files; when we collaborate, managing those files and versions can be even more difficult. It is important to develop strategies for content management, including file management.

For instance, **develop strategies for managing your secondary sources**, especially journal articles, and your notes and annotations. Consider using software like Zotero (www.zotero.org/), which allows you to orga-nize articles, search for keywords or authors, find annotations, export citations, and share your libraries or sync them across devices. I'd suggest that you immediately rename, organize, and run optical char-acter recognition (or OCR) on PDFs as soon as you download or scan them: finding an article months after you downloaded it can be time-consuming, especially if it was saved as a page image file and thus is not searchable and winds up buried in your downloads folder among other nonsearchable files with useless names developed by databases.

Develop strategies for managing your primary sources and data, whether you are working on a physical archival project, an empirical study, a digital research project, or something else. You might create a database that includes useful information about your sources, including where you retrieved them, notes about them, copyright information if appli-cable, and so forth. Develop a file-naming schema and folder structure that allows you to find materials easily: name files semantically, using all lowercase and no spaces, especially if you are creating a scholarly

DOI: 10.7330/9781607328834.c011

webtext. If your project involves digital media, keep the originals of files at the highest quality possible (e.g., a high-resolution TIFF file or native Photoshop/PSD file) and edit copies of these files (e.g., as screen-friendly, small-size JPGs or PNGs). This way, if you edit a file, you don't wind up losing your original if you make a mistake. If you are working with online sources, use a bookmarking service to assist you in retrieving those sources. Zotero can work for this, as can social bookmarking sites like Diigo (www.diigo.com/), which allow you to bookmark, tag, and annotate sites.

Develop strategies for versioning. Name your files semantically (*draft. docx* and *notes on stuff.docx* are not very useful). Create a versioning schema and add dates to file names (because you might open a file and change its save date, relying on "last modified" isn't always reliable). You might name files something like *project name date*. Version your project in case you delete work that you later want to refer to or decide you want to use—rather than it being lost, it's now in an older version. Importantly, *back up all your files*, either on a backup hard drive (typically USB and relatively inexpensive), or perhaps with a cloud service.

If you are collaborating, **discuss and develop shared strategies for workflows, file management, and writing environments**. Writers bring their own habits and practices to new projects, which can lead to conflicting practices, files spread over a variety of platforms and services, issues around versioning, and lost or misplaced files. Discuss how you want to name files, where you want to share files, what platform you want to write in (e.g., simultaneously write in Google Drive, share a folder on Dropbox), and how you plan to collaboratively write (e.g., writing sections individually, passing a file back and forth, engaging in concurrent writing sessions).

How I came to love content management: my interest in content management comes from my experiences with managing large projects, discussions with students concerned about managing the journal articles they read, and experiences collaborating with colleagues across the country. In graduate school, I rarely received explicit advice about managing projects and content. I began to learn through osmosis as I collaborated with my advisor, Stuart Selber: I picked up on how he named files with version numbers, dates, and his initials at the end to signify the version of the piece, the date on which it was last revised, and that he had been the most recent writer in the file.

But I had not yet developed my own content management strategies for my own projects. As I worked on my dissertation, I spent quite a bit of time searching for files on my computer, figuring out which version of a chapter was the most recent, and reretrieving online sources I was drawing from. This was especially true as I returned to chapters after months of being on the job market. More recently, I've been working with social network visualization software and discovered that because I didn't name versions of visualizations in useful ways, I couldn't remember which version had the most accurate and up-to-date social network data.

My graduate students are obsessed with content management regarding their scholarly sources. A few years ago, doctoral students in my publications management class asked about managing all the journal articles they were reading. Knowing they couldn't possibly remember everything they read when they turned to preparing for exams and their dissertations, they were rightly concerned about how to organize articles and their notes and annotations. We discussed tools like Zotero, but I suggested that, while their concerns were valid and important, they were considering their academic research too narrowly by focusing solely on journal articles and not content management more broadly. I was delighted a few months later when I talked to one of these students who is doing an archival project for her dissertation: she had developed a spreadsheet for all of her archival resources that included name, date, and specific location of archival documents as well as notes about the content of the documents and why they were useful to her project. This resource will allow her to more easily find resources she needs to spend more time with when she returns to the archives and to jog (and organize) her memory about the archive as she writes her dissertation.

I've also run into problems while collaborating on projects with colleagues. Some projects have run quite smoothly: one of my coauthors and I shared a Dropbox folder with subfolders for our IRB materials, older versions of our draft, interview transcripts, coding files, secondary research, and so forth. However, others are rougher: for another project, some collaborators shared individual Google Drive files with me while others shared Dropbox folders. The result of these haphazard sharing practices is that I have multiple unorganized Google Drive files that are difficult to find quickly in my "shared with me" folder, and I have multiple folders in my Dropbox for this project.

I've come to start thinking of my projects as not simply my own, where idiosyncratic file management might be okay, even if frustrating. Instead, I've started thinking of my project management strategies in a perhaps rather macabre way: if I died tomorrow, could someone pick up my project—understand where files are located, what files are what, and where I'm at in the project—and, after some work, continue the project? Of course, this imagined scenario ignores the intellectual work that isn't archived in computer files (that is, what's in my head), but it does help me in considering how I name and organize files—and it's led to less frustration when I receive feedback from an editor and need to revise many months after I last touched a project. In this way, content management serves as distributed memory for my projects.

12
STORYBOARD YOUR WRITING PROJECTS

Chris M. Anson

This method of visualizing the progress of multiple writing projects by sequencing activities can improve productivity. Project storyboarding can take several forms, both physical and digital.

Graduate students and seasoned scholars alike often find themselves working on multiple projects simultaneously: an upcoming conference talk, a paper for a seminar, a grant proposal, background research and note-taking on a topic of interest, some loose ideas that aspire to turn into an article for submission to a journal. Swirling around these projects are myriad responsibilities, such as teaching, mentoring students and colleagues, participating in committees or in administrative work, and contributing to ad hoc groups or other service responsibilities. Unless a scholarly project carries its own reminders and looming deadlines, such as a conference paper, it can disappear from view for weeks or months at a time, until it loses its currency or no longer inspires you to pursue it.

A "storyboard" is a graphic representation of your writing projects. Technically, the term refers to a series of drawings or sketches, with annotations and/or dialogue, that provides the outline for a film or TV production. I use the term more loosely here to refer horizontally to the progress status of a single project, such as an article, and vertically to represent all such projects at their various stages of development. To take a simple example, table 12.1 shows two of my writing projects, the first one showing the current status of this very chapter for *Explanation Points*, and the other one referring to a journal article nearing publication.

Storyboarding your projects serves two important purposes: first, it provides a constant reminder of where each project stands in its development. When a project is "out of sight," it's also usually "out of mind." For this reason, it's important to make sure that the storyboard, in whatever form, is always in plain view. Second, storyboarding can help

DOI: 10.7330/9781607328834.c012

Table 12.1. Sample project storyboard

September	October	December	January (due)	?	?	
invitation for *EP*	proposal	under development	submitted	revisions	publication	

February	August	September	November	January	?	?
data analysis	full MS	submit to *AW*	revise and resubmit	resubmit	decision	publication

you to allocate time to your writing projects in ways that can bolster productivity and yield success. When deadlines are imposed on you, the storyboard keeps track of them. When you impose deadlines on yourself, you'll more easily dedicate time during your day or week to work on them, moving the pieces on your storyboard forward in both time and space.

There is no "right way" to create a project storyboard. Some people organize activities by months of the year. Some list the stages of each project and annotate them with due dates or aspirational deadlines. Some track the progress of projects using various conceptual mapping techniques. Some use more sophisticated project management strategies in which subcategories of work on a project are digitally linked behind the main items on the storyboard. The goal is to find a way to organize your work with some final outcomes, usually publication, and to use that organizational chart to determine the way you allocate your time.

* * *

In 1984, I had just finished my PhD and was a few months into my first position as an assistant professor. The chair of my department set up regular meetings to talk about progress on my research and publication agenda. These helpful meetings were designed to provide formative feedback and mentoring in anticipation of my eventual review for promotion and tenure. To prepare for the first meeting, I sketched out a simple chart of my work, with a few progress notes and self-imposed deadlines. In a box, I wrote the title of a conference paper I had given a month earlier and drew an arrow to the next box, "revising for submission," and then a third box, "submit to *M/MLA*" (a journal published by the Midwest affiliate of the Modern Language Association). Below that, I had another box with the title of a revised chapter of my dissertation, then an arrow to the next box that said, "received runner-up status for NCTE Promising Researcher Award," then an arrow to a third box with "submitted to *Written Communication*." (That submission was eventually turned down, but then I put the manuscript title into a new box with "revising," and eventually it saw light as an article in a different journal.) There were two or three further chains of boxes and arrows representing the status of other projects.

When I shared this sketch of my projects with my department chair, he expressed surprise and admiration. He'd never seen anything like it. Encouraged by his positive response, I took what I'd done, which was mainly for purposes of showing him my scholarly activity, and turned it into an ongoing (now lifelong) organizational and motivational writing and publishing strategy.

After I had arrived at my present institution as a tenured full professor, I was working with an energetic, newly hired junior scholar who constantly asked me questions about how she could be productive. I shared my storyboarding strategy with her, which I was now doing digitally and leaving as an open document on my computer. But she wanted something more physical and present, so she created her storyboard on a whiteboard and hung it on the wall of her office. Figure 12.1 is a recent sample of this now highly productive (full professor's) "project board."

Notice her categories: she names each project and specifies the intended outlet (a journal or press), then indicates the current status of the project and its timeline. The last column includes the "action item" currently needed and its date or date of completion. The whiteboard allows her to easily revise the items and their dates as projects are completed, stall, or get rerouted.

A few years ago, I was visiting a university to conduct a program review, and I happened to pass by the office of a newly hired faculty member who had been a graduate student in our doctoral program and an advisee of my storyboarding colleague. Delighted to see her, I poked my head in and we talked for a few minutes. As I glanced around her pleasantly appointed office, I noticed a piece of butcher paper taped above her desk that had titles and arrows and dates on it. It turned out that my colleague had passed on the strategy and now her former graduate student was using it to further her own productivity.

A few months later, I shared this anecdote with my son, who was then finishing his PhD in political science and wanted advice about completing his dissertation. Now a second-year assistant professor at a research-extensive university, he visited us recently. When I asked him how he was doing on his research and publication projects, he showed me the storyboard he'd created on his laptop. From one of his senior (and highly productive) colleagues, he'd also learned a publication mantra, "two-two-two," which he'd incorporated into his storyboard

Figure 12.1. Project board

chart. "Two-two-two," he explained, "means that you always have at least two projects under development (such as a conference talk, a grant generating initial data, or an idea you're actively researching), two projects in the drafting stage, and two projects submitted for publication." This "production cycling" of documents, he said, guarantees that you pursue your writing and publication trajectory without interferences or procrastination. In his digital version, he color-codes the cells of his storyboard: purple for "under development," orange for "in (written) production," blue for "under review," and green for "published." When something isn't published, it gets turned orange, and the cycle continues.

Of course, whatever its name, this kind of mapping is nothing new. Tracking the flow of activity has been a staple of project management across a wide range of disciplines and industries for a very long time. But I'm always surprised to find that many members of our field—themselves interested in or studying writing practices—are unfamiliar with or don't use such strategies in their own work, especially at early stages of their careers.

Try it, then, and pass it on.

13

INVENTION AND ARRANGEMENT WHILE DRIVING
Writing for the Commute

Jim Ridolfo

When I transitioned from graduate student to faculty in the fall of 2009, I also transitioned into a commuter relationship between Cincinnati, Ohio, and Lexington, Kentucky. In the fall of 2009, Janice Fernheimer, my future wife, left Rensselaer Polytechnic University and accepted a job at the University of Kentucky in Lexington. Together, we moved to Lexington in the summer of 2010, and I began to drive from Lexington to Cincinnati. In that first fall of commuting, I wasn't able to do much research writing. The strategies that I had developed for writing and research in graduate school were not completely compatible for a long-distance commute combined with a new tenure-track job. I knew within a few weeks that I needed to develop new routines, and began to keep a calendar of my work so I could plan out what I needed to get done to stay on the tenure schedule. By winter break I hadn't accomplished much beyond driving, teaching courses, and doing some service work.

In graduate school at Michigan State University, seminars and conversations with faculty and colleagues were prompts for invention. Ideas sometimes happened late at night or early in the day, and I learned to grab a pen or computer and quickly make a note to myself. I'd pile pieces of paper on the side of my desk at work and spend the days I wasn't teaching going through them. As a commuting faculty member, my work office was out of range on the days I didn't teach or need to go in for a service-related duty. I didn't have the same frequency of conversations with faculty or graduate students. I needed to adapt means and moments of invention—and even how I recorded and processed my ideas.

I spent most of the winter break that first tenure-track year trying to finish a draft of an article, but found myself writing in circles under the compressed three-week timeline that break imposed. I had the three

DOI: 10.7330/9781607328834.c013

weeks to write, but I hadn't worked through the ideas and field conversations well enough to be productive when I finally put hand to keyboard. When classes—and my commute—resumed in January, I resolved to find another way to do my work, one that would be as compatible as possible with the two and a half to four hours I "lost" every day in the car. As I drove up to Cincinnati one day and made lists of all the things I needed to do later in the day, mentally went over my lesson plans, and tried to remember what I would do the next day, useful ideas about the article I had been unsuccessfully working on popped into my head. I pulled over to the side of the road and tried to send myself an email, but I couldn't get cell service. Instead, I recorded a voice memo on my phone.

Voice memos changed how I processed my research. For the next three years and even today, whenever I was traveling I treated those moments as opportunities for invention and future arrangement. Most recently, I've created a thread of voice memos that have helped me to conceptualize a recent project on #rhetops that I am currently working on with Bill Hart-Davidson. These memos—between nineteen seconds and almost eighteen minutes long—help me capture what I think might be a key conceptual thought or idea for the project.

During my morning Lexington to Cincinnati commute back in 2010–2013, I would think through texts I had read or arguments I was trying to make and record myself talking in as short and concise a summary as possible. These transcriptions typically resembled the following: "Okay, so I am thinking about —— and how it relates to —— and this case example keeps coming up in my head. Tonight I need to sit down and write about these things for twenty minutes. Just twenty minutes on this."

By 7:00 or 9:00 that night, I would listen again to the voice memos and instructions that I had recorded for myself. In the later hours of the day, I'd try to follow my morning advice as best I could, keeping track of progress on a Google Calendar I maintained. On the calendar, I'd plan the next few months' worth of work in gold colors, and then later check back to see if I had accomplished what I thought I would be able to finish. I still make use of this technique today.

Looking back on 2014 from 2015, figure 13.1 shows what I had done for the first half of the year. The use of mapping morning invention and voice memos, engaging in evening transcription and writing, planning my work a few months out, and then later reflecting on what I had accomplished or not accomplished and why, helped me to stay organized and focus on specific writing and research tasks. By keeping track of how I invent and arrange my time using the combination of voice

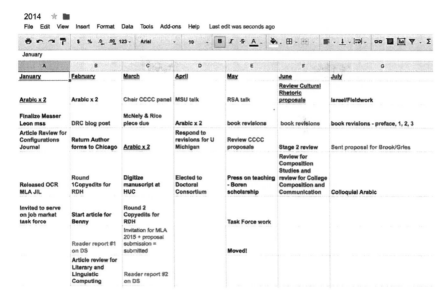

January	February	March	April	May	June	July
Arabic x 2	Arabic x 2	Chair CCCC panel	MSU talk	RSA talk	Review Cultural Rhetoric proposals	Israel/Fieldwork
Finalize Messer Leon mss	DRC blog post	McNely & Rice piece due	Arabic x 2	book revisions	book revisions	book revisions - preface, 1, 2, 3
Article Review for Configurations Journal	Return Author forms to Chicago	Arabic x 2	Respond to revisions for U Michigan	Review CCCC proposals	Stage 2 review	Sent proposal for Brook/Gries
Released OCR MLA JIL	Round 1Copyedits for RDH	Digitize manuscript at HUC	Elected to Doctoral Consortium	Press on teaching - Boren scholarship	Review for Composition Studies and review for College Composition and Communication	Colloquial Arabic
Invited to serve on job market task force	Start article for Benny	Round 2 Copyedits for RDH		Task Force work		
		Invitation for MLA 2015 + proposal submission = submitted				
	Reader report #1 on DS			Moved!		
	Article review for Literary and Linguistic Computing	Reader report #2 on DS				

Figure 13.1. 2014 work calendar as reflected on in January 2015

memos to myself and Google Calendar's version control, I was able to see if I was making slow and steady progress to the larger research objectives my job required.

This invention and arrangement for the commute, as I came to call this work, has stayed with me today and I still make use of these practices. My use of Google Calendar to project/reflect on my work and where my time is going remains the same, and I still use voice memos to help capture what I think might be a critical conceptual connection when it comes to the forefront of my mind. Since becoming a parent, new time constraints have emerged. I've once again returned to voice memos as a way to hold onto ideas as I invent and make connections.

14

CHIP AWAY

Cruz Medina

Chip away at scholarly projects by writing in small segments of time. Steal ten to fifteen minutes before a meeting or after class and make small progress while keeping ideas on the project fresh in your mind.

During my first year at Santa Clara as a postdoc, I had the chance to sit down at a roundtable discussion with the literary scholar Terry Eagleton. Eagleton is the author of more than forty books, including his well-known *How to Read Literature.* After he answered questions about Marxism that included a response about "sports as the new opiate of the masses," I asked him about his writing habits. His advice was brilliant, though simple. He said that he wrote in short periods of time between other things he had to do: "Fifteen minutes here, fifteen minutes there." I think he said that he could even write as he was being driven around. His prolific number of books attests to the success of this practice of chipping away at longer projects.

At the time, I was hard at work drafting my monograph. Because I was a postdoc, my teaching load was a mere one class per quarter; however, I was balancing my teaching with caring for my son on the days I did not teach. Writing for fifteen to twenty minutes relieved the pressure of feeling the need to complete something substantial. There were often fifteen- or twenty-minute chunks of time before classes, between department meetings, or after student conferences. I learned to be more productive in moments that had previously been periods lost to procrastination. Getting a bit of writing in here and there helped me maintain a certain consistency that I needed to keep my thinking fresh about my book, allowing concepts and relationships among chapters to evolve as I continually revisited them.

Even before I spoke with Eagleton, I found that I, like a lot of new parents, could write only during those short periods when my children napped. During the first winter break after the birth of my older son William, I traveled with my spouse for her work to Denver from Tucson.

DOI: 10.7330/9781607328834.c014

William napped regularly, sleeping every hour after every two hours awake, so I was able to use that time to respond to a call for proposals on the special issue of *College Composition and Communication*. The theme was "on the profession" and it was the first that included personal vignettes. As much as I wanted to nap while my three-month-old son napped, I realized that my only chance to write would be to steal that time while he slept. I began drafting in bursts of ideas during his first nap. I revised during the following naps. Before long, I had a draft that I sent to a trusted reader (Jaime Armin Mejía) for feedback. This resulted in the publication of my vignette "The Family Profession."

Chipping is something that a lot of new parent–scholars no doubt have to do, but it's a strategy that is applicable to not just a napping schedule but also a tenure clock.

Writing this piece about chipping was useful as I promised chapters of works in progress to different writing groups, fielded feedback from a journal submission, and followed the kind suggestions of the editors. Chipping works because you can open a document even as you tell yourself, "I really ought to be going because I only have a minute . . ."

* * *

As academics, we are asked to multitask across responsibilities divided among teaching, research, and service, with both service and teaching commitments ever encroaching on time to read, collect data, and write. By writing in short segments of ten, fifteen, or twenty minutes—even if prefaced by, "I ought to be going . . ."—you continue to think about your projects and make incremental progress that builds momentum as you become more accustomed to writing at different times. This negates feeling as though you need to meet impossible daily word or page counts.

Waiting until you have a block of multiple hours can delay starting, and keep you from resuming and revisiting projects in the works. If you tell yourself that you are going to open a piece of writing only for fifteen minutes, then you feel accomplished whether you close it after the initial fifteen or find yourself unexpectedly writing for much longer. Chipping away at a piece lowers the bar for what you expect to produce during a given session while keeping the goal of writing in mind.

You will always have multiple projects going, so sometimes moving from one to another after a small amount of progress can still be an effective use of time. Even short writing sessions can lower stress about a looming project and avoid procrastination.

Working in this way continues to ensure that there are always projects in the scholarship pipeline, an expectation for job applicants as well as promotion and tenure cases.

15

FREQUENTLY ASKED QUESTIONS (FAQs) ABOUT THE RESEARCH HOUR

Ellen Barton

What is the research hour?

The research writing hour is the one hour of the day when you are sitting at your desk writing up, writing through, or writing with your research.

Hint: It often takes the other twenty-three hours in the day to achieve the one research hour.

Does the research hour have to be of high quality?

No! The research hour is just being with your research at your desk.

Pretty soon you'll fix a sentence here, write a footnote there, add a reference now and then to the works cited, revise a paragraph somewhere else, outline the next section, and. It will add up to steady progress on your research—guaranteed!

Hint: Do not overload the research hour with other demands or expectations (e.g., word count, number of paragraphs, number of pages, number of sections in a week/month/year). The research hour is all about discipline, not structure.

Why should I use the research hour system?

Because it overcomes the primary cause of academic writer's block—starting and stopping your research. Nothing feels worse than stopping your research for a period of time, even a week, and few things are emotionally harder than starting it up again.

With the research hour, you may gradually find yourself on a more even emotional keel with respect to your writing. Writing anxiety and writing agony will be held at bay and gradually lessen their stressful presence in your productivity.

Consider forming a research hour group if you find you better hold yourself to a practice if you're participating in an activity with a group—and accountable to others.

DOI: 10.7330/9781607328834.c015

What if (oh, no!) I don't do a research hour on a given day?

Not to worry. You can make up research hours in the course of the week. You can also front-load research hours in a week if you know you won't be able to do a research hour on a particular day (administrators often have to juggle the research hours in any given week).

Hint: If you go a week without research hours, though, then something's up. You can attend to it either by thinking it through/talking to your research hour colleagues or, more simply, by starting the research hour anew the next week. A spotty week's performance is often a vestige of the conversion to the research hour system, which has to be practiced and learned. It doesn't become a work process immediately! Give yourself a few months with the research hour and that procrastination and paralysis may end.

How many research hours do I have to do every week?

Just one hour, five days a week. Don't worry that five hours couldn't possibly get you on track or back on track. The time adds up.

Hint: Again, do not be tempted to be unrealistic with setting the research hours/week schedule, which is a ticket back to writer's block. One hour is the commitment. Any extra hours of research on any given day are gravy, to be celebrated, perhaps with a post on Facebook. Those extra hours will emerge organically by using the research hour system as the basis for your work.

When should I do the research hour?

For me, the research hour works best as the first thing I do in the morning after a minimal (but necessary) amount of coffee, email, and a bit of news from the internet. If, however, you're more of an evening worker, see if you can find and protect an hour at the end of every work day.

Hint: If you can and if you're a morning worker, do the research hour in your bathrobe before you shower or leave the house. After you leave the house, you sort of belong to the world, even if you're just going to the gym, and it's harder to achieve your research hour.

What if I can't do my research hour in the morning?

You may need to get up earlier, but it's worth it. Night owls may need to stay up an hour later. Administrators can use their lunch hour.

Hint: If I couldn't do my research hour first thing in the morning at home, then I'd stop for an hour in the library or a coffeehouse or even the student center before going in to the office/department. I'd advise scheduling your research hour in your calendar each day; writing it down helps to protect it and makes it a more tangible thing.

What about weekends and vacations?
This depends. During the term, sometimes you have to use the weekend to achieve your five hours for the week. But vacations are necessary.

Hint: Don't overdo vacation exceptions, though. You'll know if you are.

Should I keep track of the research hours in a week?
Yes! It's very motivating to cross out the research hour on your to-do list or to enter it on your calendar.

Hint: I use my digital calendar, but I've heard that other people use a spreadsheet, which is a good idea, too.

Can I read the literature during the research hour?
Best not to. The research hour is a *writing* hour. If you have to consult your research notes or read an abstract, that's okay. But if you're reading during the research hour, it should be in the service of writing a sentence in your literature review or your discussion section.

Hint: Don't be afraid to start writing before you've "finished" reading the literature. Most academics are writing something all the time—a conference abstract, presentation slides, an article, a chapter, a book. Reading can be procrastination, so the research hour is designed for the writing part of your research.

What if I can only write if I have a block of uninterrupted time/I write best under a deadline/I don't think an hour is enough?
Let me repeat—an hour is enough to keep your research going throughout your career.

Hint: Trust me on this one.

Hint: You can still use these long session strategies! Just use the research hour, too, as a short session to ensure short-term progress, and then you enjoy those extra hours as they happen, whether by schedule, deadline, or any other means.

What are the benefits of the research hour?
Primarily, academic peace, happiness, and success. As I said, the research hour is mainly to keep your research going. You'll find, though, that the research hour will be the basis for more research on a daily, weekly, monthly, and yearly basis. Your mind will be thinking about

your research in a productive way, not in an anxious way. Sentences will come to mind, reorganizations in revisions will become clear, titles will become snappier, and so on.

Hint: Carry a research hour notebook or have a document available on your tablet for these great words and ideas that will come throughout the day. I can't seem to manage that good practice, so I tax my memory: I say to myself, "I know I thought of this sentence yesterday—what was it?" It will come back to you.

Are there any testimonials for the research hour?
My own! Humblebrag: I have written over seventy-five publications as of last count, one for each year of my age. And fifty-eight of those articles were based upon the research hour system, which I figured out around the time I became an associate professor.

Hint: Don't wait as long as I did to start the research hour!

Are there any independent testimonials for the research hour?
Yes! A quote from a colleague: "Ellen Barton suggested the research hour to me when I was struggling to balance research, teaching, and a new job as associate chair of a large department. What sold me was the program's very modesty; anyone, even an overworked administrator buried in spreadsheets and student complaints, can scrounge up an hour. Yet as the hours pile up, eventually so do the pages–and before long, hundreds of them. I wouldn't have written my second book without this method."

And another! A quote from a former graduate student: "The research hour saved my life as a struggling, procrastinating, tormented graduate student. When work, family, and life threatened to sabotage my dissertation, the research hour was there to buoy my writing. When overwhelming feelings of defeat surfaced, the research hour was an anchor in the stormy seas of self-doubt. Because of its simple, doable focus, I was able to persevere and finish."

Are there any final words about the research hour?
Try it, you'll like it!

16

KEEPING WITH AND THINKING THROUGH
On Maintaining a Daily Work Log

Jody Shipka

I've kept a daily work log since (at least) 2004. I cannot say with absolute certainty when, how, or by whom I was introduced to the practice, but I've always associated it, or some variation of it, with Peg Syverson. Or, more specifically, with a talk she gave—titled "Nailing Jello to a Wave: Crafting a Dissertation without Losing Your Mind"—in the spring of 2002, as part of the University of Illinois' Center for Writing Studies' Colloquium Series.

Here's how the practice unfolds, at least for me. Shortly after waking—and while I'm still groggy and have not had time to think about things too much, thereby allowing them to become overly large, scary, and off-putting—I go to my computer and open, date, and save a new work log file. Each entry begins with a reference to the time, how I'm feeling, and alludes briefly to whatever I've done thus far: "It's 4:19. Early, I know, but I couldn't sleep. Too early to get the dogs up and out, but I got dressed and started coffee." I usually remind myself where I'd left off the day before, describing whatever I'm hoping to focus on that particular day: "Have to decide which project to work on today—which file to open, what to prioritize. Would kinda love to get the —— piece done and off my plate. Start with that?" I'll usually write for a bit and then break to do something else—teach, run errands, read, go for a walk, return emails, and so on. Returning to the entry, I'll reference the time and recap what I've been doing in the meantime: "All right, so it's 10:00 a.m. I've been working on the draft since about 6:00 a.m., but still not happy with its overall trajectory/movement. Something's not hanging together, but I'm not sure what it is or how to fix it. Problem is with more than transitions. Getting increasingly pissy and my back hurts from sitting here. Should break to walk—will help me refocus before moving back again to the draft . . . Or maybe just cut my losses and end

DOI: 10.7330/9781607328834.c016

early? Maybe just not a great thinking/work day for me. Hope tomorrow's better?"

The length, tone, and content of work log entries vary considerably. Much depends on where I'm at in the overall composing process. In the earlier stages, entries tend to be longer and more idea-rich as I begin to explore my options for a project, speculating on what I might do, how, in what order, and so on. At other times, entries may run only a paragraph or two as I'm spending more time working on/in the draft itself, moving back to the work log only if I get stuck or want to make a progress update.

Sometimes entries focus on things that seem off-topic—hobbies, teaching, committee work, or relationships. Other entries might end up containing much "useable stuff"—fleshed-out and well-stated chunks of text that I can actually lift and place into a working draft. At still other times, entries may contain little that is useable or transportable, reading instead like a detailed catalogue of everything that I believe I cannot do, am angry at myself for not doing, or am afraid I will never be able to do. In this way, the work log also affords me a place to vent, doubt, whine, curse, or rage.

What's important here has less to do with whether, or how often, I produce "useable stuff" in a work log entry. Rather, as someone who has long suffered from pretty debilitating writer's/composer's block, what I find most valuable, and, indeed, what has proven most *productive* (personally, emotionally, and in terms of scholarly output) is that the work log provides me with a low-stakes, low-pressure way of *keeping with* or *thinking through* a project—whether it's one I'm just beginning, in the middle of, or attempting to remediate for another venue, audience, or occasion (e.g., turning a conference presentation into an article or the dissertation into a book). In short, while the prospect of sitting down *to actually work on* a piece of scholarship is extremely daunting—so much so, it usually shuts me down entirely, resulting in inactivity, avoidance, and panic—it feels like something else altogether to remind myself that all the work log requires of me is a willingness to sit down and *write about*, *think through* and, above all else, *keep myself connected to* whatever I'm hoping or, indeed, as was the case with both my dissertation and first book, *needing* to accomplish.

Keeping a daily work log feels very much like a *trick* (for lack of a better way of putting it) that I play on myself. I'll often begin a new entry feeling panicky, frustrated, or stuck, convinced that I've got nothing, only to find myself eventually sliding into something—and often into *many things*. And even if those things seem only slightly relevant, or appear far from usable, it strikes me that they are things I hadn't been thinking about or considering prior to starting the entry. To be sure, there are days that result in the production of long, involved, and idea-rich entries that end up leaving me feeling just as frustrated, turned around, confused, and scared as I was at the start of the day—perhaps even more so, but yet, as I also strongly suspect, *differently so.* Even if I wind up feeling turned around again at the end of the day, I'm in a decidedly different place, perhaps facing in a slightly different direction. Put otherwise, despite whatever frustration I may be experiencing, a part of me understands the project differently for having created the time and space to keep with it, to be with it—for having been willing and disciplined enough to continue thinking *about it, with it, alongside it,* and *through it.*

For more than a decade now, my work log has provided me with a decidedly more constructive and productive way of dealing with writer's/composer's block, providing me with a space and opportunity (excuse?) to speculate, to consider, to wonder—to wander to places and engage with ideas, structures, and techniques that I'd not likely explore, or even imagine, if I were working directly within the space of a draft proper. With the work log entries I'm more apt to ask myself "what if?" questions. If I sense, for instance, that something in a draft isn't work-ing, the work log entry becomes a place where I'm able to explore other ideas, options, or points of entry, and to do so without censoring myself or worrying about whether what I've just put down on the page is work-ing well, or even at all. If I happen to produce something useable, I can simply copy and paste it into the draft file. If, on the other hand, I hit a dead end or get turned around, I can hit return and begin a new para-graph where I attempt to better understand exactly why something feels like a dead end or to puzzle through where, when, and how I got turned around. And from there, I can begin again.

17

TIMING MATTERS
Focus on Achievable Tasks

Michael Baumann

I want to write about time—so, nothing new. You doubtless already know that time is something academics have little of, though it is also something we value—perhaps most. As a former copyeditor of Ohio University's literary journals the *New Ohio Review* and *Quarter After Eight*, former editor of the University of Louisville's undergraduate anthology reader *Cardinal Compositions*, current head editor of the Indiana Writers Center's imprint *INwords*, and freshly minted assistant professor racing on the tenure track, time matters to me. And if you're reading this collection, I'm confident it matters to you, too.

Both *chronos* and *kairos* signify quite a lot to us in rhetoric and composition: time to degree or to tenure, (never enough) hours in the day, rhetorical context, queer and crip time, office hours, deadlines.

Time to eat. You know, sleep. Maybe even read something that doesn't cite a critical theorist.

Here, though, I want to spend time talking about procrastination. Maybe that's a bit obvious, perhaps predictable, but I hope that my advice will (re)frame this particular marker of time that we can, in a way, associate with some publishing do's and don'ts.

Basically, don't.

Procrastinate, that is. I mean, *I* do. (Maybe we all do.) But try not to. (But *if* you do, make it some productive procrastination.) That is, while putting off that lit review, maybe plug in some works cited entries. While checking social media, try to nerd-tweet about your research topic. While waiting for your coffee to enter the blood/brain train, come up with some subheadings or a super title. Another way to avoid procrastination is to craft a list—a really detailed checklist of goals.

Here's the key, though—the takeaway: Avoid setting unrealistic, colossal goals and instead focus on achievable tasks. Once during undergrad, my advisor, mentor, and speech team coach talked to me about

DOI: 10.7330/9781607328834.c017

setting manageable goals when creating such a list. "It's great to want to become a national champion in persuasive speaking," he said. "But it's an inappropriate goal." That's because, he continued, "becoming a national champion" is a task both formidably colossal and outside of my control. That is, it's too great a leap, and the judges make the ultimate decision, not me. However, smaller goals that *are* in my domain of command include choosing to research for at least one hour every week while writing the speech, rehearsing six times every day, and so on.

I think the number one road hazard for list-makers, then, is grandeur. For me, nothing breeds insecurity—and therefore procrastination and then stagnation—like a *colossal* task. Instead, shoot for goals that are at once more possible and pullable.

Example: "Publish a book" is a *colossal* task; "Outline a chapter" is a possible task, and it's one you can control. It's not even "Do research," but perhaps "Read and annotate *this specific article*" or "Spend one hour searching the library databases."

As a graduate student or professor, add colossal goals as *categories*. Beneath those categories, add a list of appropriate *steps* (see table 17.1). Accomplish one every day (or more than one, if you can! But one at a *time*). Much better than procrastinating.

If you want to aid and abet procrastination, zoom out and fret over colossal goals. If you want to vanquish debilitating procrastination, spend time efficiently—on incremental steps.

Lists like these make me think of processes. For example, in the spirit of not procrastinating, I drafted my manuscript for *this* collection one whole week(!) before the deadline. I reread the CFP, wrote out the submissions criteria, brainstormed, outlined, enjoyed a prewriting peer-review coffee with a colleague (Ashanka Kumari, also featured in *Explanation Points*), drafted, revised, peer reviewed (again), edited, and sent this noise in.

Thinking specifically about publishing goals, the process might go on for quite a bit, depending on the scope of the project. In addition to those steps above, you might also contemplate an idea throughout a graduate seminar (either as a teacher or as a student), workshop an idea or seminar paper at a regional or national conference, spend some additional time at that conference talking with colleagues and editors about your ideas, complete a study that may require IRB approval, and so on. You will likely have several projects going on at once, and that's okay. Juggling multiple projects is probably good—for productive procrastination, for refreshing thoughts across projects, and ultimately for doing richer research.

Perhaps the number one cause of not getting published is not sending manuscripts out due to procrastination. (I have no data to back that

Table 17.1. Weekly list of appropriate steps

Monday (coursework)	read/annotate ENGL 620 articles #1, #2, #3 draft response paper revise; print pack a snack for class
Tuesday (teaching)	prep lesson plan for next week grade initial responses draft script for video lecture; revise script shoot footage for video lecture; edit footage upload video lecture revise project I assignment sheet upload assignment sheet
Wednesday (dissertation)	send an email to KK to request meeting add research articles to Google Drive folder read/annotate three articles outline meeting agenda collate IRB examples in Drive folder outline IRB proposal draft IRB proposal meet w/KK
Thursday (exams)	read feedback from committee revise reading list revise research questions send an email to committee with revised list read and annotate one book
Friday (publication)	reread and annotate manuscript for CE send an email to BH to request meeting meet w/BH spend one hour researching set up a library research appointment w/RD incorporate feedback; revise; edit

up, but it's a *strong* suspicion, certainly one couched in personal experience.) The formidable goal "get published" is so . . . well, *formidable* that of course it prompts procrastination. But the smaller steps? Cake. Maybe the worst thing you can do—and again, I know from personal experience—is to give up on a project. I once submitted an audio essay to a digitally published composition journal, and the editors asked me to revise and resubmit. I never did because I thought the revisions sounded difficult. So I said, "Bye" to a rather prestigious single-authored publication that might have been instrumental for the field. And I regret that. And this is not an isolated case. Of course, as academics we have to choose our battles: some projects take precedence, and others we may place on the back burner for later. (And some we just let quietly die and sometimes that's just for the best . . .) But for the most part, if an editor asks for a revision, respond as soon as you can—and certainly by the due date. But don't procrastinate.

Well, try not to. (But *if* you do, make it some productive procrastination.)

18

A WPA/FIRST-TIME MOM'S GUIDE TO PRODUCING THE FIRST BOOK FOR TENURE

Staci Perryman-Clark

In August 2010, I began my first tenure-track position as the director of first-year writing at a public research institution. Exactly one month earlier, I had given birth to my daughter. As a result, I needed to determine how to cope with the stresses of starting a new job, moving to a new city, and becoming a new parent all at the same time. Navigating the tenure track can be stressful by itself, but additional pressures associated with becoming a first-time parent and writing program administrator (WPA) suggest that one must also become very strategic, and perhaps tactical, in navigating productivity while balancing teaching, scholarship, and administration.

My appointment exists in a traditional English department where the single-authored monograph is the gold standard for tenure and promotion. After consulting with senior faculty and administrators, I knew the monograph as the standard for tenure and promotion would still apply to me, WPA or not, regardless of my research interests or publication orientations. Although I was grateful to have a reduced teaching load that would *assist* with maintaining an active scholarly profile, I would often feel guilty spending time on scholarship instead of doing WPA work. After roughly a month on the job, I met with my then department chair to express my feelings of guilt. He assured me I should not feel guilty at all: I needed to do whatever I had to do to get tenure and not worry so much about developing innovations pertaining to our first-year writing program. While I appreciated his assurance, I was less comfortable with ignoring or neglecting the long bulleted list of job description duties written explicitly in the appointment letter that he, our dean, and the provost had signed. I knew I needed to identify a few strategies or tactics that would provide tangible evidence of impact without taking too much time away from research and writing.

DOI: 10.7330/9781607328834.c018

I wanted to be very deliberate in how I implemented activities that led to impact and innovation, but I didn't want to embark upon a complete overhaul of our FYW curriculum for many reasons. The first reason was that overhauling any curriculum—even curricula that are obviously dated and in need of revising—requires a significant time commitment, one that is not forgiving to the tenure clock (or to the new mom). Another reason was that I wanted to consider the work, time, and contributions of current FYW instructors teaching ENGL 1050, our college-level writing course. Because our program is staffed by graduate teaching assistants and part-time instructors, I didn't want to implement any large-scale changes that would require instructors to restructure and revise their courses, given their own workload and time constraints.

Therefore, when I arrived at my institution, one of the first things I did was meet with a group of current ENGL 1050 instructors over pizza. I asked them to identify some of the things they were already doing in their courses. They identified a series of assignments moving from personal narratives to persuasive writing to research writing and genre remediation, and so I implemented a course reader of activities and apparatuses built around the assignments they were already doing. I also asked instructors to identify what they would like to see in the program and additional needs they had. Many desired more professional development opportunities and resources, so with the help of my FYW assistant directors, we planned academic year pedagogy brownbags.

After meeting with instructors, I also learned that the only textbook required was a custom handbook for which the program received royalties. I used these royalties to fund professional development seminars, guest speakers, and conference travel for any instructor presenting on pedagogical topics related to the teaching of first-year writing. These activities were featured as part of our newly designed FYW initiatives; the initiatives were posted on our FYW website along with a fresh mission statement and vision for the program, which provided written and public recognition around the activities generated by the program. In essence, a few deliberate activities with an updated web presence provided administrators with a documented profile of activities and innovations to show that I was creating and developing meaningful innovation while not embarking on activities that would consume too much time. These activities also called attention to the graduate assistants, who assisted with planning workshops and creating web-based and original content—providing much-needed program assistance while also further developing their professional skill sets.

After identifying and implementing a couple of significant changes to the FYW program during the first semester, I then turned to drafting a proposal for my first book. I decided to turn my dissertation into book because it provided me with already drafted writing, therefore expediting much of the prewriting phase that comes with new projects. Unsurprisingly, though, significant revision would have to occur for the dissertation to be suitable for publication as a monograph (see Harris's and Palmeri's chapters in this volume), which suggested that I would need significant blocks of writing time to revise. As both a new nursing mom and WPA, I quickly learned I would have to be very purposeful in how I scheduled these blocks of time. At first, I scheduled writing time around the nursing and nap schedules of my newborn; however, these schedules can often become unpredictable as routines change and babies grow. I also quickly learned that work space and environment vastly affect productivity. Placing a newborn in a crib or swing within close proximity soon became a distraction and deterrence to my productivity. Although I appreciated the flexibility, I also knew I needed a physical space where I could write alone.

Around this same period, I began developing anxiety from all of the work/life adjustments that took place within such a short time frame. I knew that in order to be productive, I needed a workable space that provided me with an essence of calm, and I also knew that I needed a space where I could write in isolation, void of distractions. To address these concerns, I decided to schedule an eight-hour writing session each weekend at my parents' house, where I could write in my childhood bedroom.[1] I decided upon this space because its nostalgia brought me the spirit of calm for which I yearned. It was in this precise space that I remember composing poetry, paintings, and drawings as a child. This location also provided me much-needed support to write in isolation. My mother and sister agreed to babysit my daughter for the day, only returning her occasionally to nurse. It was in this precise space, then, that I completed most of the entire book production process from start to finish, including the book proposal, book chapters, revisions based on editorial suggestions, copyedits, indexing, page proofs, and so on. The final book was published five months after my daughter's second birthday, and despite her growth, I still returned to this pattern of writing in my childhood room on weekends while relatives babysat. This project provided great satisfaction in seeing the side-by-side growth of one's natural child and one's professional child.

Whether or not one is a parent, time management advice on scholarly productivity is essential for tenure-track faculty, especially those who are

WPAs. While most scholarship advises tenure-seeking faculty not to take WPA positions (Dew and Horning 2007), faculty may find themselves with limited alternatives. For me, my only options were to take a position as a non-tenure-track lecturer or to take the tenure-track WPA position. I decided on the tenure-track position because I needed an assurance of job security to support my growing family. Thus, for those who find themselves in tenure-track junior WPA positions, here are three forms of advice I recommend based on my experiences writing the first book for tenure as a WPA.

Identify strategic opportunities that establish program activity with limited time commitment. I was firm in my decision not to embark upon any large-scale overhauls, regardless of whether or not pedagogies or programmatic activities were dated. For me, I determined that administrators wanted to see activity around a program, and instructors wanted evidence that the WPA considers their needs and wishes. So I developed and documented a few initiatives that were perceived as adding intrinsic value, therefore increasing impact. Establishing these, however, did not consume too much of my time. I also decided not to embark upon longitudinal programmatic assessment activities, or attempt to revise programmatic learning outcomes, even though some instructors and faculty identified these as areas for revision.

Programmatic and longitudinal forms of assessment take time, time that an untenured WPA needs to work on publications and scholarship.

Although assessment is listed as one of my assigned duties, I made the case to begin programmatic assessment activities and revisiting learning outcomes as post-tenure activities.

Establish a designated workspace and schedule that supports productivity and stick with it. In her column "Shut Up and Write," Kerry Ann Rockquemore (2010) asserts that faculty need to be very purposeful in determining their specific needs with regard to productivity, including needs that pertain to physical location: "For example, some people need to physically share space with others while writing, . . . some need solitude and the kind of support that is silent." I determined that I needed a space of solitude and inspiration, and I adjusted my schedule deliberately to accommodate these conditions so I could "shut up and write." The ability to identify these conditions sooner rather than later and then act accordingly speaks tremendously to efficient productivity while on the tenure clock.

Establish networks of support systems both at work and home. I am purposeful when thinking of networks and systems in plural forms. This is because one person, network, or system cannot fulfill every need, role, or purpose. Multiple systems are typically necessary for meeting your primary need or specific goal, in this case productivity. In my series of networks, I identified my department chair, FYW assistants, and family as key agents in my professional success. My chair could coach me on scholarly productivity, while my FYW assistants could assist with much of the behind-the-scenes work needed to design and implement programmatic changes. With regard to family, I needed a group of folks who could help with childcare. My husband provided much-needed support as a full-time stay-at-home dad while my daughter was very young, but even he needed a break. Therefore, we both needed help from my mother and sister, who assisted on weekends while I wrote. Don't hesitate to ask for help, especially with home-related duties. The worst anyone can say is no, and if (s)he does, move to the next person on the list. Being assertive and taking action to address my specific needs had a tremendous impact on my scholarly productivity and my ability to write and finish the first book for tenure. In doing so, I was successful with an early tenure bid, and I'm grateful for the network of support systems that contributed to my success!

NOTE

1. While I understand the privileges I describe here, and I recognize that support is defined and available in different ways by different writers, readers should also be aware that I come from a background of historically oppressed groups of folks who don't have many of the privileges that folks without such support actually do have. Strategize how to make a situation work and seek to find the appropriate support. For me, support was defined by family. For others, it will look much different.

REFERENCES

Dew, Debra Frank, and Alice Horning, eds. 2007. *Untenured Faculty as Writing Program Administrators: Institutional Practices and Politics.* West Lafayette, IN: Parlor, 2007.

Rockquemore, Kerry Ann. 2010. "Shut Up and Write." *Inside Higher Ed*, June 14. https://www.insidehighered.com/advice/2010/06/14/shut-and-write.

19

COMMUNITY WRITING
From Classroom to Workplace and Back

Stephen A. Bernhardt

Some of the best ideas and opportunities for research and publications come from outside the university, so don't confine your work to the academic cloister. A career in researching and teaching writing can lead naturally to engagement in communities beyond the university. Seeking research and training opportunities in business and community settings can enrich your intellectual life and give you a sense of making real contributions. Once you begin to see opportunities beyond the university, those opportunities can multiply, with one connection leading to the next, often in unexpected but always rewarding directions.

Begin by assessing who you are, where your interests lie, what particular skills you have to offer, and where the opportunities might be in your local or regional community. Ask yourself where writing has important consequences—those are your sites of possible activity. Chances are, if you enter those sites, you will connect with people who understand the importance of writing in organizational contexts, people who may well be at a loss for how to improve performance by making writing more efficient, less frustrating, more rewarding, and more impactful.

Why should we move beyond our academic settings, where we are well trained, confident, and comfortable? Such movement keeps us fresh, since new environments challenge us with unfamiliar problems and complex situations. You will find yourself among people with different assumptions about writing and how it works. You will expand your sense of working genres—how writing accomplishes work inside organizations. You will gain new perspectives on what writing does, coming to see writing as an embedded activity, part of the flow of action, and a living, organic thing, as opposed to writing being an artifact or end point, produced as an object in and for itself.

You are also likely to be appreciated in situations outside the academy. Most people write on the job, but many have no training, fail to

DOI: 10.7330/9781607328834.c019

see what is at stake in a given rhetorical situation, and follow rehearsed conventions as opposed to seeing writing as a way of solving particular problems in novel ways. We all like to be appreciated for the work we do; the satisfaction we derive from exercising our expertise is what sustains our desire to develop as a professional. Garnering appreciation from those outside the university is much more likely than from within, especially from within our own departments, where we all think we know each other and bylaws, processes, and committees have already attached a particular kind of value to the writing we produce. Perhaps the most important motivation and reward for moving in spheres beyond the academy is that everything you learn, everything you do, and each new situation and genre you encounter will enrich your teaching repertoire and underscore your expertise in the classroom.

My academic life has been characterized by movement from classroom to workplace, an oscillation that initially secured a tenure-line position at Southern Illinois University–Carbondale (SIU–C) and terrific subsequent positions at New Mexico State University (NMSU) and a named chair at the University of Delaware. In each move, my interests in writing beyond the academy were crucial to attracting interest. I first developed these interests as a graduate student at the University of Michigan. Because I had a background teaching high school English, I was appointed assistant director in the composition program and became closely involved with English Composition Board activities—writing assessment, writing center tutoring, writing in the disciplines. This was the first time I engaged with training—training TAs to teach writing and faculty to embed writing in their courses. Creating a link between teaching and training was key for me.

Because prospects for positions in literature were dim, I pursued scientific and technical communication, English as a world language, reading and study skills, and English language studies, assuming those kinds of study would prepare me to have wide utility in an English department. I settled on a dissertation in science writing, which offered me the opportunity to look at writing in various organizations: the Environmental Protection Agency, the Fish and Wildlife Service, the Department of Natural Resources, the Great Lakes Basin Commission, and other settings. In each setting, working scientists were keen to discuss writing in their organizations. The dissertation was an enjoyable, informative, engaging experience, one that deepened my sense of what writing does and how it works.

My grad school friend Ted Smith and I went on the market at the same time, and in a lucky stroke, Ted found a call for bids from IBM for training classes for information developers. Essentially, the company was asking for a writing workshop focused on process, exactly what we had been doing in the composition program. We developed a proposal—my first—and won the position. We went on to offer five to ten one-week workshops per year at IBM sites in the United States, Canada, France, Spain, and elsewhere. In addition to this enterprise being very rewarding financially, I learned a lot about how writing works, how writing supports business practices, how writing supports users in technical environ-ments, and how organizations were moving from seeing writing as a text to seeing writing as part of an information architecture. I also learned that my university would allow one day per week or one week per month of external consulting, and that my reputation was burnished by such activity. We developed the training manual for IBM as a book publica-tion, one still in use today. From what I learned, I developed a course in writing computer documentation at SIU–C, and the knowledge later informed courses I developed in writing online help systems at NMSU. Ted and I went on to deliver training to other organizations, includ-ing Hughes Aircraft, the Austin city government, and Motorola. Ted decided to make his career in training, leaving his position at UT–Austin for the challenge of building his own business. His success was another demonstration that what we know has value.

While at SIU–C, I maintained connections to secondary schools, with a continuing and remunerative contract with a local school district to enhance the teaching and assessment of writing. I and a team of other writing instructors successfully applied for grants to enhance writing in the disciplines in the public schools, and we connected with the Illinois State Office of Public Instruction to assist with curricular reform and outcomes assessment. Each of us refined our grant-writing skills, made useful network connections, achieved funding for research projects, and published multiple articles from this outreach work.

When I moved to NMSU, I had credible workplace and educational experience, with the skills to teach technical writing, grant writing, writ-ing assessment, and other useful courses. I linked up with my writing colleague Stuart Brown and professors in engineering and business to form a consulting group. Together, we were a team with skills in work-force development, literacy and writing, logistics, strategic planning, and other areas of applied research. With grants from the Departments of Labor and Commerce, we delivered a number of projects (training, consulting, development) to various tribes across New Mexico and Arizona, focused on strategic planning, workforce development, and infrastructure development. As a team, we were much more competent and effective than any of us would have been individually. We also developed a strong sense of collegiality with both engineering and business, leading to other funded projects, developing curriculum, and building labs to support teaching.

Also while I was at NMSU, Paul Meyer and I teamed up on several multiyear National Workplace Literacy demonstration projects. The funding, in hundreds of thousands of dollars, allowed us to develop worker training programs in seventeen hospitals around New Mexico to advance the career skills of a wide range of workers, many of whom were native speakers of Spanish. We were working in hospital settings with a strong sense of doing something for deserving individuals. Working with a team of grad students, we developed training courses in supervisory skills, performance appraisal, work process improvement, writing on the job, and speaking skills. We published with our grad students and produced work that led to theses and dissertations. The work we did led to contracts with other organizations, including city government, the forest service, and foundations. The work also informed development of courses in grant writing, writing in the workplace, and training and development.

All of this work led to a long-term consultancy with a McCulley-Cuppan in Salt Lake City, a group that grew out of the Franklin-Covey organization, with roots in an assemblage of English professors from Brigham Young University who started teaching courses in business writing to local companies. We've worked all over the world, delivering training courses in science writing, assessing document quality, establishing document standards, facilitating drug-development teams, coaching team leaders, and improving the documentation that keeps development and manufacturing running smoothly.

I still do this work now that I am retired from the University of Delaware. Again, it is remunerative, which is great, but it is also deeply satisfying to apply what we know as writing researchers and teachers to the challenges and complexities of industry. I get to learn from each project—about genes, toxicity, purification, cancer drugs, statistics. I am challenged in each project to defend what I recommend, addressing questions like: What does the research say? How do we know that one document is more effective than another? How do we justify the cost of changing our approach? Such challenging questions make me think continually about what we have produced as a professional body of knowledge and what unrealized potential underlies our research.

All of this work led to extremely interesting team teaching in the last few years of my career. I was a principal investigator on a National

Science Foundation grant that integrated technology and communication skills into math and physics instruction at the undergrad level. At the grad level, again under an NSF grant, I regularly team-taught PhD students in systems biology, with components of ethics, business, and communication.

Nothing in my career has been in a straight, planned line. Chance and serendipity led from one project to the next, one personal connection to a new one. Each project led me to coauthors and publishing projects. But it all depended on looking beyond the walls of the department and academy, being open to opportunities, and knowing that what I know—about writing, communication, rhetoric, teamwork, collaboration—is highly valued and of tremendous worth to those in organizational settings.

20

NOT A DRAFT BUT MATERIALS

Joseph Harris

Think of your dissertation not as a draft of your first book but as materials for it. Your dissertation is probably the longest and most important text you've written. You've put everything you've got into it, so you want to share your research and ideas. You want people to read it.

The problem with a dissertation has to do with genre: your dissertation is also the last paper you will write as a student. Your main readers are the members of your doctoral committee—who are no doubt interested in what you have to say, but who are also charged with certifying you as a scholar. They are thus legitimately invested in making sure that you've done your homework—that your review of the literature is comprehensive, your description of your methods exhaustive, your theoretical rationale laid out in full detail.

Almost no future readers of your work will ever be quite so interested in those things. The readers of a scholarly book aren't worried if you're legit. They assume as much. They want to know what they can take away from your work, what you have to offer *them*. In writing a book, then, you need to lead with your argument.

Those opening dissertation chapters that took you so long to write on theory, method, the state of the field? They are now materials for footnotes, appendices, brief subsections. Get rid of that long overview of your project as well. Or at least shorten it.

You want to move as quickly as you can to the substance of your work, to show what you have to add to the conversation of the discipline.

This may seem stern advice, but I don't mean it as such. Think of it this way: you've put a lot of work into your dissertation. Because of that work, you are now in a position to write a pointed, concise, and elegant book. Few dissertations are noted for the verve or quality of their prose, but many academic books are. This is your chance to write one.

I'm not saying to leave your dissertation behind. Of course you'll draw not only on ideas but on specific sentences and paragraphs you've

DOI: 10.7330/9781607328834.c020

written. But do so strategically. Open a blank document and start writing fresh. Go back to your dissertation only when you know there's a passage you can use. Copy and paste at the point of need. But don't try to simply repurpose your dissertation as a book. They're different kinds of texts, written for different occasions and readers.

This advice stems from my experience (from 2007 to 2012) as the series editor of the CCCC Studies in Writing and Rhetoric. I assumed that many of the proposals to the SWR series would be first books based on dissertations. In my guidelines for proposals, then, I stated that I did not want to consider unrevised dissertations. I asked authors to send me instead a very brief overview of the book they were proposing, and a full chapter that "represents your project at its most lively, consequential, and engaging." My aim in doing so was to urge authors to reimagine their dissertations as books.

This proved a hard task for many authors. Despite being explicitly told *not* to send the introduction to their dissertation, many did so anyway. The result was that I read too many chapters that felt more like a summary of a study than an actual part of it. I wanted to see writers in action—to find out how they worked with their materials, addressed their readers, and developed a line of thought. I wanted to see how their prose moved on the page. I wanted to see if the chapter made me want to read more from this author. That rarely happened if what I was read-ing was simply a rationale or background for work promised to follow.

(There is another important bit of advice here: read what editors ask for in their guidelines, and see if you can give it to them. They are trying to define the aim and tone of their series. If you feel you have to contort your project to fit their expectations, then you need to find another series or press to send your work to.)

But many other authors figured out how to write brilliant non-dissertations drawing on the materials *from* their dissertations. For exam-ples, just take a look at some recent SWR volumes. What you'll find, for the most part, are slim books beginning with pointed intros that define a question to be explored, followed by three or four chapters that do the actual work of that exploration, and ending with brief conclusions that highlight the takeaways of the study. Discussions of background materi-als and methods tend to be relegated to notes or appendices. They read, that is, like books that aim to inform their readers more than accredit their authors. The irony is, of course, that the ability to write such a book is a sure sign of a confident and accomplished author.

21

YOU WILL NOT BE ABLE TO STAY HOME
Quantitative Research in Writing Studies

Norbert Elliot

No one ever made a decision because of a number. They need a story.
— Nobel Laureate Daniel Kahneman

In 1970 I was a first-year student at the University of New Orleans. I drove my carnival float of a car, a 1968 bayou-blue Biscayne, to the campus and thought about Gill Scott-Heron. *Small Talk at 125th and Lenox* had just been pressed, and the first track announced this to an edgy bass beat: "You will not be able to stay home, brother. / You will not be able to plug in, turn on and cop out . . . / Because the revolution will not be televised." With my Black friends at the American Can Company where I worked loading boxcars in summers, I was also in the street looking for a brighter day that would not be part of wretched commercialization or cruel capitalism.

I am nearly sixty-seven now, but I am very much the same person who came to the Lake Pontchartrain campus to find out how to make a live revolution. For me, the narrative has always come first, then the aim, then the vehicle. So, here is the pattern I suggest to all scholars in writing studies: find the narrative, link it to something that moves your heart, and design a quantitative study to, as Scott-Heron wrote, put you in the driver's seat. Let's take a little ride to see if we can steer toward that brighter day.

First Stop: Find a research narrative that interests you. Contrary to the common belief of many in rhetoric and writing studies, designing and publishing quantitative research is neither contrary to humanistic impulses (to listen to our better angels) nor fulfillment of positivistic assumptions (to reduce life's complexity to mathematical proof). Rather, quantitative research is best understood as a story told with

DOI: 10.7330/9781607328834.c021

evidence. When told well, quantitative research helps us know more about who we are and, better yet, who we may become. If a research narrative—a story you will first tell to yourself and then to others—does not keep you up nights, as James M. Cain famously said, it won't keep anyone else up either.

As to the importance of narrative, I call as my witnesses Terrance Anderson, David Schum, and William Twinning (2005). These evidence scholars are explicit in their advocacy of narrative as an analytic device. Used to construct logical stories, narrative complements analysis. Taken with this idea, my colleague Robert J. Mislevy (2003) has acknowledged the role of narrative in interpretation and use models used in quantitative studies.

Although the argumentative system described by Toulmin (1958/2003) does indeed advance evidence through the familiar tune of claim, evidence, warrant, and quantification, Mislevy reminds us in the case of AP Studio Art that the psychometric model is not merely a tool for making claims about student abilities; rather it is a system for understanding evaluation episodes across time and circumstance.

Once effective argument and cohesive narration are taken as interactive threshold concepts—those discursive knowledge portals, subject to endless play (Land 2015: xiii)—doors open for quantitative research. Let's open one.

Second Stop: Recognize that hearts move in many ways. Consider table 21.1 as a thought experiment in numbers and words. If performed before research is begun, running through the fourteen phases will create a valuable way to construct a research arc that, in turn, will provide structure to the planned quantitative research.

Columns 1 and 2 identify fourteen research phases and related considerations, with column 3 narrowing those into research exercises. Column 4 identifies specific exercises for early career researchers to provide the depth of experience needed when numbers and narrative must become one. My own forty-seven years' worth of experience tells me that completing the thought experiment with a specific quantitative design in mind takes about two eight-hour days. While working, I recommend listening to Thomas Bell and Linda Creed's "People Make the World Go Round"—maybe the version by Marc Dorsey. Prepare to be kept up some nights.

At the end of that time, with your notes, materials, considerations, and tables, you will have created a quantitative research narrative—a new way to use words and numbers together, to design fresh images

Table 21.1. Phases, considerations, and exercises for publishing quantitative manuscripts in writing studies

	Phases	Considerations	Exercises
1	Embed present study in emerging research program.	Individual research studies are best understood within a scholar's current and emerging program of research.	Using the disciplinary taxonomy for writing studies developed as part of the Visibility Project (Phelps and Ackerman 2010), describe how the present study contributes to your emerging program of research.
2	Adopt construct modeling approach.	Construct modeling involves investigating relationships between and among predictors (X, or dependent variables) and outcomes (Y, or dependent variables).	Read up on construct modeling. John R. Hayes (2012) is a good place to start, identify the predictor and outcome variables in your study and describe their relationships.
3	Articulate research questions.	Precise research questions appropriately limit the investigation.	Identify a writing studies journal that regularly publishes research in which scholars articulate their research questions (e.g., *IEEE Transactions on Professional Communication*) and select an award-winning article from that journal (e.g., Schriver 2017). Analyze how the structure of the research questions will help guide your study.
4	Situate research questions within the literature review.	Locating research in the context of work by other researchers allows identification of needed scholarship and responsiveness of the present study.	Review *Education for Life and Work* (National Research Council 2012), with special attention to the three-domain model (cognitive, intrapersonal, and interpersonal). Use the construct modeling approach to identify key writing studies research articles that address your research questions and demonstrate the need for the new research.
5	Apply methodological framework.	Use of evidence-gathering systems yields principled research approaches of descriptive, correlational, quasi-experimental, and experimental design.	Review these two evidence-gathering systems created for writing studies research: Design for Assessment (White, Elliot, and Peckham 2015) and Integrated Design and Appraisal Framework (Slomp 2016). Select a system that holds the best potential for evidence gathering in your study.
6	Design sampling plan.	In the design stage, sampling plans define the target population, identify the accessible sample, and estimate potential attrition.	Read up on sample size selection (e.g., Maxwell 2000) and the U.S. Department of Education *Procedures and Standards Handbook* (2014) on attrition. Then examine the sample in your present study for its population representativeness and possible attrition rates.

(continued on next page)

Table 21.1—(continued)

	Phases	Considerations	Exercises
7	Form research team.	Multidisciplinary research teams increase research capacity.	Read up on collaboration in writing studies (see Section 2 of this collection). Define the benefits of collaboration and identify colleagues with abilities that extend your own who might be interested in your present study.
8	Identify statistical software.	Appropriate software selection is central to quantitative research.	Review the following software products: SAS, SPSS, and R. Create a three-column table comparing the products for statistical power, graphics, and learning curve. Identify a platform for this present research project (and consider identifying a longer-term platform to support work past this initial project).
9	Target representative journal.	Aligning scholarship to journal is an important stage of rhetorical analysis leading to publication (see Section 3 of this collection).	Create a table that identifies journals that publish quantitative research. Then, identify the journal that publishes quantitative research designs similar to yours.
10	Categorize evidence.	Foundational measurement categories of fairness, validity, and reliability are essential to evidence gathering accompanying quantitative research.	Read the *Standards for Educational and Psychological Testing* (AERA, APA, and NCME 2014) and determine what forms of fairness, validity, and reliability evidence you will gather.
11	Create tables first.	Creating tables before text allows you to plan data gathering and subsequent analysis.	Review chapter 5 ("Displaying Results") of the *Publication Manual of the American Psychological Association* (APA 2010) and identify the kinds of tables you will use in your study.
12	Obtain expert review.	Expert peer review allows presubmission problems to be identified and resolved.	Draw on the reviewer guidelines accompanying the representative journal you have targeted, and invite a senior scholar who has published research similar to your own to provide a review.
13	Follow submission guidelines.	Submitting required format, IRB documentation, and permissions demonstrates knowledge of targeted journal.	Use the submission guidelines accompanying the representative journal you have targeted to make sure that you have followed the checklist of required information and files.
14	Disseminate research.	Conference presentations, blogs, and podcasts allow preliminary communication of findings.	Review the Communities of Practice policy research brief (Gere et al. 2011) and create a social networking presence using platforms such as Research Gate to share your present research and expand your research team.

and new reporting genres, to craft narratives to serve and create audiences—that will move your heart and, in doing so, allow you to provide new visions for others.

Third Stop: Remember to dance with them what brought you. In graduate school, I adored the archetypal structure provided by Northrop Frye in *Anatomy of Criticism* (1957). Over a lifetime, I learned to embrace other structures from other fields, most notably those of E. G. Boring's *History of Experimental Psychology* (1957). These two scholars invented taxonomies that, if followed, revealed new ways of thinking. Table 21.1 reflects my love of structure, and this is a conceptual system that I used for thirty years in working with undergraduate and graduate students interested in quantitative methods. As I prepare to teach seminars in what, no doubt, will be near road's end, the table has been newly reassembled for you, as you experience the ontological, epistemological, and axiological transformations that accompany empirical reasoning.

Before leaving on your road trip, here is something you should know as the driver: the essence of the table is deeply humanistic and, as such, requires community to work. The methodological narrative and the empirical framework are both designed around a single aim: the pursuit of individual freedom. Each phase, consideration, and exercise implies a journey, with stops along the way for supplies and companionship. So be sure to invite others on the trip who are wildly unlike yourself—mathematicians, computer scientists, and linguistics are good companions. Your best colleagues will become those whose education and practice are unlike yours. These folks know things you do not and will help you to see that there might be another way to look that you have not yet been shown.

Used wisely, quantitative research narratives can provide rich opportunities for building a career with colleagues, for pressing back the darkness of isolation, and for ensuring that writing remains a human right central to education. While I have had to work alone in writing studies for most of my career (in this volume no other author directly addresses pursuing or publishing quantitative projects), that is no longer the case. I just had to wait for my colleagues, such as Asao B. Inoue and Mya Poe (both with chapters in this volume), to be born. Odd to think, but numbers have been a way for me to go underground, to make sure that students at their desks remain central to all I have done.

Warning: as to those big men smokin' in their easy chairs, on their fat cigars without a care: those who have come to take my place are driving to your house. They will be there shortly. They have things to tell you.

REFERENCES

American Educational Research Association (AERA), American Psychological Association (APA), and National Council on Measurement in Education (NCME). 2014. *Standards for Educational and Psychological Testing*. Washington, DC: American Educational Research Association.

American Psychological Association. 2010. *Publication Manual of the American Psychological Association*. 6th ed. Washington, DC: American Psychological Association.

Anderson, Terrance, David Schum, and William Twinning. 2005. *Analysis of Evidence*. 2nd ed. Cambridge: Cambridge University Press.

Boring, Edwin G. 1957. *A History of Experimental Psychology*. 2nd ed. Englewood Cliffs, NJ: Prentice-Hall.

Frye, Northrup. 1957. *Anatomy of Criticism: Four Essays*. Princeton, NJ: Princeton University Press.

Gere, Anne, et al. 2011. *Communities of Practice: A Policy Research Brief Produced by the National Council of Teachers of English*. Urbana, IL: National Council of Teachers of English. http://www.ncte.org/library/NCTEFiles/Resources/Journals/CC/0212nov2011/CC0212Policy.pdf.

Hayes, John R. 2012. "Modeling and Remodeling Writing." *Written Communication* 29 (3): 369–88. http://dx.doi.org/10.1177/0741088312451260.

Land, Ray. 2015. Preface ton *Naming What We Know: Threshold Concepts of Writing Studies*, edited by Linda Adler-Kassner and Elizabeth Wardle, xi–xiv. Logan: Utah State University Press.

Maxwell, Scott E. 2000. "Sample Size and Multiple Regression Analysis." *Psychological Methods* 5 (4): 434–58.

Mislevy, Robert J. 2003. "Substance and Structure in Assessment Arguments." *Law, Probability, and Risk* 2 (4): 237–58.

National Research Council. 2012. *Education for Life and Work: Developing Transferable Knowledge and Skills in the 21st Century*. Washington, DC: National Academies Press.

Phelps, Louise Wetherbee, and John M. Ackerman. 2010. "Making the Case for Disciplinarity in Rhetoric, Composition, and Writing Studies: The Visibility Project." *College Composition and Communication* 62 (1): 180–215.

Schriver, Karen A. 2017. "Plain Language in the US Gains Momentum: 1940–2015." *IEEE Transactions on Professional Communication* 60 (4): 343–83.

Slomp, David. 2016. "An Integrated Design and Appraisal Framework for Ethical Writing Assessment." *Journal of Writing Assessment* 9 (1). http://www.journalofwritingassessment.org.

Toulmin, Stephen E. 1958/2003. *The Uses of Argument*. Cambridge: Cambridge University Press. http://dx.doi.org/10.1017/CBO9780511840005.

U.S. Department of Education. 2014. *What Works Clearinghouse: Procedures and Standards Handbook, Version 3*. Washington, DC: Institute of Education Sciences. www.ies.ed.gov/ncee/wwc/Docs/referenceresources/wwc_procedures_v3_0_standards_handbook.pdf.

White, Edward M., Norbert Elliot, and Irvin Peckham. 2015. *Very Like a Whale: The Assessment of Writing Programs*. Logan: Utah State University Press.

22

PRACTICING WHIMSY

Jenn Fishman

My advice for learning how to be an effective participant in long-range collaborations boils down to a single word: whimsy. To work well over time with others on projects that have multiple goals, including scholarly publication, it is vital to cultivate not only a deliberate sense of whimsy but also a related protocol for decision making.

Each of us does whimsy differently, and the professional situations that call for whimsical stance taking and decision making are numerous. Long-term collaborative projects, perhaps especially projects that include scholarly publication as a goal, call for particular kinds of caprice management. The pace of developing a project slated to take years, whether a research study, an academic or community program, or a resource (e.g., a database or an archive), rarely resembles the pace of researching and writing an article, webtext, or book, and the socio-professional dynamics of working with a team or staff for three to five or even ten years are not the same as working solo or even working for an extended period of time with a single collaborator. Everyone involved has their own timeframe and priorities, including different needs and desires to produce scholarship.

My advice for being a good participant in such activities in any role (e.g., principal investigator, coeditor, team member) involves cultivating not only a sense of whimsy but also a related method of decision making: a procedure that is inflected with humor; buoyed by appreciation of the fantastical when it appears, usually without warning; and tempered by deliberate and pragmatic responsivity. Specifically, I recommend the WHIMSY Protocol, which has six parts:

1. Identify *why* you want to become or remain involved in a project;

2. Clarify *how* you might contribute or continue contributing;

3. At every stage, calculate what you will need to *invest* to participate effectively, whether you have the capacity to make that investment, and the kinds of returns on investment it is reasonable to expect.

DOI: 10.7330/9781607328834.c022

4. Determine what is—and is not—*moveable* with regard to the project, your collaborators, and yourself;

5. *Squint* into the middle distance in an effort to see as much as you can into the future; and

6. Know when to *yield* to others, whether to reduce your participation or to withdraw completely.

The first half of the WHIMSY Protocol involves self-evaluation, starting with scrutiny of our own motives for getting or staying involved in a long-range project. Usually the magnetism of a project is part personal and part professional. Good opportunities stoke our egos and confirm our sense of purpose. They reflect our priorities and our politics at the same time they help us (select all that apply):

- fulfill responsibility
- meet expectations
- apply expertise
- learn/grow
- advance professionally
- profit monetarily
- give back
- fulfill a duty, responsibility, or call

Clarifying how we might contribute to a new project or to the next phase of an ongoing one and calculating the merits of investing our time, energy, and attention are determinations best made in tandem. It is especially useful to distinguish between projects that ask us to contribute prior knowledge and projects that invite (or require) us to learn new things. It is also productive to consider where a project falls within a difficulty/enjoyment grid (see figure 22.1).

Once we have identified a project as "a relatively easy drag" or "a fun challenge," it is useful to ask whether and how this project relates conceptually to the other work we do. It is good to ask: Will it help us foster the kinds of relationships we want to have with our collaborator(s) and with others who are involved? In addition, it is helpful to do math. Think about the most immediate tasks and consider: Do they seem to fit into the complex working equation of our everyday lives? Do they jive with our courses, exams, and time to degree if we are students? Do they fit with our current research agendas, teaching schedules, administrative responsibilities, and professional clocks, whatever that may be? And how will they work alongside our kids' after-school schedules, our volunteer commitments, our twice-weekly life-giving running groups, and so on? To test our answers, we should ask, "*What would —— say?*" several times,

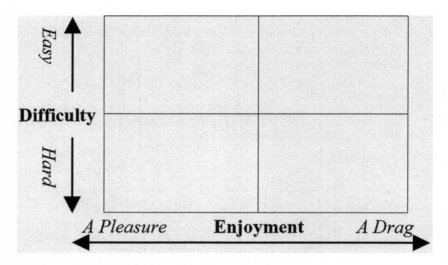

Figure 22.1. Difficulty/enjoyment grid

filling in the blank with various names: our primary graduate school mentor, our best friend, our partner, and so on. It is also a good idea to check in with our past selves, including ourselves on the best and worst days of other projects.

Each of the remaining items in the WHIMSY Protocol has its own focus. The fourth item involves scrutinizing the project and its participants, focusing on what is (and is not) moveable. This analysis is distinct from attempting to discover all the moving parts of a long-term project. That is not possible. Don't even try. However, it is feasible to distinguish known aspects of a project as adjustable, contingent on particular events or opportunities, or immoveable. Is the timeframe hard and fast—why or why not? How strictly defined are participants' responsibilities and roles? What else is or isn't apparently set in stone? It is also important to learn how others see themselves and to consider the ways in which we are and are not flexible. With these details in mind, it is time to look past immediate tasks to see what we can see in the middle distance of a long-term project. This is not an exercise in spit balling or crystal balling. Instead, this fifth prompt asks us to engage in informed conjecture about our ability to contribute to a project over time. Can we continue as active co-researchers in two years, when we are finishing our dissertations or taking a turn as our writing center's director or starting a five-year term as an associate provost? Will we participate differently during the data gathering and data analysis phases of a project given our particular resources and expertise? Can we take on new responsibilities the semester we are on sabbatical or the summer we have a research grant and thus a research assistant? And so on.

After working through the first five items in the WHIMSY Protocol and evaluating general aspects of a project, it is useful to pause and to repeat the protocol with a focus on publication. In doing so, we should ask:

1. How is the opportunity to produce scholarship part of *why* we were drawn to the project, and to date have our expectations been met?

2. To what degree is *how* we expected to contribute to a project related to producing scholarship about it, and to date have our expectations been met?

3. Especially if we prioritize scholarly production, do we consider our return on the *investment* of time, energy, and attention sufficient to meet our needs?

4. Is publishing a *moveable* or immovable aspect of the project, and does that match what we need?

5. And when we *squint* into that middle distance, do we see the project positioned to help us fulfill our long-term priorities and needs where scholarly publication is concerned?

When we fall out of sync with the ebb and flow of a project, when the answers to the above questions are no, it is time to *yield*. As the final item in the protocol suggests, sometimes the most responsible choice we can make as collaborators on a long-range project is to reduce our participation or withdrawal entirely. Too, we may need to help a project collaborator use the WHIMSY Protocol to draw a similar conclusion.

To be sure, deciding to yield rarely comes easily to most of us. However, the WHIMSY Protocol offers a tool for coming to that conclusion and for doing so in a purposefully playful way.

* * *

Even the most well-defined, well-organized long-range collaborative projects unfold in unpredictable ways, shaped and reshaped by participants' individual circumstances, the changing nature of local contexts, and the ebb and flow of scholarly and social exigences. As a result, the best collaborators are at once anchored by a clear sense of purpose and are highly responsive to large- and small-scale, short- and long-term changes. Since the late 1990s, when I co-founded the graduate-run journal *Mantis* (which continues publishing today), I have had more than my share of opportunities to learn about being an effective "co" on long-term projects. In fact, it turns out I have a "thing" not only for the scholarly possibilities that come with collaborative longitudinal projects—the breadth, the depth, the shared developmental arcs—but also for the special kind of chaos associated with duration. As a result, I have been a co-researcher, coauthor, coeditor, co-founder, co-chair, and general co-conspirator on a range of multiyear projects with publication as one of their (usually many) goals: *Mantis*, the Stanford Study of Writing, First-Year Composition at UT–Knoxville, the Embodied Literacies Project, Escuala Nueva International, REx: The Research Exchange Index, the Coalition of Feminist Scholars in the History of Rhetoric and Composition, the CCCC Committee on Undergraduate Research, *The Norton Anthology of Rhetoric and Writing*, Kenyon Writes, the Undergraduate Research Impact Project, and First-Year English at Marquette University.

Starting out, I followed my gut rather than any formal guidelines for choosing projects, and paid attention to those strong flashes of sensation that signaled "Yes, do it!!" or "Yeah, okay," or "Run away, run away, run away!" It was only gradually, through a healthy combination of good calls and bad decisions, that I began to evolve a decision-making strategy that is both deliberate and whimsical. While the combination is paradoxical, it is also well matched both to my own sense of humor and to the many unpredictable, always emerging elements of longitudinal work, whether writing research, resource building, curriculum development, program administration, or professional leadership. For example, I joined the Stanford Study of Writing based on that gut feeling: "*Yes, do it!*" Between 2001, when the study began, and the publication of "College Writing, Identification, and the Production of Intellectual Property" in 2013, I learned a great deal about how researcher roles and responsibilities can change over time. I also gained insight into how perceptions of co-work develop longitudinally, since what it has meant to others that I chose to write repeatedly for publication with a colleague who served on my dissertation committee has changed as I have progressed (not always smoothly) through the ranks of assistant and associate professor.

Another example: Joan Mullin and I regularly tell the story of how REx: The Research Exchange Index developed from an initial conversation that took place after a roundtable during CCCC 2006 to the publication of *REx 1* in May 2016. There were several times during that decade when all of us involved allowed the project to lie fallow, and at times it was hard to tell if we were merely pausing, attempting to yield it to one another, or just plain giving up. It was during the second five years of that project that I explicitly articulated for myself what I've come to call the WHIMSY Protocol. During that time, I worked on several other multiyear collaborations, each with its own pacing, promise, and

challenges. On the best days, working on projects I initiated as the president of the coalition enabled me to reflect productively on REx or *The
Norton Anthology,* or talking with Jane Greer and Dominic DelliCarpini
about the Undergraduate Research Impact Project helped me get perspective on the Kenyon Writes data I was analyzing. Other days, my cadre
of projects seemed more like a house of mirrors, relentlessly reflecting
me back to myself in various distorted forms. It was one of those days
that prompted me to resist the impulse to run away and instead very
deliberately evaluate why I was involved in each project, how I was contributing, and what I was gaining in return in relation to what I felt I
needed both for myself and to meet different professional expectations.
I also gave a lot of thought to what was and was not moveable in relation
to what I could see in that middle distance.

The WHIMSY Protocol was born as I determined which projects I
needed to yield to my collaborators in order to give others a greater
share of my time, energy, and attention. While it is by no means fool-
proof, any of us fool enough to consider leaping into work that has a
three to five or ten-year trajectory stands to benefit from the critical
reflection it promotes. So, my final advice to readers is to keep the
WHIMSY Protocol on your mantel as you might a whim-wham or some
pretty glass whimsies. But don't forget you put it there, and don't mistake it for rubbish or fiddle-faddle: all points of origin for the contemporary term. Instead, with Dorothy Sayers's Lord Peter, let your motto
be "as my whimsy takes me," and put the protocol to good use whenever
you need it.

23

TRUST THE PROCESS

Kathleen Blake Yancey

Writing for publication, like other kinds of writing but different, too, is a process. Fully engaging in the process—and *trusting that process*—can lead to a richer, more thoughtful, more carefully crafted text; it also then becomes the process we bring to other projects.

What does the phrase *trust the process* mean? It's not a naive endorsement of writing a-rhetorically. It's not a promise that all will turn out well. It's not a pretext for ignoring signs that a draft is going badly. Rather, trust the process is a philosophy about how to approach writing for publication.

Initially, trust the process is about a commitment to articulating a writing plan, including attending to purpose, audience, genre, and material; it is likewise a commitment to enacting that plan flexibly. As a text develops, its focus and shape may change, or require a change. In such a situation, it may be time for a break, which can provide an opportunity to reassess where the author is relative to both plan and draft; such reflective assessment can lead to continuing on with the initial plan or to developing a new one.

As a draft continues developing, trust the process is a commitment to reading a draft with the pen of critique in hand. Donald Murray made the point years ago that a writer's first reader is the writer him- or herself. What in the draft isn't fully explored or expressed? What may be, quite simply, a stretch—or even wrong, regardless of what we might wish to be the case? Trust the process also means inviting *and* using the responses of others, in part through asking readers about the efficacy of the whole draft or about specific moments in the draft—does the introduction set the stage appropriately; is the evidence conclusive; is the tone kairotic?—and in part through simply asking colleagues about their read of the text.

Incorporating those responses into the manuscript is also part of trust the process. Once a draft is submitted and returned, trust the process is a

DOI: 10.7330/9781607328834.c023

commitment to read the reviews as helpful notes and to make use of that help, even if, perhaps especially if, the responses don't seem helpful at all. It can be difficult to read responses that seem off-key or out of context, but it can also be enormously instructive: what can be learned from them? What in the text inspired them? (At the least, this will tell you how someone else comes to the topic and question.) And not least, trust the process signals a commitment to revise and rewrite in light of, and with the guidance, of these colleagues. If we do this, if we trust the process in these ways, we are likely to compose a manuscript speaking to multiple contexts: our intentions, what we learn in the process of articulating them, *and* the contexts and insights of others. Moreover, to the extent that we practice such a process, it soon enough *becomes* our writing process.

Trust the process, to me, also entails another step inside of the larger process sketched out above: writing a review of the submitted draft just after, or sometimes before, formal submission. I came upon this idea when a text I had sent off for publication was returned with a fairly snarky—and wrongheaded, I thought—review. As I read the review, I was more angry than disappointed because I thought the reviewer had misunderstood the rhetorical situation of the text. My frustration also stemmed from the fact that I couldn't be sure that my reaction in this case was principled. Perhaps the disagreement between the reviewer and me was a matter of principle, but perhaps it was simply emotion, a function of the fact that the text had been rejected. As Jessica Enoch notes, of course, the entire process of writing for publication is permeated with affect:

> Of course, most, if not all, of us can identify with the affective dimension of article writing: the nervousness that accompanies submission, the tense waiting for a response, the anxious reading of reviews, the eager revising, and either the elation (and, possibly, fear) of publication or the despondence and likely anger that corresponds with rejection (2013: 431).

To address the question of how to situate response, I decided that when I next submitted a text for publication, I would also literally write my own review of the text, noting what I thought worked well, what wasn't working as well, and what was absent or unobserved. With my own review in hand, I'd know if any disagreement I had with a reviewer was based primarily in principle or emotion. For me, this approach has changed the way I write. More than once, a disappointing review has come back and my first reaction is to put it in dialogue with my own review, which gives me a starting place for moving forward. And of course, what I often do now is write that review *before* I send a draft out; I use the review as a way to see what the draft might need before it is complete.

I can't claim credit for the idea of trusting the process; it was introduced to me by Michael Spooner, then editor for the National Council of Teachers of English, in the context of my first edited collection, *Portfolios in the Writing Classroom*, which he was shepherding through the publication process. As an aside, I'm not at all sure why I was working on this project because what I brought to the project was, in large part, a good deal of *in*experience: I had published only two articles and had never done editing of any kind. On the plus side, I did have both enthusiasm and energy for the project, I knew a good deal about what there was to be known about portfolios at the time, and I was convinced that portfolios had the potential to be transformative—all of which erased any chance I would be disinterested.

Still, I had an idea for an edited collection, I developed what I thought was a strong manuscript, and I had a sympathetic editor. Then the reviews arrived. The reviewers liked the *idea* of the book (that was the good news), but they didn't actually like *the book* that I'd assembled (and that, of course, was the bad news). In this context, Michael suggested that writing for publication was a process and that I should trust it. I wasn't quite sure what that meant—the outline I sketched above is my elaborated version of a philosophy and practice developed over several years—but one obvious outcome was that the project required more process than anticipated; in fact, it was almost like starting over. I reimagined the volume's focus, shifting it from assessment to pedagogy, which also involved reframing the collection; working with the chapter authors, especially to help guide their revisions; and then reviewing and revising the full text so that the chapters cohered. The subsequent reviews endorsed publication, as did the editorial board. Trusting the process in this case, then, meant moving very circuitously to publication.

I also think it is worth noting that not all dings are alike: some of them can function as a site of reinvention, thus leading to a different publication—or two. This happened to me fairly early in my career. In the early 1990s, I wrote an article theorizing portfolio assessment, emphasizing in particular the role of writing process and the new role the student plays in such an assessment. I sent the manuscript to *College Composition and Communication*, and within a few months received a lovely rejection letter from Richard Gephardt, the editor, and two reviews, one of which was helpful in noting how in (over)emphasizing process, I seemed to have eliminated student texts as a factor in assessment and explaining why, from the reviewer's perspective, this was a problem. Although I didn't agree, I understood the concern.

The problem, according to this review, was my emphasis on process, not my articulation of the role of the student in portfolio assessment as I had theorized it; accordingly, I took the issue of student-as-agent as my point of departure for my talk at the inaugural Watson Conference at the University of Louisville, in 1996, and as a chapter in the 2000 volume that emerged from it, the Boehm, Rosner, and Journet edited collection *History, Reflection, and Narrative: The Professionalization of Composition Studies 1965–1996.*

In "A Brief History of Writing Assessment in the Late Twentieth Century: The Writer Comes Center Stage," I argued that two factors in portfolio assessment increased and enhanced the role and the agency of students in assessment. First, the multiplicity of texts encourages any reader to look to the student for guidance as to ways to read and interpret them; second, the reflection in the portfolio allowed the student to articulate explicitly what the portfolio meant—arguments that I had begun to trace in the rejected article. Moreover, questions about the student coming center stage also informed my 1999 article "Looking Back as We Look Forward: Historicizing Writing Assessment," published in one of the two issues commemorating fifty years of the Conference on College Composition and Communication. As I noted early in the article, the self is always at the heart of questions about assessment, not just portfolio assessment: "First, the role that the self should play in any assessment is a central concern for educators. It is the self that we want to teach, that we hope will learn, but that we are often loathe to evaluate. What is the role of the person/al in any writing assessment?" (484). In sum, the rejection from *CCC* helped me refocus and sharpen my argument about the role of the self in assessment, leading to a talk and two publications, the latter of which has been reprinted in several anthologies. Put another way, the first ding from *CCC* ultimately led to a publication in *CCC* that people still read today.

Writing for publication isn't easy, but if we treat it as a process, if we practice it as a process, we may find that publication isn't the real or only benefit of that process: writing better and learning along the way are.

REFERENCES

Enoch, Jessica. 2013. "*College English*: The Archive." *College English* 75 (4): 430–36.
Yancey, Kathleen Blake. 1999. "Looking Back as We Look Forward: Historicizing Writing Assessment." *College Composition and Communication* 50 (3): 483–503.
Yancey, Kathleen Blake. 2000. "A Brief History of Writing Assessment in the Late Twentieth Century: The Writer Comes Center Stage." In *History, Reflection, and Narrative: The Professionalization of Composition Studies 1965–1996,* edited by Beth Boehm, Mary Rosner, and Debra Journet, 115–28. Stamford, CT: Able.

SECTION 2

Getting Feedback

Sharing Drafts, Collaborating, and (Re)Developing

24

WRITING IS/AS COMMUNAL

Trixie G. Smith

Find a writing partner or even a network of writers who will work collaboratively to listen, read, question, and offer critique and praise throughout the writing and revision process. For one-on-one feedback go to your local writing center; otherwise, form a writing group that meets regularly.

Despite romantic notions of the lone scholar in the ivory tower, we don't actually do our best writing in isolation; writing is a communication process and thus a communal process. We need other writers to read our work and we need to read other writers. There are a variety of methods you can use to get regular feedback on your writing; first is your local writing center.

Writing center tutors are trained to work with writers from across the university in a variety of disciplines, looking at global ideas related to purpose and audience, and for clear arguments and support. In particular, when working in an area they are unfamiliar with, they act as general readers who can ask questions about writing that doesn't make sense, that is filled with jargon or unclear language, that seems illogical or unsupported, that makes assumptions about readers' knowledge or background, and so on.

I myself have worked one-on-one with colleagues from fields I had no understanding of, at least at first. Not knowing the ins and outs of stem cell research or nanotechnologies in medicine has never prevented me from helping writers improve the readability of their writing or the logic of their arguments. In addition, reading work from other fields, in genres different from my own, has increased my own repertoire of writing styles and techniques, giving me new ways of supporting my theses and modeling my arguments. Don't discount ideas from other fields; their insights can be extremely valuable.

Second, many centers, as well as teaching and learning programs, also offer or help facilitate writing groups for faculty and graduate

DOI: 10.7330/9781607328834.c024

students. These small groups of three to six people plus a facilitator are designed to meet on a regular basis, usually weekly. They help keep writers focused on their work by providing regular deadlines as well as a regular audience for feedback. Groups decide among themselves how much writing to share each week: for instance, a few pages from everyone every week, or a full draft from each person once a month on a rotating basis. If you don't have any formal structures available for creating or running writing groups, form your own with a set of colleagues from across campus or across town—others who want to get regular feedback on their writing. If that still doesn't work, consider forming a long-distance group that meets regularly online; the important thing is to get other eyes on your work on a recurring basis. Look for colleagues who aren't afraid to be pushed or to push you, who will be honest with you about your work—both the positives and the negatives.

As a writing center and writing project director, it's no surprise that I'm often asked about how to improve writing, what to do about writer's block, and how to work with revision advice from editors and peer reviewers, among other writing-related questions. In response, I perpetually give the advice above to both students and faculty—in workshops, in class, one-on-one, while passing in the hall . . . and it's such good advice I follow it myself (yes, really). In fact, this short chapter has been shared with several writing center colleagues at a couple of different stages. Their ideas were quite helpful in focusing and revising.

Anyone can use the writing center I direct at Michigan State University: undergraduate and graduate students, faculty, and staff. We see some faculty, but not nearly enough, and certainly not all of those who ask for help. I stress with faculty that I use the center myself on a regular basis, making appointments to look at my writing; collaborating with our consultants on research, writing, program and curriculum design; and talking with others about projects. I try to be an example to my students, to staff, and to other faculty, urging them to rethink any stigmas or myths they may have assigned to the purposes of the center or the "proper" way to write and revise.

In our center, we also facilitate graduate and faculty writing groups; any given semester there may be twelve (or more!) groups up and running, typically with three to five members each. We also help faculty and graduate programs across campus start and run their own groups. Whenever I facilitate a multidisciplinary group, I also participate as a writer and not just a responder or organizer. One group holds a special place in my heart; the four members of this group were together for over three years, meeting weekly to share and respond to writing (and to life, which, of course, affects our writing). The group disbanded when multiple members received tenure, then took new jobs elsewhere; one launched a new research lab. I personally shared drafts of two different textbooks with this group and was able to draw on the members' expertise in various disciplines as I worked on a writing in the disciplines manuscript. They were invaluable to my thinking and revising.

All of the members of this group would credit part of their successes to the center and their writing group because here they were able to do things they didn't feel they could do in their own departments with their (sometimes competitive) colleagues: hash out new ideas—starting from really rough, half-formed hypotheses; draft multiple versions of an argument; test model after model after model of charts, graphs, diagrams, tables, images; interpret and address reviewer comments on grant proposals and journal articles; craft counterarguments for their own ways of thinking and writing when needed; test presentation slides and talks; learn about their own writing processes and habits—both good and bad; and enjoy support and comradery.

For example, one member of this group learned that she had the bad habit of using negative definitions only; always telling readers what something wasn't rather than what it was. Another had the habit of burying the thesis at the end of the paper, which didn't go over well with the STEM audiences she was writing for or the grantors in the sciences who wanted to know right away what her proposed project was trying to do. Many of these group members came looking for a group because they had been members of a graduate writing group while in school, or they had used their university's writing center while completing their dissertations and they wanted a place to regularly share their writing. They had already learned the value of getting a second (third, fourth . . .) pair of eyes on their work. In fact, all members of this group claimed that working with a community of writers from other disciplines helped them write for more general audiences in their fields, made them create more effective models and diagrams, and gave them incentive to write even when they didn't want to because the rest of the group was waiting on their work and ready to offer constructive feedback.

And when they really didn't have a draft of anything, writers would come in to brainstorm possibilities with new calls for papers or requests for proposals.

Consistently sharing your writing with a community of writers you trust leads to improvement in your own writing as well as your ability to give feedback (as a peer reviewer, as a colleague, as an instructor).

into my PhD program with a cohort that included other students of color who helped me build a community of trust and reciprocity.

Although I fully acknowledge my privilege in my PhD program, I also have to mention that the road to (and through) this program was not easy. As an immigrant Latina, I had (and continue to have) a demanding financial and emotional responsibility to my family, both in and beyond the United States. This responsibility inherently shaped my approach to work in the discipline, fueling my motivations, affordances, and limitations. Hence, by the time I got to my PhD program, with all the privileges it afforded, I was ready to invest wholeheartedly, aiming not only to create a space for me to succeed, but also committed to making active contributions to a community that works and builds knowledge together. The advice I share here is part of this effort.

ADVICE #1: TURN SEMINAR PAPER(S) INTO PUBLICATIONS

An initial piece of advice that prefaces my focus on cultivating community below was the ever-popular "Nothing you write as a PhD student should be just for class. Every paper should turn into a publication." Although I do think there is truth in this, for me, coursework was a launching point for making connections among disciplinary communities and conversations. I could not publish one side of the conversation without acknowledging the other parts and pieces, and I always had to do additional reading outside of what was assigned in class to make a coherent argument that would be accepted for publication. For this reason, my advice is that yes, all the writing you do in graduate school should lead *toward* a publication. However, it's important to spend time reading and conversing with outside content (and people) for editors and reviewers to publish your work, and also to do justice to the work that we're citing and building.

To this end, what worked best for me was to collectively turn *pieces* of *several* seminar papers in a given semester or year into a single publication, taking the opportunity to approach a topic from a wide range of perspectives that were covered in different ways *across* my classes. For instance, during my first year in the PhD program, I wrote and submitted a piece about multilingual students creating multimodal projects. This piece contains readings and writing that I completed in three different courses I took as a first-year PhD student: Histories of Composition, Digital Rhetoric, and Research Methods. The perspectives I gained through conversations and assignments in *all* of those courses helped shape my article in a way that would not have been possible if I accounted for the content only in a single course.

Because my professors allowed me to complete seminar papers related to our course but tailored to my own interests, I was able to use each class to write a different part of my paper, or to engage with scholarship relevant to different pieces of my larger project. By making connections across content and people from various courses, I was also able to strengthen my paper through feedback from professors and peers with different strengths, backgrounds, and approaches, leading to the second piece of advice I offer for publishing as a graduate student.

ADVICE #2: ESTABLISH YOUR COMMUNITY OF FEEDBACK

As I used several different courses to get feedback on a single publication, I became more comfortable sharing early drafts of my work with professors and peers. I used all course assignments and reading responses as a way to share ideas with my professors, thinking of these assignments as opportunities for *dialogue* rather than assessment. For instance, I aimed to use reading responses not just to write summaries of what we read in class, but also as opportunities to make connections between course content and the data I was collecting for my own research. In this way, assignments were a way to get feedback on my research in preparation for publication outside of a single course. It's important for grad students to consider that the faculty who read their work in classes are often also faculty who review articles for publication in journals. If you have a professor who researches digital rhetoric, for instance, it's likely that this professor has also reviewed and/or submitted manuscripts for publication in journals that include work on digital rhetoric. By taking a class with this professor, a graduate student essentially has a window into the mind of a researcher and reviewer in a specific area, as well as an opportunity to establish a relationship with this professor as both a student and a future colleague.

Although I would not advise grad students to send all their drafts to the same professors, I do think it's important to use graduate school as a way to build reciprocal collegial relationships that support successful research. For me, this means not only feeling comfortable enough to ask professors for feedback on my manuscript drafts, it also entails offering to provide that same courtesy to other professors, colleagues, and peers. I've learned that academia often runs on karma, meaning that if I ask for feedback on my work, I commit to also providing feedback for someone else. In this way, graduate students can not only get the immediate benefit of receiving suggestions and ideas to help them publish in graduate school, they also enter into a sustainable community of feedback that will only become more valuable with time. Once you leave graduate school, your professors may not be in the office right next to yours, but they (along with your peers) may still be valuable contributors to your community of feedback. This is what (in my opinion) keeps our work and our collegial relationships connected, even in the transient spaces of the academy. Since I left graduate school, the people in my community of feedback are those I turn to for ideas, encouragement, and motivation in my research and writing, even as my community continues to grow and be separated by distance and time.

26

IF YOU ARE GOING TO COLLABORATE
Three Considerations

Joan Mullin

Many publications in our field are written collaboratively with colleagues, students, and discourse community participants. When choosing collaborators for a project, authors should consider not just scholarly expertise, publishing credentials, investment in a project, or enthusiasm for an idea, but also personal characteristics such as work style, outside commitments, and cultural practices.

Having collaboratively written articles and chapters, and partnered on editing collections, a journal, and a series, I've had direct experience with all of the problems associated with writing partnerships. While I've often been the problem solver in collaborations, I have also been the problem maker—having failed and then learned a great deal from colleagues about my own intellectual, personal, and work styles.

These aren't always easy to see or to admit to. So the advice here comes from experience and reflection: (1) choose writing collaborators carefully; (2) be honest about your own interpersonal and work style; (3) don't make assumptions about how other academic cultures work, or about your familiarity with them. More about each of these below, but first I want to share a story.

Perhaps the best example of the first two pieces of advice is a case when two well-known scholars, Pat and Mike, were putting a rather unique collection together that involved timed collaboration among the contributors conducting interlocking pieces of research for a book. The project grew out of a conversation at a conference; the two had never worked together but assumed, given their publication histories, that all would be well. As the proposal came together and authors were chosen to participate, Mike began missing his deadlines. This became such a pattern that Pat asked Mike if his workload and commitments were so extensive that he couldn't participate in the project. At this point, given his publishing and university workloads, Mike should have backed out

DOI: 10.7330/9781607328834.c026

and, as Pat later admitted, she should have encouraged him to do so, but Pat was hesitant to break up this relatively new partnership, one that could be a high point in her own publishing career.

Avoiding further confrontation, Pat suggested inviting a third coeditor to distribute the work and Mike agreed. Pat subsequently called Sharon, asking if she would be a third on the coediting team, admitting that she was no longer sure Mike could pull his weight—an upfront and wise move on her part. Sharon agreed on one condition: should Mike miss deadlines, they would have to ask him to back out of the project and rethink their workloads and timelines. Mike agreed to the plan and all seemed well at first. Then he again began missing deadlines, placing more pressure and work on Pat and Sharon. During a very difficult conversation at the Conference on College Composition and Communication (CCCC), Mike admitted to Sharon and Pat that he was way over his head in commitments and he would be relieved to step down as editor—if his chapter could still remain in the collection. Relieved also, Sharon and Pat agreed, but ended up having to plead with Mike to meet every deadline along the way. His chapter barely made the last extended deadline.

Procrastination, taking on too many obligations, writing and rewriting at the infinitesimal word level, and failing to organize sources all found their way into Pat and Sharon's discussion with Mike. Deadlines always bedevil editors and publishers, so while it is important to choose writing partners carefully, it is also wise to set up early deadlines for yourself and others. If you need to give authors deadlines for a collection you are editing, set them a minimum of four weeks before the actual deadline. Someone will need an extension (and it might be you). Make those deadlines absolute at some point—two weeks before the actual deadline. If someone is continually missing deadlines, it's time to reconsider the partnership, no matter how famous or knowledgeable the author. Consider a similar strategy for your own writing (though it's harder to fool yourself by setting a fake early deadline).

If Pat could have faced Mike early on, a lot of angst, anger, missed opportunities, and a delayed publication could have been avoided. As editor of a journal and series, I have heard a lot of Pat and Mike (and Sharon) stories, where one or two people do all or most of the work and a third tags along, getting equal credit for little or no work.

Creating agreements with exit points and clear commitments is vital in collaborations, and I know this because my own private hell is paved with good intentions of what I was going to get done when. I couldn't be honest with myself about my time and workload, any more than another scholar could be honest to her coeditors when she asked to be listed as lead author because she was coming up for promotion to professor. What she didn't tell the others, both of whom did equal work on a lengthy and prestigious project, is that only the lead would be listed as editor—her coeditors' names would appear only on their chapters. They had let her make all the agreements with the publisher, cutting their own workloads in doing so, but also cutting themselves out.

Too often I have heard authors say of collaborators or of contributors to a collection, "Well, I just don't know how to tell her that her idea doesn't belong in that section/his piece isn't ready to be published/the revisions we are suggesting aren't optional." If you are the one tied to your own words and if you see collaboration as a way to "win" a conversation, don't collaborate. If you can't make credible editorial suggestions to that famous scholar or tell him that his submission needs revision, or if you start a writing collaboration with a senior colleague and find that your ideas and words are disappearing into hers, don't collaborate. Experienced writers understand revisioning, and the most rewarding end to a long collaboration over an article was when a new writer told a veteran academic that she didn't agree with the direction of the text. The veteran agreed they should write their own articles and their relationship is still intact.

* * *

Ideas for publications often happen during casual conversation, at conferences, through email, and in a number of other venues with friends and colleagues. But friends you like to hang out with or a senior colleague in the field might not be the best writing partner for an article, chapter, or edited collection. Ideally, you want to find someone who complements your own style. Are you the theorist who has trouble articulating ideas for an audience outside your immediate area? Do you have difficulty creating practices that grow out of theory, or visually representing data? Find a collaborator who pushes you to think practically, whom you enjoy exchanging concepts with, who can complement and ground you. Do you like Evernote because you can get ahead of and stay on top of data organization and deadlines? Then you may have difficulty working with someone who tends to procrastinate and work to the last minute—though that person may like working with you. Are you a broad-idea person, a visionary who sees connections? Then you'd work well with a detail person who can fill in gaps you leave or who asks questions that lead you to stronger transitions between those broad ideas.

Point #1: Find out your potential collaborator's work style and his or her expectations about what the work is, who will do it, and when and how the work will get done. Too often partnerships are created between a mentor (someone established in the field) and a mentee (someone less established), with each assuming the other will do the brunt of the work and both ending up disappointed, with a flagging project. There have been new scholars working on edited collections who are reluctant to tell established scholars that their work needs revision. I have also seen friends who, because of the nature of their friendship, can't be honest with each other about an increasingly imbalanced workload during the writing or editorial process. Difficult conversations over whose name appears first on an article can rend equitable workloads, erupt in passive-aggressive actions, or upend partnerships. Think about your own and potential collaborator's interpersonal and communication styles: are you able to negotiate language or does one of you always correct the other and hang onto his or her own language?

Point #2: Find out how personally compatible you are and how well you can disagree. Writing together is a collaboration, not a competition. Finally, collaboration naturally carries human risk. Whole projects have come to a standstill with a new appointment that overextends one of the partners; illness intervenes in other projects; academic environments or cut budgets can press on workloads; family pressures change priorities. Successful collaboration on writing projects takes not only a lot of prior thought about the partnership but also patience. The latter may be difficult to muster when a publication may make the difference in a tenure case. Thoughtful preparation, timing, and a game plan that doesn't place high stakes on a project can help create successful writing collaborations, and successful writing collaborations produce some of the richest scholarship in our field.

Point #3: Cultural differences make choosing a collaborator and spelling out understandings all the more delicate and necessary, especially if one culture is used to abrupt, straightforward interactions and the other depends on establishing social relationships, politeness, and cultural nuances. Many of us now collaborate internationally, with colleagues outside of our own known academic environments. Unless you have grown up in or spent significant time in the culture of others, you will want to carefully consider differences that may affect a collaboration. This includes cultural work cycles (including academic breaks), pressures to publish, and facility in the target publishing language. Perhaps the most important factor is to make sure you are understanding the central project's concept in the same way.

Cultural differences can range from misperceptions over how a theoretical term is "commonly" used to delays because participants and researchers are on different semester schedules and one or the other isn't available for interviewing, surveying, observing, responding, or writing. Professional or personal conflicts among distant collaborators, which might be remedied if witnessed, can unknowingly simmer and escalate, ending an entire project.

* * *

The experiences I described above, and the recommendations I've offered here, have helped me either to complete or let go of projects. They've helped guide others through difficulties they may be having with collaborators, ones they may not want to confront or don't know how to name, much less address. They've helped guide feedback about a lack of international focus in some chapters of a proposed collection to the author-editors, who subsequently took a hard look at what it was they were really interested in. They shifted the entire premise of the collection, narrowed the range of chapters, and submitted the proposal to another series. The resulting book will be more successful in the end because of the flexibility of the collaborators: their willingness to take up the feedback, to work within realistic timelines. However, the editors also came to see the difficulties of communicating cross-culturally, an issue that created the mixed focus to begin with. Whether I am acting as editor or writer, I know that everything can't be anticipated or addressed with written deadlines and defined roles; that projects and partners can change, derail, fall through; that a project can shift its focus and evolve—and that's okay.

27

FROM CHAPTER TO ARTICLE WITH COLLABORATIVE PLANNING

Linda Flower

The genre of the "dissertation chapter" seems to bring out writer-based prose in the best of us. These sample sentences reflect this approach quite well:

- "In this chapter I am going to discuss [my topic], starting with the work of [key source], which led me to look at the connection between [my topic] and [another area of scholarship] . . . I noticed . . . wondered . . . found . . ."
- "In his article 'ABC,' Professor X defines DEF as . . ."

This familiar approach uses the writer's own thinking process to structure the prose, typically topicalizing the writer as agent. Or it topicalizes an academic term from the writer's literature review, followed by description or definition. The great advantage of either move is that it offers the writer a very efficient strategy for memory retrieval—finding and organizing what she knows. Unfortunately, the reader of an article is probably looking for an engaging problem or question to motivate reading and for an argument that has relevance not just to this moment or dissertation chapter, but to a larger issue, ideally one the reader already cares about (Flower 1979).

Translating a writer-based piece into a reader-based text can start with retopicalizing key sentences to focus on issues and ideas (versus mere topics and terms) and/or replacing your writerly discovery narrative with more of an argument-based structure. Beneath that revision, however, lies the intellectual work of drawing and articulating often-unstated inferences about what you trying to accomplish here and why; how your ideas are connected; and what significance this holds for whom. That's why a writing group can give you something that good advice (about either the topic or genre conventions) can't. A reading group can force you to think for a reader and show you arguments readers might not get and/or the ones they might assume they get, but misinterpret.

DOI: 10.7330/9781607328834.c027

Yet for all their virtues, peer review and the writing groups I have seen can be tricky tools to manage. The very conventions of such review tend to produce advice based on what the commentator would do. When one is writing a genre-guided first-year theme on common knowledge, that can indeed be helpful. But turning two to three years of research into a reader-based argument may depend on figuring out how to fully articulate the rich, interconnected body of knowledge you have constructed in your mind in a way readers can—and want to—follow.

So here is where my advice comes in: **Get your peers to help you think**. Set aside part of your group time for the relatively structured practice of *collaborative planning*. By that I mean that the writer, in the role of the planner, does most of the work and talking. In a dramatic reversal of peer review, the partner's role is not to advise but to prompt you with a set of challenging planning questions—ones that you may or may not be ready to answer yet. As a practice, *collaborative planning* draws you, the writer, to explore your current thinking in three rhetorical spaces by asking:

1. What is your *purpose?* What are the goals motivating *this* article: why are you making *this* case? And at the more micro level, why are you framing *this* paragraph or sentence in the way you do? The companion question in this space is: What is your *key point?* What idea is the reader supposed to take away?

2. How might a given *reader respond* to what you have said or done here?

3. What *textual conventions* or rhetorical moves are you using—and what alternatives have you considered?

In short, a collaborative planning session actively helps you think through the rhetorical challenges reader-based prose presents.

This advice has a history. First, it found me. John R. Hayes and I were in the middle of a study on the planning process of experienced and inexperienced writers—and it was clear the "experts" were playing in a different ball field with a larger repertoire of moves (Flower et al. 1992). But I wondered, is this "novice" performance we are seeing just a matter of *can't* or *don't?* So soon I had a string of sophomores (fulfilling their "research requirement") coming into my office to do a think-aloud planning session for a paper actually due in a class they shared. To mirror the demanding concerns we had seen experts raise in their own planning, in the session I posed a variety of prompts, from "What is your point here?" to "How do you think your professor might respond to this idea?" to "So, what if someone disagreed with that claim?" The session wasn't easy or short, so I was relieved that the students seemed to be such good sports about it. That turned to surprise when they asked if their room-mate could be a "subject" in the study, because, they said, this process had been so helpful.

They were telling me that this social interaction with a partner was a potentially powerful pedagogical practice—when a partner was able to lead them into a new rhetorical space and draw out their own thinking. This became the basis for the structured collaborative planning practice sketched above, which consolidates the rhetorical moves seen in good writers into three key areas and foregrounds this distinctive relationship between the planner and the partner. (For details on the practice itself, see Flower 1998.)

It was clear that under these conditions, sophomore writers could indeed do some inventive rhetorical thinking. But the next surprise was seeing what first-year students, in a large multisection study, actually did with this good advice when they practiced and recorded this process on their own as they met in a dorm or coffee shop. The result was good news from a researcher's perspective (Flower 1994). Collaborative plan-ning did indeed prompt a dramatic increase in the amount of *rhetorical* planning, in the construction of new ideas (that turned up in central places in the final texts), and in students' reflective awareness of their choices and process.

But from a writer's perspective, the story is not all a bed of roses. It seems that that when writers set meaningful goals for themselves, plan-ning is also a site of conflict, of what I would call useful disturbance. Writers discover that ideas and approaches compete with one another; the logic of one section doesn't connect with the previous one; multiple kinds of readers pop to mind, raising different expectations; or it sud-denly becomes clear that the writer, in fact, doesn't actually know how some of his ideas are connected. Planning becomes a space in which writers rise to more conscious *awareness* of these conflicts and learn to *negotiate* them. That is, good writers—or writers with good partners—do.

Because translating a dissertation into a work people will read and cite is not an editing task but an intellectual challenge, you will want a partner who is up to the task, that is, a planning partner who:

- Is supportive, not with free advice or just positive feedback, but with insistent curiosity, asking questions like: "Okay, I hear that, but what is your real *point* here?"
- Resists your own probably persistent tendency to review your topic knowledge in response to such questions.
- Draws you to face the rhetorical problems posed by articulating your purpose and key point, projecting an audience response, and

considering textual options, and recognizing and rising to reflective awareness of conflicts.

- And, with sweet insistence, encourages you to build a more self-consciously negotiated meaning.

For this reason, I see collaborative planning as a rather systematic practice. Even better, when writers record and review the session they often gain new insight into their habits of mind, including their own brilliant and/or unproductive strategies.

As a graduate advisor, I also think my most productive meetings are when I ask these hard questions, follow up points of tension, and—listening hard for the writer's logic—take good notes to let the writer see what she has constructed over the course of our conversation. The test of a good collaborative planning session will be addressed by the question: Have we both learned something?

REFERENCES

Flower, Linda. 1979. "Writer-Based Prose: A Cognitive Basis for Problems in Writing." *College English* 41 (1): 19–37.

Flower, Linda. 1994. *The Construction of Negotiated Meaning: A Social Cognitive Theory of Writing.* Carbondale: Southern Illinois University Press.

Flower, Linda. 1998. "Making Plans." In *Problem-Solving Strategies for Writing in College and Community,*" by Linda Flower, 81–126. Fort Worth, TX: Harcourt Brace College Publishers.

Flower, Linda, K. A. Schriver, L. Carey, C. Haas, and J. R. Hayes. 1992. "Planning in Writing: The Cognition of a Constructive Process." In *A Rhetoric of Doing: Essays on Written Discourse in Honor of James L. Kinneavy,* edited by S. Witte, N. Nakadate, and R. Cherry, 191–243. Carbondale: Southern Illinois University Press.

Flower, Linda, D. L. Wallace, L. Norris, and R. E. Burnett, eds. 1994. *Making Thinking Visible: Writing, Collaborative Planning, and Classroom Inquiry.* Urbana, IL: National Council of Teachers of English.

28

WHAT'S THE WAY IN?
Some Lessons and Considerations about Inventing as a Collaborative Team, from a Collaborative Team

Julie Lindquist and Bump Halbritter

Invention is a peculiar and difficult phenomenon in any event, as a rhetorician or two in the past couple of millennia may have noted. When you invent as part of a writing team, the peculiarities and difficulties of inventive work are both more and less peculiar and difficult. Working within a long-term partnership has special affordances, we have discovered, and (we believe) this experience delivers lessons that may be useful for anyone working to get an idea into print—but especially for those who write, or who are thinking of writing, with another (or others).

In what follows, we hope to share a few things we have learned from our experience as long-term collaborative partners. At the center of our story is one piece of writing in particular, an article we published in *College English* a few years ago. This piece represented our first major publication together: through it, we learned not only what it means to write collaboratively, but about what it meant to work collaboratively as *us*—two people who had been collaborating in other ways, who had come into our partnership with different areas of interest and scholarly identities, and who were at different moments in our careers. The lesson here, we believe, is that invention in a partnership is a different sort of process than invention alone—that it has its own rhythms, affordances, constraints, and surprises—that it is not simply additive or subtractive (twice the ideas! half the labor!). We learned what it means to write collaboratively *as us* by doing it, but we hope that our story can better help you imagine what it may be like to collaborate as *you*.

The article we reference developed from a long-term research project, Literacy Corps Michigan: "Time, Lives, and Videotape: Operationalizing Discovery in Scenes of Literacy Sponsorship," published in the November 2012 issue of *College English*. In this article, we elaborated a methodology for a scaffolded program of inquiry for discovering experiences

DOI: 10.7330/9781607328834.c028

of literacy sponsorship, one in which video and phenomenological interviews played a central role. Through this article, which developed over several years from and following our involvement in LCM, we learned many things, some of which had to do with what it meant to work together as writers. The piece had several versions and iterations, went through a difficult and attenuated review process, and ultimately, won NCTE's Richard C. Ohmann Outstanding Article in *College English* Award in 2013. The process of inventing this piece of scholarship helped us understand how we discovered and worked through ideas. Each of the lessons that follow is an articulation of something we have taken away from our work together so far—but since the particulars of our situation may be, well, particular, we pose a question for you in each case—a thing you may, in establishing or maintaining a writing relationship, want to consider for *your* case.

In a later chapter, "What's the Way Forward? Some Lessons and Considerations about Revising from Feedback as a Collaborative Team, from a Collaborative Team" (see Halbritter and Lindquist, this volume), we offer some advice for working with and through feedback at the post-editorial (review) end of the process.

Lesson #1: There are different kinds of collaborations, and each has its own way of behaving.

Q: WHAT ARE THE SPECIFIC TERMS OF YOUR COLLABORATION?

In a recent *New Yorker* piece, Cass Sunstein and Richard Thaler described the long-term collaboration of psychologists Daniel Kahneman and Amos Tversky. Of the pair's habits of invention, Sunstein and Thaler write:

> Kahneman and Tversky were in constant conversation. They worked intensely in a small seminar room or a coffee shop, or while taking a long walk. The sessions were private; no one else was invited to join. As they began to produce work together, each sentence would be written, rewritten, and rewritten again, with Kahneman manning the typewriter. (Tversky never did master the art of the keyboard.) On a good day, they would write a paragraph or two (2016).

The essay is primarily about the joys and heartbreak of a lifelong friendship, but it is also about what happens when people with big ideas come together to produce even bigger ideas. It goes without saying that there are as many kinds of collaborative partnerships as there are partners (though there may be some recurring types): long-term partnerships or shorter-term, more occasional collaborations; those who work at a distance or those who work in parallel or in sequence; those who mostly sit together and work out every idea together in conversation (like Kahneman and Tversky). The choice of *how* to collaborate depends on institutional location, institutional position (and stability of these), available human resources, career trajectory and moment; affective, labor-related, and creative compatibilities—the list goes on. We have to come to think of the kind of collaboration we have as (in some ways) analogous to being in a band.

Bump spent many years in and out of bands before finding his way to graduate school in his mid-thirties. In many ways, his ongoing collaboration with Julie is just another band. In fact, the metaphor is especially productive in thinking about the life cycle of a collaboratively written article. In the beginning, writing that first set of tunes, all you have are each other and your ideas. And while one or two of those first tunes may make it into the main catalogue eventually, what truly lasts is the band itself—the relationship between the band members. And the stronger that bond is forged in the early moves, the longer the band lasts—the better the band is able to weather the inevitable storms of the music business: "The band is great, but your drummer sucks"; "The drummer is great, but your singer sucks"; repeat ad infinitum.

When we worked together on "Time, Lives, and Videotape," we spent a lot of time composing in the manner of Kahneman and Tversky, at least in their earlier years—sitting in a room together, hashing out the terms and implications of every idea. One of us would deliver a riff, and the other would play along, or hear it as the seed of a melody. Ideas that found no purchase were demoted from the record, or bracketed off for use at a later time. Having a commitment to an inventive team allows for a different relationship between process and products, immediate and potential. There's a greater investment in the productive capacity of the team over the long term, so the false starts, digressions, and inefficiencies aren't relegated to the trash heap, but very likely become productive in a later moment.

Lesson #2. The scene of work determines the nature of the invention.
Q: WHAT HAPPENS IN THE VARIOUS SCENES OF YOUR WORK TOGETHER? WHAT KINDS OF INVENTION ARE LIKELY TO HAPPEN IN WHAT KINDS OF SPACES, AND HOW CAN (AN UNDERSTANDING OF) THIS RELATIONSHIP OF SCENE TO INVENTION BE TURNED TO YOUR ADVANTAGE?
One of the things we've learned as we've worked together is that *scenes* of writing matter: that a particular inventive process emerges within each space, and that part of learning how to make a writing project most productive is to learn which scenes of invention have which affordances, and to begin to predict how a routine of *place* (as well as *time*, which we

will also say a few things about) can be as generative (and productive, if all goes well!) as possible.

We produce notes and maps and jottings—or, as musicians in a band, lots of riffs and bits of melody. Later, or on other occasions, we work by composing chunks separately, and then working to effect syntheses of these chunks later, when we're working together. More recently, we have been working in Google Docs (which we didn't do in the process of making "Time, Lives, and Videotape" but which, we have found, also has its distinctive potentials). With Google Docs, we can compose from different sites in real time, and pose questions back and forth as we write (we have even begun to do so while sitting in the same room). And yet, we are finding that the first step, for us, is often a conversation—or several—in which we discover our purposes. If we were to take different jobs that separated us geographically, our routines would be radically altered—as would, no doubt, the nature of the products. In any case, our collaborations are as much a story of spatial mobility as anything else.

What kind of invention task can be best accomplished in which scenes? Finding a productive writing routine, we have found, is as much about finding the right places—and the right forms of togetherness and apartness—as it is about finding the right time(s).

Lesson #3: Timelines can feel difficult to predict and control under the most controlled circumstances, but working with a partner can augment that unpredictability.

Q: HOW MIGHT WORKING WITH A PARTNER MAKE IT MORE DIFFICULT TO PREDICT OR KEEP TO A TIMELINE?

Under the best of circumstances, and as a general rule, a thing you're writing for publication will take much longer to get into print than you imagine, or will likely predict. This is even more true, we have found, in writing collaboratively. Thus, prepare to entertain the affordances (and perils) of time. Working together makes the difficult business of predicting timelines and adhering to schedules even more difficult, especially in a new partnership when you're discovering the habits, predilections, and work routines of your partner. You have a lifetime of experience observing how you yourself work, and you might expect that your own habits and routines are more or less the same as those of others: who *wouldn't* want to write first thing in the morning, when the day is fresh and the inner critic dormant? Who *wouldn't* be inclined to begin a project months before the deadline, to allow for myriad low-stakes interventions? When you work closely with another person, especially over a period of time, you not only see but *feel* the constraints and possibilities

of different orientations to, and uses of, time. One partner may habitu-
ally compose as if painting a wall—adding a layer, letting it dry, adding a
layer the following day, and so on (Julie)—while the other may compose
in protracted, intensive bursts of productivity (Bump). Part of the work
of establishing a productive partnership, then, is to figure out how to
honor and sustain what seem to be incommensurate habits, at the same
time as finding a routine that is viable for both.

And all of this work takes—you guessed it—time.

However, there is good news: what you lose in efficiency, you often
recover in generativity. Our experience has been that when things
have taken longer, it's not only because any given writing project has to
accommodate the demands and vagaries of two people's divergent lives
and schedules, it's often because brainstorming can be stormier when
there are two weather systems in operation: you get both more pre-
cipitation and more wind. In the case of "Time, Lives, and Videotape,"
we found that our common investment in, and experience with, the
research project out of which this writing emerged kept us in the space
of invention for a very long time (years), as we continued to learn new
things from that project even after we stopped actively collecting data.

**Lesson #4: In a collaborative relationship, each person takes on a peda-
gogical role.**
Q: HOW CAN YOU IMAGINE YOUR PARTNERSHIP IS A PEDAGOGICAL
ARRANGEMENT? WHAT ARE THE TEACHERLY MOVES THAT SEEM TO MAKE
SPACE FOR THE BEST IDEAS TO EMERGE?
If you've never written as part of a team, you might expect that an intellectual partnership formed for the purposes of producing scholarship
would be both additive (you get twice the intellectual stuff, an enlarged
disciplinary geography), and subtractive (having two people on the job
naturally reduces the sheer labor). While this may more closely describe
certain provisional or shorter-term collaborative relationships, what
has happened in our situation is that we have grown as concerned with
longer-term, transferable knowledge as with short-term predicaments of
invention. To put it another way, we have found that when you work as
part of a long-term partnership, you find ways to facilitate each other's
intellectual growth. You become each other's teachers. We have discovered that we often take on these roles in conversations—one of us functions as facilitator for the other's ideas-in-progress. Each of us came to
our partnership with a particular intellectual history and body of knowledge, and working together has been a process of learning what the
other knows: in Julie's case, audiovisual writing; in Bump's case, literacy

and cultural studies. "Time, Lives, and Videotape" is a disciplinary synthesis. However, rather than predictably supplying, in every case, what was a needed idea in any given moment, we have helped each other to learn the commonplaces of the less-familiar field.

What does it mean to become a teacher within a collaborative relationship? Like any pedagogical situation, learning happens best through induction, problem solving, and discovery, and not through direct didactic intervention. In other words, teaching and learning happen best when you are each working to address a common problem (strange that we have found John Dewey's work to be so productive, isn't it?). Good teachers invite their students to explore, take risks, work with ideas that are not yet formed. That means that, when you're generating ideas together, you need to trust that you will eventually hear something you don't yet hear—and that what you do hear, when you hear it, will have value.

If the collaborative relationship is strong, ongoing, and predicated on faith in each other's potential to offer contributions, you can afford to wait. The most valuable response to an idea is likely to be something along the lines of "Say more about that!" Of course, who is in the role of "teacher" most immediately depends not only on the expertise of each person involved, but on the institutional roles that each partner has (e.g., grad student, junior faculty, senior faculty). In our case, Bump was pre-tenure faculty when we began working together; Julie was senior (since then, Bump has been promoted to associate professor with tenure, and Julie to full professor). This meant that, when we first started out, the role of mentor naturally fell to Julie, who had been at MSU longer, and who was further along in her career. But over time, these roles became less distinct. In the case of a shorter-term collaboration, it might be less efficient to invest in the longer-term learning of your partner. But if the partnership is ongoing, your priority will be to make sure that the band is tight, healthy, and likely to produce viable tracks not only this time around, but for the next record(s).

Lesson #5: Your voice is not your voice, until it isn't, and then it is.

Q: WHAT IS YOUR RELATIONSHIP WITH YOUR WRITERLY VOICE, AND WHAT WOULD IT CHANGE FOR YOU IF THAT RELATIONSHIP WERE TO BE DIFFERENT? Just as single authors' voices evolve over their writing careers, within an extended partnership, the collaborative authorial voice changes over time. When we first began writing together, it was very clear to us (and would, we imagine, be clear to any reader) which parts of a resulting product were crafted primarily by one or the other of us—each had distinctive affectations of voice and style (in returning to earlier drafts of "Time, Lives, and Videotape," for example, we notice more distinctive shifts in voice to signal shifts in primary authorship of parts). Although some of this persists, more recent work we've done seems to be written primarily in a "third voice," a new synthesis of voices that belongs to both of us, and yet to neither of us. Julie, who had always been in the habit of finding content through particular stylistic moves and affectations of voice, has had to learn to lean on other things as inventional resources.

At some point in a collaborative relationship, it can be really difficult to know or remember exactly who said what, exactly who started an idea, exactly who finished an idea, or whose words are whose. At some point, these things have a tendency to blend together. The bits and pieces begin to lose their individual integrity. What's more, within a strong collaborative arrangement, maintaining the integrity of origin, development, and expression becomes, in many ways, less important than maintaining the collaborative arrangement itself. Once each collaborator has contributed, it can be nearly impossible to separate those raw contributions out again later. We have found through experience that the trust collaborators find in each other as they navigate the early challenges of give-and-take during the invention and initial drafting of a project, when each person's work is still primarily her or his own, will pay great dividends in the ongoing lifecycle of the work.

You may ask yourself: How do you predict that your voice may change as part of a writing team? What changes would be welcome, and which would feel like losses?

Generally speaking, what role does your *voice*—a thing with which you have had a long relationship, and which you experience as uniquely your own—play in your writerly habits and identity?

Concluding (and Continuing) Thoughts. We hope to have offered, via the particulars of our own situation and what we've learned from it so far, some ideas for what it means to work as part of a team—to write as a member of a band. Both of us have had writing lives outside the band (we've both been solo artists), so we know that the process of finding ideas and putting them to work in a collaborative relationship can feel like a different experience—and we also know that there's no better way to learn how you work, and what you value, than to put it in relation to another set of routines and values. We hope that what we're leaving you with is a heuristic of sorts: what might it be a good idea to ask and pay attention to when it comes to *invention* in forming and sustaining a writing partnership.

REFERENCES

Halbritter, Bump, and Julie Lindquist. 2012. "Time, Lives, and Videotape: Operationalizing Discovery in Scenes of Literacy Sponsorship." *College English* 45:171–96.

Sunstein, Cass, and Richard Thaler. 2016. "Two Friends Who Changed the Way We Think." *New Yorker*, December. https://www.newyorker.com/books/page-turner/the-two-friends-who-changed-how-we-think-about-how-we-think.

29

PLANNING THE PERFECT HEIST
On the Importance of Assembling a Team of Specialists in Your Writing Group

Ben McCorkle

When soliciting feedback as part of a writing group or informal collection of peers, it's important to recognize the unique skills, perspectives, and focal points each reader brings to the process. A better understanding of the unique position each colleague occupies in your writing group will potentially allow you to more effectively utilize everyone's talents when soliciting their feedback on your writing.

* * *

Indulge me in this rather odd analogy, if you will. Since I was a kid, I've been a fan of the heist film: classics like *Thief*, *The Hot Rock*, and *Dog Day Afternoon* as well as more recent popcorn fodder such as *Reservoir Dogs*, *The Town*, and *Ocean's Eleven*. Part of the genre's appeal for me has to do with the attention that these films often pay to planning and logistics, particularly when it comes to assembling a crew of disparate personalities with specialized skill sets to come together in common purpose. The master of disguise, the weapons expert, the elite hacker, the getaway driver, the femme fatale—each played his or her role in pulling off the seemingly impossible caper. Even if everything ended up going sideways, which often happens in these films, seeing the interactions among these big, often conflicting personalities would draw me in. Depending on the prize, I often wanted to be part of the action myself (although, I should hasten to add, my talents as a career criminal are woefully underdeveloped).

Bringing a work of scholarship to the printed page or pixelated screen of an academic publication feels a lot to me like organizing a heist; the product is often the work of many covert hands, eyes, and minds other than who is ultimately credited with authorship at the end of the process. This behind-the-scenes labor is often provided by a writer's co-conspirators, that merry band of ne'er-do-wells otherwise known as a writing group.

DOI: 10.7330/9781607328834.c029

Mind you, I am not exactly advising that you go about manufacturing an artificial writing group with complementary skill sets—far better to feel comfortable with the people and personalities with whom you share your not-quite-ready-for-primetime writing, because that can be a vulnerability you don't necessarily want to expose to perfect strangers. What I am suggesting, though, is that when you find yourself part of a writing group, recognize what each member brings to the table, including yourself. A clear assessment of the individuals in your writing group will allow you to utilize their individual skills more effectively, allowing them to work together as a cohesive team that will help improve your writing projects. Moreover, by better understanding your team's strengths and assets, you can offer directed requests to your group members so that they can provide you with focused feedback based on those strengths.

This is a lesson I personally came to learn as I was writing my dissertation years ago. I fell into a writing group at the time, partly as a measure of accountability, partly because dissertation writing can be one of the loneliest stretches of one's academic career. While I was part of that group, I came to realize that each member of our intrepid crew read my work in a slightly different way that, taken together, offered me a fairly comprehensive blueprint for revision. Back then, my crew looked like this:

- **The Philosopher Queen**: This member, well versed in critical theory and fundamental philosophical works, asked the big questions that challenged the fundamental assumptions of my argument, making it much clearer in the process.
- **The Stranger**: This member was outside of my field of rhet/comp (an Americanist, actually), but asked probing questions about research that would send me back to the stacks to locate sources to back up my claims.
- **The Dandy**: This member was a consummate stylist whom I would consult on matters of phrasing and flow. Even today, I'm mindful of his advice to watch my penchant for overusing embedded clauses and strings of prepositional phrases.
- **The Big Kahuna**: This member was actually my dissertation advisor, and not a regular member of the crew, but obviously I shared my work with her regularly (although maybe not as regularly as she would have preferred). This member was a career veteran with a deep disciplinary knowledge and critical insight for figuring out how to situate my work within the field. Also, having overseen several of these projects before, she was much more familiar with the genre of the dissertation.

This ragtag crew helped me immeasurably in making the big score: completing a defendable dissertation (and, by extension, the book that would evolve out of it a few years later). Without their help, not to mention the sense of camaraderie engendered back then as we met on that drafty, seldom-occupied top floor of Thompson Library, I'm not sure I would have finished. Beyond that, though, they've imparted to me lessons about my own writing process that I carry with me, even when I take on projects in isolation.

Even today, I find myself thinking similarly about the new people I share my work with, how our dynamic *as a group* functions. Beyond simply identifying the particular skills and talents of your readers, your job as the organizer of the heist is to lead, to offer direction to your crack team of specialists. Don't simply throw your writing at your group and ask its members to tell you what they think; rather, play to their strengths. That means asking them questions from the outset designed to elicit the kind of feedback you're needing from each individual: Can you come up with counter-arguments I haven't addressed? Are my examples adequate, or should I consider alternatives? Where does my writing seem imprecise, rough, or lacking in style? What research and scholarship have I overlooked? Of course, you shouldn't be overly prescriptive to the degree that you stymie your readers' ability to read the way that they would prefer, because you then risk negatively affecting the necessary trust and flexibility your crew needs to carry out the plan.

To the question of whether or not there is honor among thieves: I found the members of my dissertation writing group to be incredibly charitable and generous as they helped me with my dissertation, and I can only hope that I at least in part returned the favor to each of them (well, they all defended successfully, so there's that). More than the immediately practical advice they offered me, they've also given me a model for how a group could interact that I've since carried with me into my subsequent relationships with writing peers.

30

"OKAY, YOUR TURN"
A Dialogue on Collaboration and Editing

Kyle D. Stedman and Courtney S. Danforth

Even though we're teachers at two different institutions, Kyle at a small liberal arts university and Courtney at a large community college, we've nevertheless worked for more than three years (so far) on collaborative publishing projects: two digital edited collections on soundwriting pedagogies, including seventy-one total authors, coedited with Michael Faris. Because our work is so collaborative, it makes sense for our chapter of advice to be collaborative as well, in the form of a dialogue. We wrote this chapter together synchronously in a shared Google Doc.

* * *

KYLE: So this is weird. Typing here in the same document. Kind of to each other, kind of to readers. And readers are seeing only the final, clean version, not all our messy drafts.

COURTNEY: And our chat window. And our comments. Do you think any other chapters will get written like this one?

KYLE: Unlikely! We should go ahead and explain—we are writing in dialogue because we want to talk about why collaboration is such a valuable option for scholars with heavy teaching loads.

COURTNEY: Yes, or maybe for people who need to spend their time on family or other passions. People for whom research and publication are not top priority. But we're not just talking about collaboration as a smart option for scholarship; also we've found editing to be a manageable choice for teacher-scholars.

KYLE: At my four-year teaching school, it's really important for tenure that I prove I'm an awesome teacher, and I have to do *something* to show I'm participating in my scholarly community. But we're coediting two collections for university presses back to back. It's way more than is necessary for me. It's tough—I love teaching, but I love scholarship too!

COURTNEY: I'm at a two-year school and I don't really have to do any scholarship as far as my campus is concerned. For me, collaboration is attractive partly because I teach 450 students a year so I literally

DOI: 10.7330/9781607328834.c030

don't have time to "do research." But scholarship helps me be a better teacher. Collaboration is a way of involving myself in that part of academia, but in a manageable enough chunk that I can make it work with the rest of my responsibilities.

KYLE: When I've told people I've collaborated on a scholarly project, often they'll say, "That just seems so hard." You know—the "isn't it easier to just sit down and work on your own schedule?" thing. But when they say that, I think they're thinking of the ease of working alone versus the complexities of working together. For me, though, it's more trying to work alone and never getting it to happen versus working together and egging each other on with deadlines and meetings and interpersonal motivation, and thus actually producing something.

COURTNEY: It seems pretty efficient, really, because sometimes we're working on different pieces at the same time, but then we're also able to work in relay so one of us has a few days to grade while the other one's drafting and then we switch off. Either way, collaboration can keep the work moving along. I teach multiple sections of first-year composition every single term and that can feel like a perpetual-motion teaching machine—audience, exigence, citation—but I'm also super-invested in teaching composition and I want to grow my understanding of exigence or whatever and teach it better every time.

KYLE: Yeah, my tenure and promotion committee always wants to know how everything improves my teaching. I'd say that's a big reason why the edited collections we're working on focus on pedagogy: because it fits so naturally into our day-to-day professional lives. And editing work is perhaps the best work I'm able to do, busy as I am with all the teaching. Like, I can't keep up with every new book or article in my field; I just can't do all the reading. But I can coach authors who have read more than I have. That's something I loved about my podcast: I was learning overviews of all these interesting subfields by interviewing experts instead of actually needing to do all the reading. It was a shortcut that fit the needs of my job.

COURTNEY: Right. And working with a partner or team lets us distribute the tasks and knowledge and networks. Speaking of efficiencies, I want to add that my editing supports my teaching, and my teaching also supports my editing. The elements of writing I coach students in my classes on are exactly the ones I find myself working on with professional writers. Editing is a way of reading while also contributing.

KYLE: Oh, definitely. Whether responding to students or authors in our collections, we read/listen to/experience texts by others and help them understand how it sounds to a reader/listener/audience. I absolutely feel like a teacher when I write to authors in our books.

COURTNEY: One of the things that's challenged me while editing is feeling bashful about responding with the same vocabulary or with the same questions I might ask my student writers. I hesitate to insult colleagues with the same peer-review prompts I provide my students or to reference rhetorical fundamentals, but the same stuff applies!

KYLE: Right. Working with any writer is tough when there's a power imbalance, perceived or not. And with editing it can feel both ways: authors might see us as more powerful than we sometimes feel, or we're working with authors who have been in the field a lot longer than we have. I think, though, that one of my favorite things about our field is the ways that those imbalances ultimately mean less than I originally think they do. At least that's been my experience: whenever I write to editors or meet senior scholars at conferences, I've felt welcomed. (I get how privileged a statement that is, of course; society situates white men to feel welcomed everywhere.) I think we're good at extending that kind of welcome to others. At least I want to be.

COURTNEY: Exactly. I want my classroom to be welcoming and diverse and available to everyone who wants to participate, and we really try hard to do that with our books too. It's about friendliness, but it's also about nurturing a functioning and productive and supportive environment for work. It's a little like reading groups in grad school—group accountability plus an efficient combination of social and scholarly work.

KYLE: Yes! The people I've published with or presented with at conferences have often been part of my life for a long time, or I can at least trace how an early decision to be friendly to someone led to opportunities down the road. For instance, you and I "met" when you emailed me wearing your hat as a section editor at *Kairos*, asking if I wanted to start a podcast. But I think one way you knew about me was because you were working with Harley Ferris. I met Harley because we started tweeting after going to the same panels at Computers and Writing 2011. Those early informal conversations with Harley dripped down into the present work you and I are doing.

COURTNEY: Yes, that's true, but also I cold-called you because I'd worked with Steph Ceraso on a conference presentation and when I wanted to talk to somebody about podcasts and pedagogy, she recommended you.

KYLE: And you know how I met Steph? I was at a Conference on College Composition and Communication (CCCC) presentation in 2011 where she and Kati Fargo Ahern were on a panel together. I didn't know either of them but it was like the best panel of all time, and I forced myself—despite being actually really shy deep down, even if I pretend I'm not—to walk up after the panel, get their cards, and suggest we work together at next year's CCCC. I emailed them pronto when I got back home, we put on a panel the next year, and now we're professional and personal buddies. Those little decisions pay off.

COURTNEY: Right! And we're working with all these people still.

KYLE: I guess our advice is to meet smart people and then collaborate or work with them.

COURTNEY: Even when it doesn't feel easy to meet them or to find ways to work with them.

KYLE: Yes! Take this chapter here in this book, *Explanation Points.* Even our process here has felt kind of like a risk, kind of like something we'd never quite done before.

COURTNEY: I started us off by pasting the CFP into a Google Doc. Then I added a ton of comments to the document, saying anything about my experience or history that might be useful to say.

KYLE: Yes, and then I added my own comments, and then tried to clean up our mess by summarizing the main, most interesting points in an outline of sorts.

COURTNEY: Then we both got into the doc and used the chat window to discuss what was most interesting about that outline, and then we just kind of started typing. With the chat window open. Writing to each other in the main doc, in this dialogue, but also *really* writing to ourselves in the chat window.

KYLE: We typed out a whole draft in one go, and the next day we took turns refining the draft over and over and over.

COURTNEY: What's funny is how nonspontaneous you're making it sound. This reads as a dialogue—it *is* a dialogue—but dialogues aren't typically planned that way. At least when you sit down with a friend and talk about something. You just talk. And this text sounds a little like we just sat down to talk about this.

KYLE: I know, I know. But that's partly because of our spontaneous process and it's partly a literary conceit; we're faking a spontaneous sound on purpose. And I think we're telling this whole story to make a point for our readers: that when you read a finished-looking text, you never really know what kind of messy, collaborative drafting went into making it. (For instance, who can really say how many of your lines I wrote and how many of mine you wrote? Maybe I just took over and am pretending to be both of us.)

COURTNEY: It's not like we haven't written lines for each other before, in other projects.

KYLE: Seriously. I don't even know what my own writing voice sounds like anymore.

COURTNEY: I wouldn't go that far. And I hear what you're saying: you're suggesting that readers just be willing to try things out.

KYLE: Yes, especially when we're talking about collaboration. To be creative. To say, "This might sound like a weird way to do it, but let's give it a shot anyway."

COURTNEY: I've got seventy-five annotated bibliographies to grade, so can you handle the submission process for this one?

KYLE: I'm on it.

31

CONFERENCE TO PUBLICATION PIPELINE
Making Work Work for You

Katie Manthey

I want to start by introducing myself and my positionality. I am a white, middle-class, cisgendered, able-bodied, fat, queer femme. I have depression, anxiety, OCD, and unspecified bipolar disorder. I have a PhD in rhetoric and writing from Michigan State University, where my concentration was in cultural rhetorics. A Venn diagram of my research would contain circles with fat studies, dress studies, cultural rhetorics, queer theory, and composition pedagogy. I am currently a writing center director and assistant professor of English at a women's college in North Carolina, where I teach professional writing and women and gender studies courses. This is my first job out of graduate school.

I'm telling you this so that you understand the context of my advice. I have had a relatively privileged academic experience, and I have a lot of embodied privilege that I exert both in my institution and in daily life. That said, my relationship with my mental illness permeates everything that I do. What I want to talk about in this chapter is a way that I have found to work around/with/through my depression and anxiety to keep my writing going and hold on to relationships with colleagues.

* * *

I've always been better talking to people than writing—which might seem odd for a rhetoric and writing professor, but I think this is more common than we may want to admit. Writing sucks. It's hard. It's often lonely. It's easy to get overwhelmed when you try to write alone. For me, my depression keeps me in a cycle of procrastination guilt last-minute writing not my best work self-fulfilling "Imposter Syndrome" prophecy.

The funny thing is that as a writing center scholar I *know* that writing is inherently a social process. I also *know* that I do my best work (hell, any of my work) when I'm not alone. This "not alone" writing can take the form of writing in a public space (airports, coffee shops, etc.), being

DOI: 10.7330/9781607328834.c031

part of a writing group, or collaborating on a publication or presentation. I want to share an experience that combines all three for me: academic conferences.

I want to make it clear: conferences can be *very* problematic. They are expensive, both emotionally and monetarily, but for some (especially people in tenure-track positions) they are currently a necessary evil. Conferences require participants to make the hard parts of travel and networking invisible: show up, look sparkly, chat with people, share your ideas. Pretend like this isn't putting you in debt, or that you won't have to be alone for three days when you get home to recover from your introvert hangover. Monetarily, I've found that conferences cost about $1,000 per trip. After registration fees, hotels (even with three roommates), travel expenses, and meals . . . needless to say, they had damn well better be worth it. And there are usually parts of conferences that are great: those moments of connection, the discussion at a panel that you really put yourself into, meeting the two other people in the world who think about things like you do. But I've found that even with the best intentions, by the time I get home I'm usually too exhausted to find that business card from someone who asked me to email, let alone continue working on my project, although I am still excited by all the possibilities.

To combat this conference fatigue and general feeling that I was throwing my money and energy into the abyss of academic global consumer capitalism, I started thinking about conferences as part of a publication pipeline. The pipeline (ideally) moves from conference abstract to 2,000-word talk to article outline to draft article or book chapter book manuscript. The key to all of this, for me, is to not do it alone. I've found that working with other people and setting shared deadlines helps me manage my depression and anxiety. With conferences, this can mean proposing whole panels instead of individual submissions. The collaborative preparation before the submission and then before the presentations allows me to stay on track, not feel isolated, and always results in richer ideas. It's also easier to keep momentum for collaborative publications with panelists who have already been working together.

Starting a conference proposal as a group isn't always possible, though, and sometimes even when it is, other directions for collaboration come up as a result of the presentation. To harness the potential of academic conferences, I started to formalize my process of the conference to publication pipeline by posting materials from my conference presentations to my personal website (http://www.katiemanthey.com). I share a link to the updated page after every presentation and have found that this is a really great way to get conversations started and to keep them continuing. And thus the digital "conference to publication pipeline" was born.

At the heart of the pipeline are two ideas:

1. The necessity of making everything work for us as much as possible. Side projects and other ideas spin off from this process, and are sometimes richer than the original idea. It's all good stuff; we just have to tend the garden of ideas, and not dismiss things that may initially look like weeds.

2. The centrality of collaboration. The ideas that I have for panels are usually developed with my co-panelists (at least initially in the proposal stage). The conference presentation is a moment of collaboration between myself and the audience. The pipeline invites people to talk with me and bring their own work to a project.

Since 2015 I have had multiple collaborations come from sharing materials on my website, including a book-length project currently under contract with Computers and Composition Digital Press (CCDP), multiple journal articles, and a series of media installations with another scholar doing embodied community-engaged activism. The pipeline has also helped me stay connected with colleagues at other institutions. As the "only lonely" composition person at my college, maintaining connections through collaboration has been vital to my mental and emotional health. This process also helps me practice the things I preach to my writing students: peer review, the importance of talking through ideas, the benefits of group work. Sometimes I wonder if I'll ever wake up one day and be happy writing on my own—but if that never happens, I'm glad I have a process that works for me.

32

BE OPEN TO FEEDBACK
Separate Yourself from Your Writing

Janice Cools

I was working on a paper in which I discussed using oral presentations as a valuable part of the prewriting process. During lunch I showed a draft to my husband, a writer and fellow academic, well published in his own right. He started reading, and, as usual, I started becoming defensive, expecting the worst at every step. As students often do, I was trying to explain what I "was trying to say." After he read my paper, he said, "This needs a lot of work." My heart sank, and I recalled Nancy Sommers's *Shaped by Writing* video in which one of the Harvard students comments that he was told his writing needs a lot of work, but "there are programs for people like you." Like the student, I was floored. I had thought I had written a good piece.

Noticing my despair and defensiveness, perhaps bordering a bit on hostility, my husband said, "You need to separate yourself from your writing. It's something I had to come to learn." For me, my writing is very personal and I have tended to equate a "rejection" of any part of my writing as a rejection of me. A deadline was looming, so that afternoon, out of desperation, I decided to try his approach. I listened to his suggestions and every time I slipped toward defensiveness, I crossed my fingers or took a deep breath. I tried to engage in the same critical distance I ask first-semester students to take when they write and respond to each other's auto-ethnographic essays.

I went back to my office and looked at my writing with less defensive eyes. I could indeed see the validity of the comments I had received. I privately acknowledged that my writing had not been great, and began addressing the issues. By the time I sent off my final draft I could see how the feedback helped me write a better essay.

The next essay I had to write was on rhetoric and national identity. And this time, I was a little more open to receiving feedback that I did not want to hear, to dealing with disappointment. I shared my proposals

DOI: 10.7330/9781607328834.c032

and my drafts for that essay and was less defensive when doing so. This, in turn, helped move the writing process along.

One of the obstacles to defamiliarizing myself, to separating myself from my writing, had been the fact that I was always judging myself in my head. Perhaps like some other academics somewhat new to the publishing world, I had anxieties, like pondering whether the person I ask to review my work will think my writing is horrible and is appalled that I'm a writing teacher. I seemed to have subscribed to the view that *because* I was a writing teacher, any writing that I showed anyone had to be flawless.

What I was doing was, in fact, undermining the very writing process I was teaching in my composition classes.

I've come to realize that the anxieties I experience are no different from those I place on students when I ask them to peer-review assignments. When they write about the peer-review process in their reflections, many students describe the pressure they feel. At the beginning of the process they fear how their classmates, whom they hardly know, will judge them on their writing. They fear that their writing will not be good enough; they are afraid that fellow classmates will read their writing and will not want to be friends with them. Yet these same students write about deciding to be brave and determining that they will not take feedback personally. They write about how this decision and an open-minded approach in the end made for better writing. I've been inspired by my students. I tell myself that if students can do it, then I too can be brave enough not only to solicit feedback but to receive criticism.

As well as seeing the tangible benefits of incorporating feedback, my sense of desperation to meet my deadlines and my commitment to getting more work published also helped me to realize that the first step in the feedback stage is being mentally open to receiving feedback, even in the form of criticism. Since then I've been working on seeing me and my writing as two related but different entities: Janice the teacher of writing is knowledgeable about the elements, such as style, organization, and so on, that need to go into writing that is rhetorically situated and targeted to particular audiences. Janet the writer, despite her knowledge about and teaching of writing processes, is not immune to the challenges all writers face in trying to communicate in various rhetorical contexts.

33

EMBRACE THE OPPOSITION

Asao B. Inoue

Before you submit your manuscript to a journal or publisher, seek feedback from readers who seem most opposed to your views or position in the draft, then practice compassionately listening to what they say, not merely to use the feedback, but to understand it as a gift. Ask these colleagues for the chance to listen to them talk about your draft. The point is not just to get feedback from adversarial readers in order to bolster counter-arguments in your work, but to practice compassionate listening—to hear carefully and listen nonjudgmentally.

One might think of this kind of listening as similar to what Krista Ratcliffe (2005) has described as rhetorical listening, a way of hearing what others say in the ways they say it, letting those different ideas and cultural logics "stand under" and next to your own (28). Compassionate listening will expand us—help us grow and be fuller people. In compassionate listening practices, it is important not to evaluate or apply the feedback you receive, at least not initially. The practice is about *hearing* all that is being said and how those words are spoken/written.

Central to practicing compassionate listening is being in the right frame of mind, one that is humble and respectful toward others, and one that prioritizes receiving, not responding. It may help to set the stage with your colleagues by asking them to give you feedback and promising them that your first priority is to listen to it carefully. From a Buddhist perspective, one might say this is a small way the writer might practice suffering with the other, with the reader. Many define compassion as suffering with others, meaning simply being present during moments of suffering. In this case, being present means being fully in the presence of the feedback, the words and their sounds in the air, listening to the words and how they are given, without judgment or rebuttals. So whether it is through email or in person, being fully present, listening carefully to your colleagues, and accepting fully the gift of their words without judging their usefulness (at least initially) is a hard

DOI: 10.7330/9781607328834.c033

job—an arduous one, one that takes full concentration, a compassionate stance toward others, and a set stage that tries only to understand.

Why should we not judge the feedback initially and immediately?
There are lots of good reasons. I'll give you one: because your colleagues
have just given you a gift composed of their words. And as we all know,
our words are intimately a part of us. Responding too quickly can feel to
your colleagues like a rejection of the gift, and keeps you from being able
to listen to them fully and carefully, which ultimately prevents you from
fully receiving and using as much of their words as possible. A good friend
of mine, Frankie Condon, gave a faculty workshop on my campus a while
back in which she quoted a former colleague of hers on feedback. She
told us that feedback is a gift to the writer. And when someone gives you
a gift, it's rude and disrespectful not to accept it and appreciate it, or to
question its value upon receiving it, especially when you've asked for it.

Once you've been given the gift of feedback, be sure to thank your
colleagues and tell them what you heard them say. You don't have to
tell them how you'll use the feedback. In fact, I don't think that is a
good idea at this point. The point is to practice, for both their and your
benefit, gratitude for their gift of words to you, and show that you've
received them humbly and respectfully. Part of this practice is explaining in a nonjudgmental way what you heard them say. It's a crucial part
of compassionate listening. Voicing others' ideas is as close as we can
come to walking around in their skin, seeing with their eyes, and hearing with their ears.

* * *

Seeking advice from likely adversarial readers is not advice I ever got
from anyone directly, but I've done it because it helps me see and hear
my blind and deaf spots. I have a good friend and colleague who is a
professor at a public university (let's call him Dr. Z), and he is an explicitly anti-theory guy when it comes to what he values as good academic
writing in rhetoric and composition. He simply finds all the referencing
to others that is obligatory in our journals and books to be unnecessary.
He values the personal in texts more than other features, finding truths
and insights there that do not require much referencing or abstracting
of ideas in the ways that one finds in most composition theory today.
In fact, I can see my good friend enjoying this book quite a bit for its
conscious attention to praxis, or rather to the practical (he'd hate that
term *praxis*). He is also a white, heterosexual male who is conscious of
his biases and privilege to a degree, yet he is resistant to thinking too
consciously about race in writing pedagogy or the evaluation of writing. We've had many conversations on these topics. Because of these

dispositions, I wanted him to give me feedback on a middling draft of my book manuscript "Antiracist Writing Assessment Ecologies," in which I argue that conventional systems of evaluation and grading in college writing classrooms are racist, among other things.

Now, I knew that Dr. Z would likely disagree with my manuscript's ideas and with the heavy theorizing and referencing I was doing in the first half of it. So I knew he'd not like some of what I was saying, nor how I was saying it. I emailed Dr. Z and asked him for a favor: to read and give me some feedback on my manuscript. Here was my rationale to him in the email—and it's important to the advice I offer:

> Would you be willing to read a manuscript of mine for a book I'm completing this summer and offer me some feedback on it? I know this is a big favor, but I value so much your pedagogical eye, and I really could use someone I trust and respect, like you, to help me make sure this draft is the best it can be . . . I thought of you because in many ways, you are the kind of audience I'm writing to, in that you are a writing teacher but don't necessarily have a background in writing assessment theory or race theory. So while it is a book about writing pedagogy, it's really one that argues that writing teachers must think first and foremost about writing assessment, not pedagogy. Pedagogy flows from the ways assessment exists in our classrooms, the way assessment contextualizes pedagogy and forms learning in the ecology. Thus I argue that we see our classrooms as writing assessment ecologies and that doing so can help us form antiracist practices, which I demonstrate in my own classroom.

At the risk of belaboring this point, I offer part of my email to my friend because I want to highlight my initial stance to him: one of a friend who wants to humbly hear what he has to say because he has a position other than mine. I like to think of this as a compassionate stance, one that seeks to *suffer with* the other in front of me. A stance like this means I must be willing to be humble and listen only to hear, to put any intentions to respond to what I get back on hold. I think, in situations like these, when we have so much on the line professionally, when we give our words to others, words we've pined over and are a part of us, it is very difficult not to be defensive or upset or mad when we don't hear agreeable evaluations of our writing, when we hear our readers disagree with us or tell us things we don't want to hear. But if we go into the situation asking for the disagreement, expecting it because we sought it out, anticipating it as the most optimal outcome, then it's easier to hear what the other person is saying. Part of my own practice of compassionate listening is reminding myself that I'm asking for disagreement from someone unlike me in many ways, and the other part is listening without judging or responding, listening only to accept.

Once Dr. Z agreed, I thanked him and sent the manuscript along. In a few weeks, he returned an annotated electronic copy of the draft. Dr. Z's reading was, in his own words, "cranky and resistant" but "very engaging." He resisted exactly the aspects of the draft I thought he would, but in a generous way. He showed me how a reader like him would experience my book. For instance, I don't know if I would have gotten feedback that aggressively talked against my claims about most conventional evaluation systems as racist, which made me rethink how, or even if, I was backing them up. Dr. Z's comments in that draft's version of the introduction offered this helpful perspective:

> In a way what I resist is the clarity and directness of your charges at the beginning. They get my back up. So I'm wondering if that's necessary or rhetorically deft and if maybe you couldn't get the theorizing about race up there earlier. I guess the claims about race at the beginning are less sophisticated for me than they are later in the introduction—although it doesn't seem that any of this is demonstrated yet. I don't see yet how race is the key issue. Of course, this is the introduction. The book is going to do that.
>
> I also have to confess to a kind of fatigue when it comes to these issues and questions, whether from feminism or race studies or any other quarter in writing and literary theory. This is the kind of thing we're always saying, about everything. We're against absolutism. Of course. Of course it's all true, in a general and obvious way. It's so true as to be a cliché . . .
>
> A final general idea, and it's funny coming from someone who is so narrative and autobiographical himself in approach, but one of the things I struggle with in writing studies is how almost everything we write is grounded in a narrative about our own teaching, in these representative anecdotes, and that seems really limited to me.
>
> Always has. There's something intrinsically self-serving here, I think, unavoidably, partly because these narratives always suffer from the pressure to tell a story of redemption or recovery, right? Once I was lost and now I'm found? So I always feel set up. Once I did it this way and now I'm doing another way and everything is fine. I always resist that.

I needed to hear this at this moment, and I didn't get it from the others who had read my manuscript at the time, all of whom were more ideologically and politically aligned with my project. As a consequence of this feedback, the introduction changed. I had started with a personal anecdote from my classroom, a rhetorical strategy, ironically, I had picked up from Dr. Z years before, which he alludes to in the above comment, but because of his own reading, I took it out. Before I could do that, I had to hear what that story did to him as a reader just as I had to hear what all the quoting, citing, and theorizing did to him.

Now, I don't think I could have heard the above feedback if I hadn't had a good relationship with Dr. Z, but I also equally needed to walk into the situation with an open heart and attuned ears. I needed to take on a compassionate stance and realize that the feedback that Dr. Z gave, the time and labor it took him to read my manuscript and write up feedback, then respond to me, was a real gift, a gift that needed to be acknowledged, not just for Dr. Z's sake but my own. Giving thanks to others is a way we also help complete the gift exchange. Here's part of my long reply to Dr. Z, which mostly summarized what I heard him telling me in his initial feedback:

> Thank you so much for your time and reading, your comments and thoughtfulness. I know you mean well. I can hear through all your comments how much you care that I write a good book, that it be more than preaching to the choir, or more than assertions. I want it to be so too. I asked you because I do believe firmly that you are central to my audience, and I don't think I made that clear in the introduction, and if you are an important part of my audience, then all of your concerns about the first five chapters are important. And I understand your reading, so this email is a way for me to say back to you what I think you're telling me, and what I think I need to do.

The details of my retelling of what I heard are not important. What is important in my follow-up email is that I tried to exercise a compassionate hearing of Dr. Z's words by telling him what I heard him saying and doing because it shows both of us that I'm working at listening carefully to him, taking it in, letting it sit next to my initial ideas. I did this very consciously by reading his comments and feedback out loud to myself. I wanted to hear his words in the air, even say them as I think he might. One of the best ways to let ideas sit next to each other in a nonevaluative way is to do this kind of hearing of feedback, then redescribing it to your reader. However, getting and using editorial feedback from others isn't just about improving a draft or manuscript—at least this is what I've always believed. It is about forming connections and exchanges, being human in this very human word activity. Feedback and editorial advice can be about practicing compassion and suffering with one another.

REFERENCE

Ratcliffe, Krista. 2005. *Rhetorical Listening: Identification, Gender, Whiteness*. Carbondale, IL: SIU Press.

34

TO HEED OR NOT TO HEED
Evaluating Advice

Marcia Bost

If you're like me, you've received a lot of advice about your writing and career. At various times, I've been told the following:

- You're too old to be in college.
- You can't write about *that* topic.
- You can't organize it *that* way.
- You can't write *that* kind of book.

Obviously, if I had followed that advice, I would not have completed my doctorate and transitioned, after sixteen years as an adjunct, to a tenure-track full-timer with a few publications. In fairness, I've also received excellent advice and encouragement. But how does one evaluate advice in the midst of challenging writing projects? Instead of laying down a list of hard-and-fast steps, I suggest three principles and a series of questions and follow-up questions to use in evaluating advice. There are three principles I have found to be helpful: voice, positionality, and community.

Suggested Principles. VOICE: First, you have a unique voice. Jacqueline Jones Royster argued for the importance of the writer's voice in "When the First Voice You Hear Is Not Your Own." "Subjectivity as a defining value pays attention dynamically to context, ways of knowing, language abilities, and experience, and by doing so it has a consequent potential to deepen, broaden, and enrich our interpretive views in dynamic ways as well" (1996: 29). She was writing in context of the iconic Kenneth Bruffee article that effectively declared that everyone wanting to be an academic had to think in the same way. At least that's the way I interpreted it when I read "Collaborative Learning and the 'Conversation of Mankind,'" in which Bruffee suggests that academics agree on "interests, values, language, and paradigms of perception and thought"

DOI: 10.7330/9781607328834.c034

(2009: 555). However, in addition to Royster, others have opened the way for all sorts of voices. Now, if you're thinking that you don't have a voice yet, I can relate. I didn't think I had or could have one when I received back a heavily edited submission (due to publisher constraints) and did not recognize it as my words. So, keep writing. You will find your unique voice.

POSITIONALITY: That voice will also be dependent on your past experiences and your position as an adjunct or junior faculty. If you, like myself and many other adjuncts, are on the front lines of teaching writing in first-year composition courses, the virtual interface between students and the monolithic university, you see problems, gaps, triumphs, and strategies that others in the field may have missed or forgotten.

COMMUNITY: In that position, you are actually a part of a broad community of adjuncts, graduate teaching assistants, and non-tenure-track faculty. The American Association of University Professors (n.d.) estimates that more than 50 percent of all faculty are not full time and that approximately 70 percent are not tenure track. That number is the hidden foundation of college writing and the teaching of writing. The field of rhetoric and composition needs to hear from those like you embedded in that community.

Guiding Questions. Based on my experience of transitioning from being an adjunct, I suggest the following guiding questions. (Feel free to disregard any that do not help you reach your goals. In fact, the idea of goals is the basis of the first question, although the others are not necessarily in any order.)

HOW DOES THIS ADVICE HELP ME REACH MY GOAL(S)? Of course, this question presupposes that you have one or more goals. My goal, when I enrolled in a doctorate program, was to become the English department chair at the institution where I was then an adjunct, which was dependent on two factors: (1) the university enrolling enough undergraduates to have an English department, and (2) my getting my doctorate. That university still does not have an English department, but I do have that doctorate and a full-time position elsewhere. Thus, I am further along than if I had not had any objective. Being told that I was too old to be in college obviously did not help me reach it. If I had been less stubborn, I might have just quit. Instead I saw it as a challenge and persevered even when the economy tanked and no one at my house had a full-time job.

HOW DOES THIS ADVICE HELP ME FIND OR EXPRESS MY VOICE? As suggested above, you do have a unique voice, but finding it can be a journey. Being told that I could not write my dissertation about the subject that most interested me was not helpful in finding that voice. For me, the most interesting and challenging topic was the intersection of imagination and the four means of knowing as articulated by Samuel Taylor Coleridge. If I had written on someone else's topic, I don't think I would have found my voice. I had to lay that theoretical foundation for myself to proceed with future writing and publication.

WHAT OTHER PATHS CAN I FIND? There's an old saying in my community that there's more than one way to skin a possum, meaning that there might be multiple ways to achieve a goal. When faced with a comment that does not seem to be helpful, ask yourself if you can find or blaze another path through more research, more credible or flexible models, and/or a better argument. When advised to write the traditional dissertation formula of literature review, methods, research, and results, I tried it—but then I looked for other writers who had used the more controversial model I thought would better fit my topic. Providing that additional research to frame my approach convinced my committee to approve my proposal.

HOW DOES THIS ADVICE CONSTITUTE "TOUGH LOVE"? Yes, occasionally we need to hear corrective advice. Although I did not heed advice that might have led me to quit or write in someone else's voice, I (like every writer) needed to hear responses from readers. What we thought we said may not be what readers understand. Our tone may be too declarative and not properly hedged. We may not have explained position or theory, or connected the dots enough. We may have missed an important source or idea. I needed "tough love" in all those areas to help me reach my writing goals.

WHO HAS ALSO FACED THESE CHALLENGES? You are not alone in your writing even if you don't have the entire field peering over your shoulder, or the entire "canon" of rhetoric and writing studies at your elbow. Others have made this journey. Hopefully, you will get that sense from my brief recounting. When I was writing my largest document to date (the dissertation), I found great encouragement in reading *The Authority to Imagine: The Struggle toward Representation in Dissertation Writing*. In this edited volume by Noreen B. Garman and Maria Piantanida (2006), several doctoral candidates share their struggles in finding a voice and discerning new or existing paradigms.

Although their field is education, I could relate to their journey. Robert P. Yagelski, in *Writing as a Way of Being* (2011), described the difficulties of writing in a coffee shop about a moment of clarity experienced while hanging on the side of a cliff. I found all these writers to be encouraging mentors, even when only reading about their journeys.

WHERE CAN I FIND OTHER ADVISORS? Sometimes the most likely-looking advisor may not be helpful. After being told by a seminar leader that I did not have the authority to write a book based on my dissertation, I talked with one of the other would-be authors. She advised me to start my book where my dissertation left off. That turned out to be the best takeaway from the whole seminar. I'm still working on that one.

Follow-up Questions. When you realize that the advice you are getting may not be helping you reach your goal, find your voice, or otherwise forge ahead, here are some additional questions that you could ask.

CAN YOU HELP ME BETTER DEFINE ——? Fill in the blank: audience, rhetorical situation, argument, and so on. Nothing is better than discussing the structure of a potential work with another interested writer. Draft a colleague, or make an appointment with a writing center.

CAN YOU GIVE ME AN EXAMPLE OF WHAT YOU ARE TALKING ABOUT? WHO HAS ALSO WRITTEN IN THE WAY THAT YOU ARE SUGGESTING? Actual models can be helpful, even if you vary the presentation. Yagelski used the pattern of development that I wanted to use, even though I varied it somewhat to create better flow within my writing.

In conclusion, let me urge you to see yourself as a unique voice who has much to add to the field of writing and writing instruction, based on your experience, positionality, and community. Ask tough but generative questions—about yourself, your goals, and your work. Don't heed any advice (even mine) that might keep you from achieving your writing goals.

REFERENCES

American Association of University Professors. N.d. "Background Facts on Contingent Faculty." https://www.aaup.org/issues/contingency/background-facts.

Bruffee, Kenneth. 2009. "Collaborative Learning and the 'Conversation of Mankind.'" In *The Norton Book of Composition Studies*, edited by Susan Miller, 545–61. New York: Norton.

Garman, Noreen B., and Maria Piantanida, eds. 2006. *The Authority to Imagine: The Struggle toward Representation in Dissertation Writing.* New York: Peter Lang.

Royster, Jacqueline Jones. 1996. "When the First Voice You Hear Is Not Your Own." *College Composition and Communication* 47 (1): 29–40.

Yagelski, Robert P. 2011. *Writing as a Way of Being: Writing Instruction, Nonduality, and the Crisis of Sustainability.* New York: Hampton.

35

FEEDBACK FROM TWO SIDES

Amber Buck

No one can write (well) alone. Do not be afraid of feedback, and choose two people to whom you can send your writing who will serve different roles, one as a coach, and one as a critic.

Asking for feedback on your writing can be daunting and nerve wracking. As much as we are our own worst critics at times, it can be stressful to send your writing out into the world where it can be judged by others. Feedback, though, is a crucial part of the writing process. It's the means through which we can gauge how well our ideas were communicated to our intended audience, to measure whether what sounded right inside our heads makes sense to others also. It can also make us better writers. Think of it a bit like crowdsourcing or collective intelligence. We're smarter together than we are apart, so take other people's ideas and use them to make your own work better.

When you solicit feedback, it's important to think strategically about whom you will ask to review your work. It is, of course, natural to send it to instructors or colleagues familiar with what you're doing and part of your intended audience. But it might also be helpful to consider the results of their feedback. Who will help you, in specific and general ways, move your project forward? Is this a moment where you need a cheerleader? Or is this a moment where you need a coach? A critic? Sometimes you might select someone based on your relationship with that person, or perhaps his level of expertise, or maybe your awareness of the time she could potentially contribute to helping. I am suggesting here, however, that you also consider the emotional impact of others' feedback on your project. Pick a coach, and then pick a judge.

Some people like to surround themselves with what can charitably be called yes-men (and women). They want advice and support that confirms their status and reaffirms their ideas. Others take a Lincolnesque "team of rivals" approach. They want to be surrounded by the smartest people in the room who also disagree with them, because it makes their

DOI: 10.7330/9781607328834.c035

own position stronger and more thoughtful. My advice here is to take a middle approach and to use a little of both.

You don't want a yes-man/woman so much as you want a coach, someone who can see the positives in what you're doing and to point you in the right direction to make it work even more successfully. For me, coaches are important because they help reduce my anxiety about sending my work out in the first place. We all need a bit of positive affirmation sometimes. Coaches can offer valuable feedback, but they also can encourage your work and tell you what is working well. When I choose a coach, I pick someone who is familiar with my subject but also someone I know will be positive about my own approach to the topic. You might think of this as if you were a gymnast. A coach will help you improve your technique, but he'll also cheer you on when you nail that vault cleanly.

After I've chosen a good coach, I look for a critic or a judge. This person should be someone who can provide a bit more of a critical perspective on your work. A critic is not necessarily someone who disagrees with your approach; if you know that this person does not approve of your methodology, theoretical framework, or the fundamentals of your argument, you probably don't want to choose that person. You don't want someone who is diametrically opposed to your approach. You do want to choose someone you know to be thoughtful but discerning, who might approach your work with a critical eye and understand it from a different perspective you had not yet considered. She can help you address counterarguments and other perspectives you may not have considered, but she can also make your work stronger by encouraging you to strengthen your core positions. To take my gymnast metaphor a bit further, this person is the judge critiquing your form, measuring you against an ideal, and adding up your score. These individuals might have a more critical eye, but they are still helping you to succeed.

I am a professor, so I completed a dissertation, have published several articles, and received many acceptance and rejection letters. I critique student writing and provide them with a good deal of feedback. Yet I still hate to send my own work out for feedback. It produces a great deal of anxiety in me, to the extent that I will often put it off for weeks. When I finally do send it out and receive feedback, though, I am always glad I did. Knowing the outcome will be helpful, however, doesn't get rid of my anxiety and antipathy.

This feeling is the reason I try to choose at least one friendly in nature person to provide me with feedback. This practice is something that I have continued since I was first forming my dissertation committee while I was in graduate school. There were two faculty members I liked and respected whose expertise matched with my dissertation's subject matter. I had taken classes with both of them and knew the types of feedback they typically provided. Another graduate student told me that writing a dissertation was an isolating and emotionally draining experience. Not only was I going to need committee members who were able to critique my work in a productive way, I was also going to need professors who were able to provide some positive feedback for those more difficult moments.

I chose both these types of professors for my dissertation committee, and I found that the feedback of each type complemented the other's in productive ways. I always sent my work to the person I saw as more of a coach first. Her feedback helped me strengthen my writing, but it also was supportive in its tone and provided me with the reassurance I needed to send my dissertation out to the rest of my committee.

The committee member who served in more of a critic role was also incredibly helpful. I always sent my work to him after I had received initial feedback from the coach committee member. He had an invaluable, incisive way of getting to the heart of my work and asking essential questions from a different perspective. Addressing his questions and concerns was always important for justifying the overall purpose of my project. "Is this really an issue?" he would ask. "Why should we care about this?" In all of these instances, my responses to these questions required me to take a step back, to situate my research in larger concerns within my field, and to justify its importance.

These rhetorical moves are the ones I make every day as a faculty member to explain my research to students and to others, to situate my work to faculty tenure and promotion committees, and to explain its importance to grant-review committees.

There is nothing wrong with having a bit of healthy anxiety about sending your work out into the world. I have found the coach and then critic model helps me reduce those concerns while also strengthening my writing as a whole. And it certainly helps me stick the landing.

36

THE *WHEN* OF SUBMITTING AND PUBLICATION

John Gallagher and Dànielle Nicole DeVoss

Consider not only what and how to submit publications but also when you will submit and the timeliness of your submissions: have a publication pipeline (see also Manthey's chapter in this collection). Writing with a "pipeline" in mind is an excellent practice to adopt. Think about your pipeline as having three interconnected pieces: incubating ideas, processing ideas, and producing ideas.

The activities and happenings in the first part of the pipeline might emerge in graduate seminars or courses directly related to your research (that you're taking or teaching). Ideas might also emerge from seeing conference presentations or having hallway conversations. A spark for a writing project might appear as you wrap up another project and still have questions or possible directions to pursue. The second aspect of the pipeline is where the heavy lifting happens. This is where you take those ideas and get them down on the page, migrate them into manuscript format. You might also pitch, prep, and deliver a conference presentation on your ideas. This aspect of the pipeline involves getting feedback and input about the next steps in the project. The third chunk of the pipeline relates to production and includes all the steps across publication—sending a piece out for consideration, receiving and addressing reviewers' comments, checking page proofs, providing a biography statement, and so on.

There are two key problems that we see posing challenges to the pipeline. First, both of us have seen colleagues who excel in one particular area. For instance, they're idea generators, constantly brainstorming and imagining projects. Or, for example, they're perennial presenters: they present work maybe two or three times a year. But in these unfortunate cases, those people live in either part 1 or part 2 of the pipeline.

Second, both of us have also seen colleagues—and ourselves—fall victim to the linear and one-at-a-time pipeline approach. You have an

DOI: 10.7330/9781607328834.c036

idea. You nurture it. You present it. You send it out for publications (or, if you're Andrea Lunsford in this collection, you write and then present). Frankly, if you're heading toward the tenure clock or you're on the tenure clock, then this is moving too slowly.

Our advice is to avoid getting stuck in one spot on the pipeline—think carefully about when your materials move through the pipeline. Cultivate multiple streams across multiple pipelines. At any one time, you want to have ideas in development, presentations coming up, *and* publications moving through the production processes. Part of a successful publication pipeline has to do not only with maintaining multiple flows across a pipeline, but also with the *when* of each moment of the pipeline, especially the when of production.

For instance and perhaps most important, when you have a piece heading out of phase 2 into phase 3—you've drafted a piece, one that's sharp, cogent, and refined—consider when you'll submit it. Likewise, consider what is in the pipeline of a journal by asking journal editors or individuals who recently published in the journal. *When* considerations include aspects like:

- How long will it take for this piece to come out?
- When will I get an initial response?
- If I get a revise and resubmit, about when will this fall? When will I need to turn around a revised piece?
- How will the publication date impact my career at that particular moment in time?

This advice is useful for at least three phases of a career: going on the academic job market, ensuring productivity in the first year of a tenure-track position, and creating a sustainable publication record for securing tenure. Deciding on when a publication appears with respect to marketing yourself is important: you want the piece to be officially out when you enter the market—not under review but either out or forthcoming. Page proofs are an effective way to gauge this. You also want to remember that a publication counts with your institution at the time it comes out. If you are hired and have a piece forthcoming in the fall or spring of your first year, you want to change your institutional affiliation and get, hopefully, credit for it while on a tenure-track job. And finally, consider a pipeline as a sustainable approach to publishing consistently. One publication per year is better than three publications every three years!

SECTION 3

Finding a Foothold

Identifying Audiences, Targeting Presses, and Situating Scholarly Fit

37

BE BRAVE AND BE BOLD

Shirley Rose

Be brave on behalf of your scholarly work. Believe that if you have been care-ful, thorough, and honest in your work, it is worthy of the attention of others. *Be bold* in advocating for your work so others will believe in it too. *Be vigilant* in your efforts to help your work reach its audience.

During the process of doing scholarly research—exploring, draft-ing, and writing it up—as authors we often have a sense of immersion in our work and feel that it is a part of us or we are part of it. But at some point, the work must be circulated to others. Managing its cir-culation is our own individual responsibility, because as academics we don't, as a rule, have literary agents. Managing it successfully requires that we see it as no longer part of ourselves, but rather something that has taken on a life of its own. It still needs our faith in it, our work on its behalf and, in some instances, our protection. We must be brave on its behalf.

What does being brave on behalf of your scholarship mean?

First, BELIEVE IN YOUR WORK. Have confidence in the value and worth of your work. Have faith that if it address a topic or issue that is impor-tant to you, it will be important to at least a few others. If it has been worth your effort to do the research and write about it, it is worth the effort to get it published.

Second, BE BOLD ON BEHALF OF YOUR WORK. Aim high when you seek a publisher and pitch to the audience you really want for your work, whether that is a small but specialized audience or a large, more generalist readership. If it's been worth your best efforts, it's worth the attention of the best possible audience. Be an advocate for your work by calling attention to it when appropriate. Don't think of it as "shame-less self-promotion" or "marketing," if those marketplace metaphors are problematic for you. Think of it as an awareness campaign or an infor-mation strategy intended to bring knowledge and ideas to audiences who are in search of them.

DOI: 10.7330/9781607328834.c037

Third, BE VIGILANT ON BEHALF OF YOUR WORK. Stay watchful for opportunities to circulate your work. Watch for calls for conference proposals, calls for contributions to edited collections and special topics issues of journals, invitations to join special interest groups or other places where you will have a chance to bring your work to the attention of readers who will value it. Keep up to date on changes in editorial leadership of journals and scholarly press series that might signal a change in topical focus or direction and a new opportunity for circulating your work. Keep track of the circulation of your work by maintaining detailed, accessible records of the process of review for all the work you have in circulation and following up with editors so you know the current status of everything you have in circulation. Editors and reviewers are busy people, but they expect contributors to hold them accountable. If a journal editor has held onto your submission for weeks longer than the authors' guidelines suggest, contact the editor.

For example:

November 8, 2016

Dear Professor Jones,

I am writing to inquire about the status of my essay "What I Know about Writing," which I submitted for consideration for publication in *Journal of Academic Writing Studies* on September 1, 2016. Thank you for your email confirmation (forwarded below) on September 8, 2016 acknowledging receipt of my submission.

Your confirmation message indicated that I could expect to hear from you within six weeks regarding your interest in publishing my essay in *JAWS*. Eight weeks have now passed since I heard from you and I'm eager to know the response my submission has received from *JAWS* reviewers.

Please let me know the status of my essay "What I know about Writing."

Cordially,
Shirley Rose

If an editor takes even longer to get back to you with reviewer comments, it's okay to withdraw the essay from consideration. A good general rule is to allow roughly double the amount of time the journal has announced as its typical timeline before withdrawing. You can withdraw your work from consideration at any time, however.

December 1, 2016

Dear Professor Jones,

I am writing to let you know that I am withdrawing my essay "What I Know about Writing" from consideration for publication in *Journal of Academic Writing Studies*.

I submitted the essay on September 1, but I have not yet received any referees' reviews or any other indication of your interest in considering my essay for publication in *JAWS*. I am withdrawing it from consideration in order to seek publication in another venue.

> Cordially,
> Shirley Rose

If you've submitted a chapter for inclusion in an edited collection, and it's been months since you received a progress report from the volume editors, don't hesitate to contact them for information about its status.

January 2, 2017

Dear John and Mary,

I'm writing to check on the progress of your planned edited collection, *Writing about What We Know*, in which you indicated you plan to include my chapter "Writing about Singing." I am updating my CV as part of our department's requirement for submitting materials for our annual review and evaluation, and I need to provide as much information about the status of my chapter as possible. Have you found a press that is interested in the project? Is the collection under contract? Do you have a projected date of publication?

Please let me know if you need any additional information or further revisions from me in addition to those I sent on November 1. Looking forward to seeing this project in print!

> Cordially,
> Shirley

Keep your message short and straightforward and include key information about your submission (such as title and date of submission) to provide any necessary context.

* * *

Throughout most of the first decade of my postgraduate career, I was often too timid in working on behalf of my scholarship to get it circulated. I naively thought that if my scholarship was worthy, it would get published. Believing this meant also believing that the corollary was true: if it didn't get published, it wasn't worthy of publication. This belief led me to make some big mistakes. In my second year on the tenure track, I submitted an article for publication in a journal devoted to feminist studies that was just getting started. I failed to follow up with an editor when I didn't hear back from her about my submission for months. When I finally wrote to her to ask about the status of my essay, she returned it with a note saying that my essay didn't fit the editorial focus of the journal. If I'd contacted her after two months, I could have sent the essay to at least one other journal for consideration in that amount of time.

I also made the mistake of waiting too patiently for the editors of a volume of essays to find a publisher and complete the work of putting together a coherent collection. Just out of graduate school, I was unfamiliar with the steps in the process of publishing an edited collection and didn't realize that submitting work for an edited collection on the broad topic of "literacy" could be taking a higher risk than submitting it to an established journal. I was also unaware that the publication process spanning from my submission of a proposal to the volume's appearance in print could take more than two years, even when the editors work quickly and efficiently, due to the length of the "in-press" process after submission of the final manuscript. I know now that, after a year had passed without word of the project's progress from the editors, I should have withdrawn my chapter and submitted it in response to the CFP for another proposed collection, one with a much tighter focus on gender and literacy.

Looking back, it's hard for me to understand why I didn't follow up, but I suspect it might have been because I was afraid of irritating or offending the editors or afraid that it would be out of line to withdraw my submission. But I know now that I should have been brave and been bold on behalf of my work.

38

QUEER/ED RESEARCH
Disrupting the Unending Conversation

Jacqueline Rhodes

My practical advice? Take that idea and queer it up (and down). Be the square peg. Treasure your excess.

For the first sixteen years of my career, I worked at a teaching-intensive university, teaching three classes each quarter—nine courses a year. During my formative professor years, I found myself pushing constantly against limits of time and energy to join the unending scholarly "conversation" we all learned about reading Kenneth Burke. But that conversation has limits, too—structural ones—and queer theory could and should help disrupt those limits. Queer work has, ironically (or not?), offered me a deep connection to research, to view it as hungrily as I would a lover. But that lover is promiscuous, collaborative, affective, and embodied. It pushes me to engage in what Rosi Braidotti has called the task of critical theory today, in our ironically embodied posthuman world: to create adequate representations of our situated historical locations (2013: 2). Current research on materiality and the historical moment falls short because it *analyzes* rather than *performs* materiality and historicity. What would happen if you composed to be interpreted rather than to interpret? What does it mean to create material, embodied, affect-infused research?

Answering those questions led me to winding, overlapping yellow brick roads of experimentation with multimodality, installation rhetorics, and queer meditations on multiplicitous subjectivities. Those roads have been generative; but more important—because research does not have to always be *procreative*—they have been playful, serious, fun, exasperating, and expansive. They have ranged from one-night stands to encounters with multiple partners to enduring connections. And they have increasingly become richly inappropriate to conversations in the Burkean parlor. I hear stories from my grad students (current and former) about being "forced" (gently) to always cite the appropriate

DOI: 10.7330/9781607328834.c038

names and conversations before they can speak in our journals. Taking queer ideas—of interrupting, playing with, and challenging instrumental reason and the gentle, hegemonic force of Burke's "unending conversation"—I began to see our treasured metaphor of the parlor as restrictive. It's not true that we will be free, will advance, will transform through always already "appropriate" action. In fact, ironically, sometimes the only "appropriate" acts in those staid academic conversations *are* interruption, play, outrage, anger. And those acts—those very *queer* acts—are necessarily disruptive and potentially revolutionary.

To some great extent, I'll argue, the parlor metaphor is about disciplining the subject—both the subject discussed and the Subject discussing. The queer challenges such disciplining—such *assimilation*—and resists the demarcation of "acceptable" and "unacceptable," "appropriate" and "inappropriate." Queer researchers researching queerly struggle against the confines of this guiding metaphor, which is governed by a logic of mastery, of individual attainment, and of disciplinary assessment of that attainment.

What might queering research look like? What might it mean to play in the Burkean parlor? Some thoughts:

- Looking slant at researched material. Not just trying to find negative space to fill.
- Embracing failure as purposeful and generative activity.
- Having side conversations that do not necessarily add to existing ones, but that talk over, whisper, layer, overlap, diverge.
- Paying attention to bodies and affect: where does the conversation straighten you out?
- Courting your own slippage of signification: when the researcher becomes the research(ed), self-referentiality is okay, even encouraged.

My work lately—blending personal reflection/anticipation with critical theories—plays with a yearning and a potentiality indicative of what J. Jack Halberstam has called "queer time," a sort of temporality in which "futures can be imagined according to logics that lie outside of those paradigmatic markers of life experience, namely birth, marriage, reproduction and death" (2005: 2). What happens when those paradigmatic markers of *straight* temporality are set aside? What happens when we inhabit time that is not heterogenerative or reproductive? We remove a knowable future and replace it with a radical uncertainty—queer futurity is uncertain because it cannot be reproduced *toward*.

I also take my sense of queer time from José Esteban Muñoz, who distances himself from the antirelational bent of contemporary queer studies and argues for a "utopian function" of queer futurity. That is, it's not the case that queer futures are necessarily atomistic landscapes of antirelational, local, subjective experience. Rather, through a sense of utopia as a critical and collective longing, "queer futures" are a radical belonging that takes into account critical differences in race, class, and other identity markers. As Muñoz writes, "Queerness is not yet here. Queerness is an ideality" (2009: 22). We look at, simultaneously, "what merely is" and what could be. Longing, failure, possibility all crash together into an ecstatic sense of queer time, linking affect, *eros*, and discourse in such a way that we will surely (albeit politely) be asked to leave our treasured Burkean parlor.

And so to extend the idea of queer futurity to research: what happens when we distance ourselves from the paradigmatic markers of the straight Burkean parlor?

I find myself looking slant at my own research, searching for the possibilities of playfulness, tomfoolery, and even failure. I do not have, then, a narrative of progress. Starting with my Bakhtinian-focused master's thesis, continuing to my dissertation (and then my first book) on radical feminist print culture, to all my collaborative work, and now circling back to multimodal archiving of lesbian lands, I can't say for sure that my research is *better* now. It's that I'm older, and queerer, and more tired of waiting to join conversations "appropriately." *I've been in too many parlors.* I'm a bit jaded.

This confession is itself a sort of failure. And I'd like to talk about that failure as generative and resistant. As Halberstam writes in *The Queer Art of Failure*, under some circumstances, "failing, losing, forgetting, unmaking, undoing, unbecoming, not knowing may in fact offer more creative, more cooperative, more surprising ways of being in the world" (2011: 2–3). Those queer acts destabilize what appears to be inevitable in conversation. Those acts are necessarily failures—purposeful ones. They fail to perform as expected. And in failing publicly and purposefully, they point out the constructedness of those conversations in the parlor, and in so doing allow for the possibility of subversion (Wilchins 2014: 149).

Halberstam, in his discussion of failure, argues that we should *resist mastery* and that we need to *privilege the naive or nonsensical.* He references in particular Eve Sedgwick, who said once that ignorance is "as potent and multiple a thing as knowledge" (quoted in Halberstam 2011: 12). Indeed, the energy in queer research often comes from our failure in the conversation, and the discomfiting, uncentered, unstable joys within and without the subject. As I wrote this essay, thinking of the joys within and without the subject, I found myself listening to an *NPR* interview with the poet Jane Hirshfield (2015), who in her most recent book of essays talks about "window moments" in poetry. In the interview, she describes the moments this way: "Some poems and not all poems, and it's not necessary for a poem to be good to do this—but some poems have a way of, sometimes quite literally, looking out a window. They change their focus of direction, they change their attention. And by doing that, by glancing for a moment at something else, the field of the poem becomes larger. What's in the room with the poem is bigger." As I listened to Hirshfield, I thought of window moments in my own research—which probably really are failures, when I look out the window toward the playground, toward recess, toward play. In that turn outside, in that glance at something else, in that looking slant at research, we become bigger.

Or maybe we just want to play. To this discussion I might add Muñoz's forwarding of *disidentification* as a form of serious play: "Disidentification is about recycling and rethinking encoded meaning. The process of disidentification scrambles and reconstructs the encoded message of a cultural text in a fashion that both exposes the encoded message's universalizing and exclusionary machinations and recircuits its workings to account for, include, and empower minority identities and identifications. Thus, disidentification is a step further than cracking open the code of the majority; it proceeds to use this code as raw material for representing a disempowered politics or positionality that has been rendered unthinkable by the dominant culture" (1999: 31). Research often trades in identification, or failed attempts at identification. This economy of identification counts on research as necessarily *procreative*, as *reproductive*. Where is the room in our conversations for purposely *disidentifying?* For play? Certainly not all research must be procreative. Sometimes we do it for fun.

I'm not saying, "If you build it, they [readers/editors] will come"—rather, I'm encouraging you to take that idea, own it, twist it, hold onto it, and let it gather editorial comment like a hermit crab piecing an im/perfect shell. Queering research means making sure there are windows to turn to, places where we get a radical sense of identification *and* disidentification. It means, ironically and queerly and foolishly, losing the subject to find it.

REFERENCES

Braidotti, Rosi. 2013. *The Posthuman.* Cambridge, MA: Polity.
Halberstam, Jack. 2011. *The Queer Art of Failure.* Durham, NC: Duke University Press.
Halberstam, J. Jack. 2005. *In a Queer Time and Place: Transgender Bodies, Subcultural Lives.* Durham, NC: Duke University Press.
Hirshfield, Jane. 2015. "Windows That Transform the World: Jane Hirshfield on Poetry." *NPR,* March 14.

Muñoz, José Esteban. 1999. *Disidentifications: Queers of Color and the Performance of Politics.* Minneapolis: University of Minnesota Press.

Muñoz, José Esteban. 2009. *Cruising Utopia: The Then and There of Queer Futurity.* New York: New York University Press.

Wilchins, Riki. 2014. *Queer Theory, Gender Theory: An Instant Primer.* New York: Riverdale Avenue Books.

39

REMIXING THE DISSERTATION

Jason Palmeri

Your dissertation is *not* a book; it is *source material* for a book that you will remix, extend, and resee over time (see also Harris's chapter in this collection).

This can be hard advice to hear, especially at the moment when you have just spent years of your life carefully revising and editing a book-length dissertation into polished form. When I finished my dissertation, I was left with the sense that it was not yet a book, but I also just couldn't look anymore at the text I had written and see how it could be any different. I was completely and totally stuck. To quote my mentor Kate Ronald (riffing on Flower and Hayes 1981, 371) the "text written so far" is one of the hardest obstacles to overcome in revising the dissertation into a book. In this essay, I share five brief pieces of advice that helped me push past the "text written so far" to radically revise my dissertation into my first book, *Remixing Composition*.

1. It takes a year to recover from writing a dissertation. Beverly Moss told me that it is okay to put your dissertation away in a drawer for a year to recover from the process—as long as you are working on other research. This advice was just what I needed to hear and just what I did in my first year on the tenure track. In your first year, I suggest working on pieces on topics broadly related to *but clearly distinct from* your dissertation. This is a great way to get some distance from your project and continue the transition from being a student jumping an institutional hoop to becoming a scholar participating in an ongoing conversation.

2. Your best book material may come from the roads not followed in the dissertation. Your book will arise more from the *process* of writing the dissertation than from the final *product* that you deposit with the grad school. Some of the best material for your book may come from the phantom chapter you never had time to write, the archival source

DOI: 10.7330/9781607328834.c039

that just didn't seem to fit your argument, or perhaps the question one of your readers asked you that you just couldn't answer at the time. For example, I did a lot of research on Ann Berthoff's multimodal pedagogy for my dissertation, but never could figure out how to fit her complex work into my chapter structure (organized according to Berlin's classic taxonomy). So in my first year on the tenure track, I proposed a conference presentation on Berthoff that ultimately led not only to much new material for the book, but also to a new remix methodology and chapter structure that I think made the book project stronger.

3. Embark on deep, radical revision that messes everything up (in a good way). When people talk about revising a dissertation into a book, they often think of adding a new section or a new chapter to be dropped right into the manuscript as it stands. These kinds of revisions can be useful, but I think it's even more helpful to embark on a plan of *deep* revision that requires you to do new writing and thinking about every part of the manuscript. For example, deep revision might mean bringing in new methodological frameworks, new sources of data, or a new organizational structure that necessitates shifts in the argument of each chapter. It's scary to embark on such a deep revision process and there are no guarantees that it will work out, but the act of taking on an ambitious revision plan will help free you from the limits of the "text so far" so that you can see your project in new ways.

4. Write all parts of the book proposal from scratch. Sometimes one of the best ways to move past the dissertation is just to open a blank page and start writing. The power of the blank page is especially useful for one of the most crucial steps of the book process: the proposal to a publisher. When I was working on the first draft of my book proposal, I largely followed this advice and wrote all parts completely anew except for my first two paragraphs, which I copied and pasted directly from the introduction to my dissertation.

When I shared the book proposal draft with my aforementioned dear friend and mentor Kate Ronald, she invited me over for wine at her kitchen table and laid some truth on me with love: "Honey, this book proposal is brilliant and exciting, but the first two paragraphs are dull as dirt; they don't tell anyone why they should be excited by what you have to say." Kate was right; the parts of the book proposal I had written from scratch had voice, energy, life. The parts copied from the dissertation lit review were dutiful, plodding, dead. To move past this impasse, Kate advised me to throw out those paragraphs, open a new document, and just start writing why my work mattered without worrying so much about what other scholars had to say. This is how I went from a book proposal that started in a plodding way—"In recent years, numerous scholars have advocated for a multimodal turn in the field"—to a proposal that began more pointedly: "The history of composition is the history of forgetting." This kind of bold declaration was nowhere to be found in the hesitant academic prose of my dissertation. I needed to open a new page and start again to find the words to succinctly explain why my work mattered to the broader field.

5. Seek out generous, critical readers who work in different subfields than you. Your dissertation is written first and foremost for specialists in your subfield; in contrast, the most successful academic books move beyond a narrow conversation to reach scholars throughout rhetoric and composition studies (and beyond). After all, academic editors want books that will sell to as wide a scholarly audience as possible. So it's crucial to seek out mentors (both peers and senior colleagues) who can read your drafts and help you articulate why your work matters beyond your own narrow scholarly area.

To this end, I often kept Kate Ronald in mind as my ideal reader for *Remixing Composition*—because Kate offered me a vision of an open-minded, generous reader who nevertheless was deeply skeptical of all things digital and multimodal. If I could write clearly and persuasively to Kate, then I knew the stakes of my argument were finally coming clear. Similarly, I sought advice from grad school friends not just in computers and writing but in other areas of rhetoric and composition too—focusing especially on making my work legible and engaging for those friends not working directly in my area.

Postscript. It takes at least another year to recover from writing your first book. So you finished the first book, and now you need to write the second book. What do you do? I'm still figuring it out myself, but I have a few thoughts. First, chill the fuck out. Take a summer off from writing and have fun; then start reading and writing about something totally unrelated to your book topic just because it fascinates you. And finally, once you have gained some distance from your first book and hopefully rekindled your love of scholarly writing, keep in mind that the seeds of your second book may once again be found in the roads not taken in your previous work. For example, my current collaborative book project in process arises in part from my previous research when I encountered a massive 100-year archive of new media pedagogy in *English Journal* that was just too unwieldy for me to engage at the time. Yet my fascination with the *English Journal* archive stuck with me and I eventually sought out a collaborator (Ben McCorkle; see his contribution in this volume) and new methodological frameworks (distant reading and data visualization) to help me make sense of it. And now, as Ben and I are embarking on writing a digital book proposal based in part on the *English Journal* archive, I know for sure that we need to seek out the advice of friends beyond our scholarly area who will tell us with love when our book proposal has voice and when it's "dull as dirt."

REFERENCE

Flower, Linda, and John R. Hayes. 1981. "A Cognitive Process Theory of Writing." *College Composition and Communication* 32 (4): 365–87.

40

READ THE JOURNALS, THEN MOVE THE FIELD

Kristine Blair

I've had the opportunity to serve in a range of diverse administrative and editorial roles during my career: from graduate educator to journal editor to department chair and now dean. While these roles have enabled me to approach scholarly production from a disciplinary, editorial, and institutional perspective, my overall advice is actually very consistent across those roles: know your audience! Thus, what follows are some audience-awareness pointers, specifically for graduate students but appropriate for all, as you (re)develop your scholarly identity in rhetoric and composition.

Often there is intense pressure for graduate students to publish early, in part because of the demands of the academic job market to be as professionalized as possible. As my own dissertation director Janice Lauer wrote two decades ago:

> Scholars of tomorrow need to develop a sophistication that entails becoming critical readers of rhetoric and composition studies in different modes of inquiry, understanding their assumptions, methods, limitations, issues, and interdisciplinary connections . . . Pushing students to publish early in their doctoral work may promote expedient but not well thought-out decisions about the kind of inquiry they choose to undertake (1997: 230–31).

What I myself have learned as both a graduate educator and an editor is that early drafts of work, such as those completed in a doctoral seminar, are too often tilted toward the literature review, proving to yourself and your instructor that you've read all the relevant scholarship—usually to find out that you haven't by the time you actually submit to the discourse community that a scholarly journal represents. By the time such a project reaches my inbox as an editor, the result is typically a submission that's heavy on other people's ideas but light on your own, calling for a better synthesized manuscript that aligns theoretical frames with your own focus and argument and offers readers implications for future

DOI: 10.7330/9781607328834.c040

research, theory building, or curriculum development. What Janice Lauer and other mentors taught me is that you're joining a conversation, a discourse community in which you do more than summarize the conversation in either overly positive or negative ways—you add to the dialogue and help the field move in new directions or apply canonical discussions to new contexts as one of those "scholars of tomorrow."

* * *

One of the great blessings of publishing in rhetoric and composition is that there are many options for both print and digital publication, including some options related to the subdisciplines of the field, such as writing program administration, rhetorical history, and my own specialization, computers and writing. Despite these possibilities, it's important to understand, as Lauer's long-standing advice suggests, the preferred modes of inquiry and other discourse conventions that govern scholarly dialogue. The best way to understand these conventions is to actually regularly read the journals to which you plan to submit your work. This may sound like a "no-brainer," but as an editor I've been surprised to receive submissions that not only are not formatted according to our standard in-house style but also are not aware of the existing scholars or recent publications in the journal on the proposed topic. It's often clear in such submissions that a manuscript may have been originally intended for publication elsewhere but has been redirected after a negative editorial decision. Understanding a journal's expected methodological and theoretical frameworks goes a long way to ensure that your work is taken seriously by both the editor and the peer reviewers.

In working with graduate students, I have developed a "journal forum analysis" assignment for use in a doctoral seminar titled Research and Publication in Rhetoric and Composition. I based this assignment on James Porter's (1992) Foucauldian heuristic included in his *Audience and Rhetoric* for helping students understand the discourse conventions, as well as the power relationships behind them, of specific forums. Such an analysis applies equally well to academic publications, as students apply questions about the typical topics, methods, authors, and format and citation practices that a journal appears to privilege. I then ask students to apply this analysis to three relevant journals in the subfields in which they hope to place their work. While this work begins in a graduate seminar, I genuinely believe this type of close reading of text and context is something both new and established authors should embrace, as many times, the primary reason for a piece being rejected has to do with the overall fit and relevance for a journal's audience.

One concern among graduate students is that in some cases they don't find many graduate student authors in the publications they research, which leads to questions about their ethos and the peer-review process. Peer reviewers of journals are most typically appointed editorial board members who possess relevant subject expertise, have likely published in the journal, and are well aware of the journal's expectations. The peer reviewer can and should be an invoked audience on the part of would-be authors, who are establishing a conversation with a knowledgeable member of the discourse community they are entering. Common feedback to authors, regardless of their rank and longevity in the field, includes consistency of purpose, clarity of methodology, organization, appropriate scholarly citation, and significance for readers.

In my own role as a reviewer, editor, and graduate faculty mentor, I have stressed the collegiality of the peer-review process; nevertheless, there's often a myth that circulates of a review process that eviscerates both the manuscript and the author with either too much feedback or too little. Admittedly, sometimes the slightest critique, however constructive, can sting. But it's important for both authors and reviewers to view peer feedback as a collegial opportunity for mentoring, and in the majority of cases that's how it plays out.

To help graduate students see this process in action, I have, with permission, provided sample confidential peer reviews of manuscripts ranging from an *accept with revisions* to a *revise and resubmit* and even a *decline*. In the context of the graduate seminar in scholarly publishing, this has helped students see not only the potential for mentoring that occurs through peer review but also the typical types of issues that are important to journal readers to convey audience expectations. Based on those samples, I have also had students draft similar peer reviews of their colleagues' work to understand the need for constructive, collegial feedback. It's imperative that both author and reviewer embrace the audience-driven nature of the editorial process, and such practices help graduate students as those future scholars of a not-so-distant tomorrow.

Part of developing a scholarly identity involves articulating the intellectual questions your work addresses and recognizing similar scholars and publication venues that undertake those questions as well. I often give this advice to both graduate students and pre-tenure faculty in the hope that it fosters a research trajectory of conference presentations and publications that align those questions with a supportive and engaged scholarly audience. This also helps explain to future hiring committees as well as future tenure and promotion committees why you have made the publication choices you have, why those discourse communities are the ones you need to be a part of, and how those communities and conversations advance knowledge in the field.

REFERENCES

Lauer, Janice. 1997. "Graduate Students as Member of the Profession: Some Questions for Mentoring." In *Publishing in Rhetoric and Composition*, edited by Gary A. Olsen and Todd Taylor, 229–35. Albany: SUNY Press.

Porter, James. 1992. *Audience and Rhetoric: An Archaeological Composition of the Discourse Community*. Englewood Cliffs, NJ: Prentice Hall.

41

LISTEN FOR A WHILE, THEN PUT IN YOUR O(A)R

David Blakesley

In *The Philosophy of Literary Form*, Kenneth Burke describes the drama all writer–artists face with his now-famous anecdote about the unending conversation of history going on at the point in history when we are born. "Imagine that you enter a parlor," he proposes. Like everyone else, you arrive at a disadvantage. What do you do? "You listen for a while, until you decide that you have caught the tenor of the argument; then you put in your oar" (1973: 110–11).

Advice about how to write well is ubiquitous, sometimes inspiring, and usually anecdotal—going all the way back to classical times when Plato's Socrates claimed that everyone's advice was wrongheaded. He was right that there are no recipes for writing well that will work universally, so I don't presume that any advice I offer will work for everyone, or even anyone other than myself. Still, here we are.

I've been a writer my whole life and a magazine and journal editor since I first started teaching writing thirty years ago. For the last fifteen, I've also been a book publisher, having written a number of my own and published more than 250 by others in my work with Parlor Press. I mention this experience only because you'd think I'd have plenty of advice to offer. I do, but I don't want to create the illusion that there are secrets to learn or recipes to follow that will do the trick. There are no shortcuts. You have to put in your time, know what you're talking about, and care enough about it to share it with others. The assembled advice in this collection will certainly help as well. These writers, editors, and publishers know what they're talking about because they've been there—listening, collaborating, developing, responding, publishing. Taken together, their "explanation points" transcend the advice any one of us might offer.

In short, my advice is to listen for a while, then put in your oar by writing what you know and care about to others who need or ought to know and care about it, too. Let me break that advice down.

DOI: 10.7330/9781607328834.c041

* * *

Listen for a while. Be curious about what people are saying and why they are saying it. Listen rhetorically, in other words, to the conversations in your areas of interest. Read the latest scholarship in journals and books, of course, but also join the fray at conferences, especially the more intimate ones that give you the chance to go beyond casual conversation with people you may not have known before. The scope of your listening should include the insights of editors and publishers. What kind of scholarship do they say they want to receive? What have they published lately? When it comes time to submit your work to them, you'll want to show that you've been listening.

Catch the tenor of the argument. That may take some time. It may take years. Or a lifetime. If you listen attentively, you will know when you are ready to put in your oar because you should feel some exigency, some passion for saying/writing what you know and a desire to identify with those who probably want to know as well. But don't wait too long. You have to jump in eventually.

Put in your oar. Sometimes, you catch the tenor of the argument only after you've made your own. You don't need to paddle with the current, however. ("Oar" can imply "or" in Burke's pun.) Like everyone else, invent arguments and try them out to see if anyone else listens, if anyone comes to your defense or wants to push your argument even further. Imagine argument not as a destination but as a form of inquiry and invention. One of your greatest satisfactions as a writer will come not when someone agrees with you, but when they take what you say and carry it somewhere exciting and new. With that in mind, and rather than merely repeating the ideas and arguments of others to bolster your own, elaborate what you learn. Take what others say and run with it into new territory. After all, in one sense, rhetoric is an art of invention, the elaboration of ambiguity.

Write what you know and care about. To really know something, you need to care about it. There should be some exigency or felt need, almost as if you can't help but write about it. Someone needs to say it, so it might as well be you. However, try not to let your passion overcome good sense or even your craft, which can temper enthusiasm without erasing it.

Write to people who need to know and care. Who are they? This is the looming question about your readers, those you imagine need to know and care about your work. Readers are not some unified collective, but certain readers will and probably should influence what you say. Imagine that you're writing to readers who genuinely care about the subject and, at least initially, what you might have to say about it.

Some of your readers won't care much initially, and their motives for caring will be tangential to the act of reading for knowledge or entertainment. Ignore them!

Readers on your tenure and promotion committee, local colleagues, or even family members may not care much about the subject, but they still care about you. Don't feel that you need to demonstrate to a tenure and promotion committee, editors, or peer reviewers that you're serious, that you know what you're talking about. When you write solely to display authority (the prestige ethos), people will know and probably be bored to death.

Instead of writing to prove that you're worthy of attention and admiration, write about what you know to others who want to know, other people with whom you might identify, who do care, as you do, about the subject. Imagine smart people reading your work because they want to. When the people who don't know or care much about your subject hear you address your readers this way, they'll listen closely. They'll learn, and want to learn, about your subject. Give them the feeling that they're spying on a deep and interesting conversation or hearing some secret revelation. Invite them to identify with you on that level. If your exigency is in the subject, theirs will be, too. All things, explored deeply and sensitively, are interesting in the end.

REFERENCE

Burke, Kenneth. 1973. *The Philosophy of Literary Form: Studies in Symbolic Action.* San Francisco: University of California Press.

42

LOCATE FIRST, INVENT SECOND

William Duffy

Not long into my first job out of graduate school, I realized something that has since grown into an observation I frequently share with students and colleagues: it's easy to have a good idea but it's hard to write a good manuscript. All of us are capable of developing interesting arguments worthy of an audience, but translating these arguments into texts ready for publication is something else altogether.

For example, I remember the first time someone told me I should consider publishing something I had written. It was a seminar paper for a graduate course written on a topic I was particularly excited about. When the instructor returned her comments, they concluded with the suggestion that I should try to publish the piece. For the next couple of weeks I was ecstatic, but the excitement soon waned when I realized I didn't know where to actually submit my work. I asked my instructor for advice and she gave me the names of several journals, but I was still a relative newcomer to the field so my familiarity with those journals was at best cursory, as was my experience with scholarly writing. In short, I didn't have the disciplinary know-how needed to transform the paper into a publishable manuscript.

A couple years later when I was in my last semester of coursework, I had an idea for a paper that I knew could have a future beyond the particular course for which I was writing it. This time around, however, the first thing I did before starting the paper was to investigate possible venues *for this idea*. In other words, I thought about what journals would publish an article about this topic, and from there narrowed down several possible titles to one journal in particular. Then, as I started doing research for the paper, I was also reading the latest issues of this journal and taking notes on the form and organization of its articles. When I eventually submitted the draft to my instructor, it still needed a lot of work (I was doing a lot of throat-clearing before getting to key arguments, there was too much lit review, certain lines of inquiry needed

DOI: 10.7330/9781607328834.c042

development, etc.), but I had a fairly clear picture of what the paper could be and what it needed to do. In addition to the feedback I got from my instructor, I gave the draft to several peers and used their comments to revise the paper. I submitted the manuscript to the journal I had in mind throughout the drafting process, and after an invitation to revise and resubmit it was eventually accepted for publication.

I share these two episodes from my experience because they illustrate the piece of advice I want to share: *locate first, invent second.* Even though it's a cliché from the real estate industry, the mantra "location, location, location" is no less relevant for scholarly writers who aspire to publish. Location matters when writing for publication because *where* you want to publish something should be reflected in *how* you write it. Here I'm not just talking about issues of form and style, the surface features of writing, but also scope and content—that is, the things that determine what makes a piece of writing appropriate for publication in a specific venue.

Consider, for instance, a journal such as *Pedagogy* compared to the *Journal of Teaching Writing.* Each of these venues publishes scholarly essays about pedagogical theory and practice, but it would be hasty to assume that just because you've written a piece about the teaching of writing that it would be appropriate for either of these journals. Moreover, even if the topic is appropriate, the scope of your argument might be too broad or too narrow; the style of your writing might be too dense, or the draft might have too much narrative; the examples used as illustrations might be too general, or the reach of your claims might be too modest or perhaps too provocative; not to mention, your references could be too dated or too few in number or from sources that aren't recognized authorities for readers of these journals. The point I'm making should be obvious: *If you want to write for publication, it pays to know ahead of time not just what you want to write but where you aspire to publish it.* This is not to say that you will always have a clear idea of how the content of your writing will take shape, but if you are familiar with what types of manuscripts get published in particular venues, this knowledge can steer your writing process in ways that are more deliberate and goal-oriented.

Of course, research and writing can be and often are unpredictable. Our ideas change and develop, as does what we are writing as it progresses from draft to draft. Indeed, what you might have originally envisioned as an article for *Rhetoric Review* might reveal itself to be more appropriate for a journal like *Present Tense.* So I'm not suggesting that to *first* locate a venue for a project and *then* engage the work of writing is a straightforward process. In fact, sometimes we have to messily draft for a while just to discover what it is we are actually composing. Nevertheless,

I'm convinced that even for novice scholars who have no immediate plans to publish, to *locate first, invent second* is a helpful approach that can assist you in developing the kind of rhetorical awareness that will make writing for publication a more realizable endeavor once you are ready to undertake it.

43

SELECTING A JOURNAL

Erin Jensen

I vividly remember finding out that my first journal article was going to be published. I read and reread the email and then jumped out of my chair and danced around the office screaming that my article had been accepted for publication. It was very validating to realize that an academic journal believed enough in my ideas to actually publish them. My excitement carried me down the hallway and through the rest of a hard semester. I still smile when I think of how incredibly excited I was about my work being published. Although I have been appreciative and happy about other articles being published, none of those emotions can rival the pure joy and excitement of my first publication.

The same day I received that acceptance email, I had a meeting with one of my dissertation committee members. I excitedly told her my news, but then began to internally doubt myself and if I should even have told her. My dismay was because the article was being published in a small and relatively unknown journal and not one of the more prestigious rhetoric and composition journals. My professor could tell that I had conflicting emotions and she interrupted to give me a piece of advice that I have never forgotten. She said, "Erin, what matters is that you got published. The journal doesn't matter as much. Getting a first publication is what really matters. You'll have plenty of time to get published in higher-ranking journals in your career."

Her advice has had a long-lasting impact on what journals I choose to submit to and the counsel that I give other people. She recognized how important it was for a beginning researcher to feel accepted by the academic publishing world. I continue to follow her advice as I mentor graduate students and new faculty through the publishing process.

I used the emotional excitement of getting my first publication to start planning out other articles to submit to journals. Knowing that a journal cared about my ideas gave me a much-needed boost of confidence. The next article that I submitted for publication went through a

DOI: 10.7330/9781607328834.c043

much more rigorous review process and took several years to finally be published. Knowing that I had already been published helped me keep revising my second article and continue to believe in myself enough to make it through the much longer process. I've often wondered if I would have kept resubmitting my second article if I had not already been published. I honestly don't know the answer, but I do know that having a positive first publication experience made a difference in how I viewed academic publishing and gave me more confidence in submitting to other journals.

When I embarked on the publication journey, I felt alone and isolated regarding the process of how to actually get published. When I started even thinking of what I needed to do to get published, I received some advice from my professors about targeting the most prestigious journals first. As I read through several such journals, I became more and more discouraged that I could never produce that level of prose. I had very little knowledge about the dozens of rhetoric and composition journals that exist. I found the journal that eventually published my first article by seeing a call for papers on an online message board. After being published, I began to do more research and discovered multiple websites that list rhetoric and composition journals by their rank and tier. I began to understand how to use the ranking and tier system to aid me in choosing journals to submit to.

One important detail that I mention to anyone interested in publishing is to stay away from predatory journals. I often share my personal story about accidentally submitting to a predatory journal that had a similar name and similar-looking website to the journal I was intending to submit to. Unfortunately, I did not realize my mistake until after the article was published. Look up lists of predatory journals and then avoid them. Some of the warning signs of a predatory journal are having a fast publication process (e.g., publishing an article within a couple of weeks) or publishing articles that do not fit within the journal's stated and supposed scope.

When you have selected a field-specific, nonpredatory journal, the intimidation of the publishing process can often be reduced by following a few steps:

1. Identify what you plan to submit; if you've recently presented at a conference, consider transitioning that presentation to a manuscript. If you have a piece that's been percolating for a bit, see if it's close to ready to submit. If you have a newer project you're working on, imagine the shape it will take and when you might have it in submission-ready format.

2. Look through lists of rhetoric and composition journals and look at calls for papers (or CFPs) posted on social media sites, journal websites, and via email lists.

3. Focus your search by choosing four or five journals to look at in more depth.

4. Read through the current issue and through the archives; skimming the tables of contents for the past few years is a really useful process for getting familiar with a journal and the conversations happening within it.

5. Choose a journal and follow *all* of the author guidelines related to layout, style manual, delivery format type, and so on.

6. Submit!

To elaborate: my first step of selecting a journal is to actually figure out what article or academic work I plan to submit. Because all journals have target audiences and mission statements, it is important to first think about who would be interested in what I have. Going to the websites and reading the mission statements and publishing goals of a journal is incredibly helpful. An article on best practices of facilitating online peer-reviewed writing workshops might not be as good a fit for a journal as a multimedia piece on the rhetorics of silence in the writing classroom. Knowing what you plan to submit and what audience you imagine for that piece is a helpful starting point in selecting a journal.

I often remind myself when determining which article or work I plan to submit that the work does not have to be perfect. My first article was not an example of the best writing that I have ever done. However, my first article was on the requested topic for a special issue of the journal, and that is why it was selected to be published. I find that I often talk myself out of submitting an article because I think that it is not quite good enough to be published. I then remind myself that it is impossible to have a perfect manuscript and part of the process is to realize that the topic is more important than trying to reach an unattainable level of perfection.

I then spend time looking at lists of rhetoric and composition journals. There are several very detailed lists available online. I prefer lists that rank journals and includes their impact factor and the number of times the journal is cited. I find this to be helpful information in selecting a journal. I usually spend time reading through the various article titles to see if any sound relevant to what I am planning to publish. Another technique for finding journals is to ask colleagues what journals they would recommend. I've also found calls for papers posted on social media sites, the websites of journals, and email lists. (I saw the call for this chapter on a writing center email list!)

My third step is to choose four or five of the journals and do more in-depth research on them. I will go to each journal website and look up its mission statement to get a better sense of who the target audience for each journal is, what the journal seeks to do, what sort of editorial philosophy the journal articulates, and so on. Based on reading the mission statements, I have a better idea of the journal and its focus. I will also look at the author guidelines to get a better understanding of the required topics and formats; these guidelines often include what citation style is required and specifics on formatting.

My fourth step is to read through past issues of the journal to get a better sense of the topics of articles that have been published and to understand what format the journal is looking for. Some journals want research reports, while others prefer a more traditional essay. By reading through past issues, I can also see typical article length, tone and style, types and quantity of citations, and more. Reading through past issues can be an invaluable technique to gain a better understanding of the journal.

My fifth step involves choosing a journal based on the information that I gathered in the previous steps. Once I have selected a journal, I focus on preparing the work to fit the parameters set by the journal.

The sixth step is by far the hardest part of the process. I have sat and stared at the computer screen with my hand hovering over the mouse as I try to convince myself to just press "submit." The fear of rejection is hard to overcome. In mentoring students and faculty who aim to publish, I remind them that even if their work is rejected by the journal, at least they tried. If they decide not to submit to the journal, they have no chance of publication at all.

Selecting a journal is an important part of the process of getting published, but the task can feel overwhelming. This step becomes more manageable when broken down into the smaller steps of taking time to research a journal and examining its format. The ultimate goal is to publish in one of the dozens of different options for rhetoric and composition journals.

44

IT'S ALL ABOUT FIT
Finding Your Particular Publication

Kathryn Comer

Academics have a messy relationship with publication. So much of our focus—in graduate school, in professional development, on ShitAcademicsSay—is on the pressure to produce, to publish in order not to perish. We know we need to write, and that's complicated enough, so we often pay more attention to production than distribution. Publishing can therefore seem like *South Park*'s underwear gnomes' business model:

> Phase 1: Collect underpants
> Phase 2: ?
> Phase 3: Profit

We talk a lot about Phase 1, and we dream of Phase 3. The process in the middle can be murky and intimidating, but it's also where a lot of magic happens, and it begins with familiarizing yourself with target publication venues to determine where and whether your work belongs before submitting it for review.

Successful (by multiple metrics) publication all comes down to fit. Despite disciplinary commonalities, publications are particular. Your work will be best served by finding the right match between a particular journal's ongoing conversation and your potential contribution. Does your piece belong within this publication? Is your rhetorical agenda compatible with the conversation already going on among the editors, reviewers, contributors, and readers? Do your writing choices align with their expectations? Will they respond as you hope? Below, I provide some tips to help you identify and adjust for fit, whether that means revising your work or reconsidering your target venue.

These recommendations are based on ten years of the *Harlot* project. *Harlot* isn't a conventional academic publication, but its particular case highlights issues that I suspect are common. *Harlot*'s mission to

DOI: 10.7330/9781607328834.c044

engage nonacademic audiences, and our resulting variation on peer review (which includes at least one reader from outside academia) has been its signature pleasure and challenge. Contributors have been eager to participate in *Harlot's* public-oriented project, but they often struggle to put that into practice: some submit seminar papers, many assume audience interest, and most maintain a distinctly academic, not-so-inviting style.

On our side, the editors have struggled over the years to articulate our mission and help authors align their work within it. The conversations and revisions throughout have been, for me, a wonderful education on publication (among other things).

Actually, perhaps my best advice would be this: become an editor. It effectively demystifies the path to publication, highlighting the common pitfalls along the way. Of course, it's also rather laborious. And so, for now, I offer these recommendations on finding the right publication for your work.

Figure out the publication's personality. *Don't just scan the submission guidelines; do some research to understand the editorial agenda and how successful submissions perform that mission.* The *Harlot* project's goal is to reach beyond the academy, and it was created as an alternative to discipline-centric journals. That history and purpose is articulated in policies, review criteria, and editorial letters. We discourage submissions about rhet/comp as a field unless the takeaways are relevant to other readers. We do publish work that connects educational situations to broader contexts and concerns, and authors often acknowledge and negotiate their academic identities. But regular readers of *Harlot* know we're not aiming for "academic discourse." Out of ninety-four articles published to date, only one focuses on rhet/comp as a field (and it's really relatable).

Yet we regularly have to reject pieces—often very good ones—about rhet/comp as a field. More than any other weaknesses in a submission, such an indication that the author hasn't taken the time to get to know *Harlot* leads to outright rejection. Another common scenario is less dramatic but more disappointing: An issue or argument *could* be fascinating for diverse readers, but the author doesn't articulate its value or significance. Many seem to assume interest from other specialists and therefore don't invite new audiences; others successfully sell the public interest angle, but then direct their implications back toward scholarship. In such cases, we often request revisions after a preliminary editorial review, because we don't want to waste the precious resource of reviewers' time and commitment. Both cases result in squandered energy among an already overextended editorial staff—and they slow down progress toward publication.

Find the tenor of the conversation. *Listen for tone in editorial communication and reviewer feedback, as well as within published articles. Harlot,* as the name would suggest, doesn't take itself too seriously. We built the project over many happy hours, and relationships among participants are remarkably friendly. This dynamic reflects the mission and is reflected in the criteria for review as well as published pieces, which tend to be playful, personal, and passionate. Nevertheless, we regularly receive submissions that adhere to scholarly conventions that, outside of academia, become academese: style is formal and syntax is complex; every other paragraph begins, "According to [theorist or critic] . . ."; few headings or media break up the text; and the length is twice our recommended maximum (and five times most online readers' attention).

Harlot's reviewers have consistently demonstrated distaste for these moves, recognizing them as exclusionary. They also notice when authors who have been nominally addressing a public audience let slip a "we" that clearly refers only to other scholars. Reviewers point to these moments as a clear sign the piece isn't really intended for *Harlot,* and their recommendation comes down to whether it's likely to be worth the amount of work it would take to get the piece nearer its target. Many rejections—again, often of quality work—result. Meanwhile, almost every revise and resubmit request we send asks authors to lighten up, to adopt an inviting and inclusive style appropriate to *Harlot.* Spending more time getting a feel for the journal's personality could save you an entire cycle of review and revision.

Become a part of the community. *If you've done your research and decided that a publication fosters conversations you want to be a part of, consider introducing yourself.*

Harlot's quite friendly, and we love to hear that people dig what we're doing. So when a prospective contributor reaches out with a question or suggestion, we try to be receptive and responsive. Many authors have contacted us to pitch an idea or gauge our interest in their work, and these brief exchanges can be incredibly efficient. I'm not suggesting you contact editors with unnecessary questions to raise your profile; this won't make you popular. But a genuine inquiry to assess fit can save everyone a lot of work.

For the longer game, consider getting involved. We often tell people that becoming a reviewer for *Harlot* is the best way to get to know the project from the inside. Look for internship or assistantship opportunities. Follow your favorite journal on social media. Chat with the editors at conferences. If this publication is where you believe your writing belongs, chances are you'll belong there too.

Welcome to Phase 2.

45

WHAT'S THE PAYOFF?

Marilyn M. Cooper

When I was editing *College Composition and Communication* (*CCC*) and working with graduate student interns reading manuscript submissions, I kept asking them, "What's the payoff? What did you learn from this piece? What can you use from this piece?"

Payoff is one of the most important things journal editors (and book publishers) look for in a manuscript. When you are drafting or revising a manuscript to submit, what strategies can you use to discover and develop a real payoff? Getting feedback from readers, whether colleagues or reviewers or editors, will help. Almost all published journal articles have been initially returned to the author with suggestions for revision before acceptance, and often the suggested revisions focus on payoff. It is this feedback that most often inspires the hard thinking about the implications of what you are offering that will produce payoff for your readers and for you.

Payoff is more than a "contribution," which could just be a synthesis of theories, a description of practices or an approach, a report of results of a case study or a pilot study. Payoff is a new approach, insight, practical directions—something that helps others see something in a different way, helps them redirect their research, helps them transform their teaching. Transforming beliefs, redirecting research, or transforming teaching requires that you discover the problems hiding behind seemingly irresolvable paradoxes, interrogate the nuances of your concepts, and spell out precisely what's new about the directions you recommend, with reference to other directions that have been taken. Even if in your revisions of your manuscript prior to submission you have expanded your explanations and added discussions of more related research, you will usually find that developing the payoff of an article requires further substantial revisions. That was certainly the case for me when at the request of the editor of *College English* I revised and resubmitted the manuscript of "The Ecology of Writing" (published in volume 48 in 1986).

DOI: 10.7330/9781607328834.c045

   This article originated as a job interview talk that was, frankly, not well received. Faculty at the institution where I was interviewing asked many puzzled questions. The question I remember best was "What's in this approach for me?" My concern in the talk was to challenge the cognitive process model of writing that was dominant at that time. I argued that it was too narrow, focused on the "solitary author" who produced texts introspectively rather than through interacting with others. I proposed an ecological model of writing as an activity through which a person is continually engaged with a variety of socially constituted systems, dynamic interlocked systems of ideas, purposes, interpersonal interactions, cultural norms, and textual forms. I distinguished this ecological model from other contextual models in that ecological systems are not static constructs to be analyzed but rather are dynamic webs of influence that are made and remade by writers in the act of writing. I offered hypothetical examples of how these systems worked. What I did not do, however, was explain how anyone would find this model useful—what, for example, it implied for how we teach writing.

   I was nonplussed when the faculty member asked, "What's in this for me?" I thought the implications of the ecological model were overwhelmingly obvious and that they could and should be worked out by teachers as they applied the model in their own situations. This response, however, made me realize that clearly they weren't obvious, that the model needed further explication, and that I needed to do a lot of revising. Before submitting the manuscript to *College English*, in addition to adding at the beginning more context for my proposal of an ecological model, I rewrote the last third, trying to demonstrate some ways the model would be useful. I can't remember now what I tried, but it didn't work: the *College English* editor said the first two-thirds of the manuscript was promising but the last third didn't fulfill the promise—in short, no payoff.

   So, after a couple of days of totally undeserved fuming at the failure of the editor and the reviewers to understand what I was saying, I deleted the last third of the manuscript, leaving me with only seven print pages. Over the next few weeks, I wrote a new section analyzing the then current and seemingly irresolvable problem of audience as addressed or invoked: in other words, should writers analyze their audiences or invent an audience in their writing? I argued that the problem could be resolved by realizing that whether the writer is urged to address or invent his or her audience, the audience is always considered to be a mental construct, and that the ecological model enables teachers to understand that writers don't just think about their audience, they actually know and communicate with real audiences. This realization could inspire teachers to instead focus on helping students develop the habits and skills involved in finding readers and making use of their responses. Having explained in a more concrete way how the shift from seeing writing as a dominantly cognitive activity to a dominantly real-world social activity might redirect teaching practices, my manuscript finally provided a payoff and was accepted for publication.

My story doesn't end here, however. Considering the implications of ideas presented in manuscripts and successfully published articles provides a further benefit in that it helps you develop a long-term research agenda that offers further practical contributions (payoffs) to the field of rhetoric and composition. Over the thirty years following the publication of "The Ecology of Writing," I have developed my thinking about the ecological model in an article published in *College Composition and Communication* and in several book chapters and a recently submitted book manuscript. I expanded the ecological model with reference to other projects influential in humanistic fields—continental philosophy, complexity theory, posthumanism, and new materialisms—and proposed new understandings of the rhetorical concepts of agency, techne, persuasion, and ethics. And I suggested revisions of the habits of mind presented in the *Framework for Success in Postsecondary Writing* and the *WPA Outcomes Statement for First-Year Composition* in line with an approach to teaching writing that focuses on the creative process of writing rather than on critical reading and writing.

Developing the payoff of your ideas is a way of making your work valuable to others as well as to yourself, as Carolyn Miller memorably suggested in an interview with Dylan B. Dryer (2015). She attributed her persistent revising of her "Genre as Social Action" article to the "intuition that there was something here, and maybe this is the experience of every writer: the fact that I could write about it made me think it was real."

REFERENCE

Dryer, Dylan B. 2015. "Interview with Carolyn R. Miller." *Composition Forum* 31.

46

ACHIEVING VISIBILITY THROUGH STRATEGIC PUBLICATION

Christie Toth and Darin L. Jensen

Not Quite a Radioactive Spider. Every team has its origin story. Ours begins in a 2014 snowstorm in Lincoln, Nebraska. Christie was finishing her doctorate and "on the market," and Darin was a full-time community college English teacher in working on his PhD. We drank coffee in the nearly empty student union and bonded over our interest in community colleges, which often makes us feel like academic mutants. We didn't discover superpowers that day, or get matching spandex, but we did become collaborators who share a commitment to the democratic promise of community colleges, the distinctive professional roles of their writing faculty, and the often structurally disadvantaged students they serve.

Community colleges teach half of all composition courses nationally, but it's often hard to get scholarship about these institutions heard in writing studies.

We're perhaps a little *too* inclined to imagine ourselves battling sinister forces together, but we know ours is not a superhero saga. It's more like a buddy story about the nerdiest of road trips: our three-year, cross-country effort to raise awareness about the need to reform graduate education in English studies to better account for community colleges and their students. On that journey, we learned a lesson that might be useful to others who dwell in less-heard parts of the field and are seeking to make change within our disciplinary community: Plan a campaign, not just a publication. Hustle to create opportunities to get heard. Collaborate wherever and whenever possible. Understand publication as a by-product of the work, rather than the work itself. Cosplay is optional.

It's the Journey. This buddy story has also been a kind of hero's journey. Our call to adventure came in 2015, with an invitation to serve on the Two-Year College English Association (TYCA) taskforce authoring

DOI: 10.7330/9781607328834.c046

the new "Guidelines for Preparing Teachers of English in the Two-Year College." We found ourselves traveling in the company of several seasoned TYCA sages: Carolyn Calhoon-Dillahunt, Howard Tinberg, and Sarah Z. Johnson. Parts of the journey were comfortably mapped out. The "Guidelines" would be published on the TYCA webpage and in *Teaching English in the Two-Year College* (*TETYC*), where we knew they would reach many two-year college readers. However, we also realized that we couldn't stay in the Shire. We were not the first to undertake this quest: our archival research had uncovered half a century of largely unheeded calls from two-year college English faculty for relevant graduate preparation (see Jensen and Toth 2017). If the new "Guidelines" were going to be heard by the university colleagues who controlled graduate programs, we would need to yell from different mountaintops. And so we embarked on what we took to calling "the roadshow."

We hit both the virtual and the physical pavement. We circulated the "Guidelines" through professional email lists like TYCA, WPA-L, and CBW, as well as personal and organizational social media outlets. We talked with whoever would listen and presented wherever we could, including at several TYCA regional conferences, the Conference on College Composition and Communication (CCCC), the Watson Conference, and the Modern Language Association (MLA). In our travels across these different locations, we worked together to figure out which answers to which riddles would open which doors. We honed our arguments with challenging questioners, and we met new friends who gave us unexpected gifts. We helped spur critical conversations about graduate preparation in spaces where it otherwise probably wouldn't have happened. Those conversations fed directly into our writing. So, lesson 1: Plan a campaign, not just a publication.

In a campaign, publishing should be strategic. Our strategy involved calling on many fellow travelers. We contacted Kelly Ritter, then editor of *College English*, and told her about the new "Guidelines" statement. We explained our sense of the need to circulate it in a high-profile journal with a readership across English studies, and offered to write a contextualizing companion article. We lucked out when another manuscript dropped off the slate for the July 2017 issue, freeing up space for the article we titled "Unknown Knowns: The Past, Present, and Future of Graduate Preparation for Two-Year College English Faculty." Ultimately, our publication strategy worked: we got the new "Guidelines" in front of a much wider audience of university faculty, we carved out more space to develop our arguments about graduate education, and we had a publication that "counted" for Christie's tenure committee. Lesson 2: Hustle to create opportunities to get heard.

As these conversations were unfolding, we approached Holly Hassel, incoming editor of *TETYC*. We proposed the idea of a special issue on the topic of preparing two-year college English faculty. Holly liked it, and we agreed to coedit a symposium for the special issue that responded to the "Guidelines." The symposium allowed us to reach out to other community college colleagues we'd met on our journey. We received insightful contributions from former *TETYC* editor Mark Reynolds, developmental education and ESL specialist Emily Suh, two-year college CWPA leaders Mark Blaauw-Hara and Cheri Lemieux-Spiegel, and Jeff Andelora, current TYCA chair and leading historian of two-year college composition. These short essays extended the insights—and addressed some key oversights—of the "Guidelines." Lesson 3: Collaborate wherever and whenever possible.

Framing our work as a campaign to bring awareness to the issue of graduate preparation helped us reach multiple audiences. Our multi-journal publication strategy was, of course, dependent on the responsiveness of the editors, their ability to see the importance of these conversations, and their willingness to think outside conventional publication procedures. Holly and Kelly wrote about their cross-journal coordination in an October 2017 NCTE blog post titled "Textual Collaborations: Preparing Two-Year College English Faculty." That post was yet another way to gain visibility for the new "Guidelines" and the polyvocal companion pieces they have inspired. In fact, the discussion of our campaign that you're reading now—the last stop on the roadshow—is another strategic publication, one more way we're amplifying calls to reform graduate education to better serve community college faculty and students.

Publication Is the By-product. These narratives are supposed to culminate with advice for academic publication. Here's ours: articulate the changes you want to see and labor for them across multiple genres and media. Consider different professional subcommunities, publication venues, and arguments that will make your message audible. Don't limit yourself to conventional methods for submitting journal manuscripts. Propose ideas for linked articles or special issues, and consider how to reframe your work to fit existing CFPs. In queries, proposals, and submissions, articulate the *moral* case for why your perspective should be represented in whatever conversation you're entering. When possible, write collaboratively. Collaboration cultivates shared intellectual understandings that help sustain your network and further collective goals.

Seek to create spaces not just for your own publications, but for those by other scholars who can extend—and productively complicate—your thinking.

Most important, know what your real work is. In her incisive critique of "the academic game," Carmen Kynard (2018) advises us to distinguish between "the job" and "the work." Christie's student co-researcher Nathan Lacy gave us a gift of moral clarity when he asserted that academic publication is "but a by-product of the real work." As we return from our roadshow journey—a little older, a little tired, a little sorry we *weren't* bitten by radioactive spiders—we feel this lesson in our bones. The real work was devising a campaign, creating new opportunities to discuss a pressing social justice issue, insisting that community college colleagues' voices be heard in that conversation, and making friends and common cause along the way. The by-product was a set of publications that continues the rhetorical work (and satisfies the requirements of the job) as we plan the next stages of our journeys.

REFERENCES

Calhoon-Dillahunt, Carolyn, Darin L. Jensen, Sarah Z. Johnson, Howard Tinberg, and Christie Toth. 2017. "TYCA Guidelines for Preparing Teachers of English in the Two-Year College." *College English* 79 (6): 550–60.

Hassel, Holly, and Kelly Ritter. 2017. "Textual Collaborations: Preparing Two-Year College English Faculty." *NCTE.* http://www2.ncte.org/blog/2017/10/textual-collaborations -preparing-two-year-college-english-faculty/.

Jensen, Darin L., and Christie Toth. 2017. "Unknown Knowns: The Past, Present, and Future of Graduate Preparation for Two-Year College English Faculty." *College English* 79 (6): 561–92.

Kynard, Carmen. 2018. "Academia as a Hustle; or, How Everything I Know about Academia, I Learned from Rick Ross (Part I)." *Education, Liberation, and Black Radical Traditions for the 21st Century*, January 9. http://carmenkynard.org/academia-as-a-hustle -part-i/.

TYCA. 2017. "TYCA Guidelines for Preparing Teachers of English in the Two-Year College." *Teaching English in the Two-Year College* 45 (1): 8–19.

47

U CAN HAZ FAIR USE!

Timothy R. Amidon

Envision an epigraph in this space. The epigraph you envision might be lyrics derived from a 1990s hip-hop song about other people's copyrightable intellectual property (OPCIP). Those lyrics haven't been included in this space because this is a true story of a make believe epigraph picked to demonstrate what happens when people stop understanding fair use and start using other people's wonky interpretations of it.

—Super Rad, 1990s hip-hop artist

Recently, I was talking with a group of friends at the Conference on College Composition and Communication when I overheard a colleague tell this wack story about fair use. It kind of (but not exactly) went like this: Colleague 1: "Duuuude, I am totally writing this awesome scholarly thing about a band, but the editor just told me I can't use lyrics in the article." Colleague 2: "Whoa. That totally sucks. What are you going to do?" Colleague 1: "I don't know."

At that very moment, a meme began continuously looping in my head: U can haz fair use!

If you've written or designed a text that makes use of other people's copyrightable intellectual property (OPCIP), the chances are you've probably had an experience that kind of went like this. You were like, okay, *who's down with OPCIP? I'm down with OPCIP* in this article/chapter/webtext/essay, and you went rambling on that yellow brick road to the magic land of fair use. But then that inner voice kicked in.

You know the one. The voice of that professor, peer reviewer, colleague, mentor, student, or editor who once told you: *Oh, no, copyright prohibits composers, designers, and researchers from integrating OPCIP.* But then you were like [record scratch]—*but wait. hold up.* What about fair use? Doesn't fair use say I can use OPCIP in my scholarship?

Yes, but it's complicated—predominately because the fair use provisions of copyright law (Section 107 of 17 USC) are written in statutory

DOI: 10.7330/9781607328834.c047

language and enacted through case law that can be wicked confusing
to interpret unless you have a legal degree. This chapter offers insights
on fair use composing that I've gleaned from hanging out with folks
like Kyle Stedman, Renee Hobbs, Martine Courant-Rife, and Dànielle
Nicole DeVoss. Channeling them, I repeat, u can haz fair use. You can
use OPCIP in your scholarship. Do it. Go forth and be awesome. To
help you navigate this terrain, I offer six brief strategies that I've used
when incorporating OPCIP into my own scholarship. My hope is that
you might use them to help you feel more confident about integrating
OPCIP in your scholarship.

* * *

Get used to being a little bit uncomfortable about fair use. Most of the
intellectual property (IP) that academic authors create is regulated by
copyright law (Title 17 USC). The fair use provisions (Section 107) enu-
merate situations under which you can use OPCIP in your own work.
However, only courts can determine if a specific use is fair or infringing.
That's the uncomfortable part you have to learn to accept. When I first
started remixing stuff and integrating OPCIP into my own scholarship,
this freaked me out. It's totally cool for you to freak out, too. It's a normal part of the process. Still, it's exactly this fear that can cause writer-
designers to make overly conservative decisions about whether they
incorporate OPCIP in their own work, avoiding even the types of legitimate fair uses directly protected within copyright law. Consequently, it's
also a good idea to follow these other strategies.

Learn about the four factors courts employ to make fair use rulings. If
you're using OPCIP, it's prudent to learn a little bit about how fair use
works. It can be confusing, but once you get the gist of how courts apply
the four factors to make rulings on fair use, you'll feel more comfortable in thinking through how it impacts the ways you are using OPCIP
in your own work. Rich Stim's "Measuring Fair Use: The Four Factors"
(2010) is a quick and accessible starting place. In fact, before I began
reading the stellar scholarship on fair use in rhetoric and composition
(e.g., Hobbs 2010; Rife, 2007; Rife, Slattery, and DeVoss 2011; Westbrook
2009), I used Stim's explanations as a basic, simple heuristic for making
independent fair use assessments. It won't give you 100 percent certainty that OP might not get grumpy about the ways you used their CIP,
but it might help you build comfort knowing that what you are doing
with OPCIP in your scholarship is (definitely not, maybe, probably, or
mostly) okay.

Avoid fair use entirely by using content in the public domain. This is the play-it-safe approach. If you use content that isn't protected by copyright, you don't have to worry about copyright or make a fair use argument. You can do this by using works that are in the public domain, which means that members of the public have a right to make use of them. Although there are different ways that works enter the public domain, the three most common types of public domain works that I like to use are (1) works whose copyright has expired (currently copyrightable works published before 1923); (2) works created by federal employees acting within the scope of their positions within the U.S. government; and (3) works released to the public domain through Creative Commons licensing, a website that functions as a digital clearinghouse that allows creators to say how other composers might use their work. When I am searching for public domain content to remix, I tend to go to sites such as PublicDomainArchive, The Public Domain Review, Wikimedia Commons, Vintage.com, Pixabay, ccMixter, and the New York Public Library Public Domain Collections.

Use and transform small parts of many original sources to create something new. One of the four factors that courts use to make a fair use ruling involves determining the "amount and substantiality" of the original work integrated within your own. In other words, if you're using a very small part of a larger whole, it's more fair than less fair. When I composed "Spotlight on Intellectual Property (IP): An Interview with Members of the CCCC IP Caucus" (published in *Kairos* in 2012), I created eight thumbnail images to serve as navigation buttons in the webtext. I used found images—those either in the public domain or those licensed by Creative Commons for remixing (as long as I attributed the creators). However, my general practice as a composer is to select small portions from larger works and combine them. To create the thumbnail images, I layered and feathered elements from the images I had found using photo-editing software. Through these edits, the elements of the original images I had selected were transformed into a new whole—an amalgamation of distinct, derivative elements drawn from original sources.

Compose fair use statements to frame or initiate dialogue with editors about your use of OPCIP. Different editors or publishers will have different interpretations of copyright and fair use, which means they will apply them in ways that are more and less liberal. There are good reasons editors take conservative approaches: not wanting to get into time-consuming legal battles or discussions about how to clear permissions that can threaten an edited collection or an issue of a journal. If you're making use of OPCIP, it's good form to initiate conversations with editors well in advance to make sure that they are onboard with what you are doing or hope to do.

One way to initiate that dialogue is to compose a brief fair use statement that describes how and why your use of OPCIP should be interpreted as a protected fair use. I like to adapt the fair use statement that The Critical Media Project (n.d.) created for use with my projects.

Reach out to the CCCC IP Caucus. Finally, use your networks and human resources. If I have a question about working with content that is copyrighted—I'm not sure if it's safe or ethical—I go right to my colleagues on the CCCC IP Caucus. I've found that they are a generous and receptive group whose members have helped me think through a variety of fair use questions that I've encountered as both a writer–designer and an associate editor at *Kairos: A Journal of Rhetoric, Technology, and Pedagogy*. There is usually at least one member of the group who knows exactly how to respond to different types of IP issues or can point you toward someone who might be able to help you think through the questions you have.

With these six pieces of advice in mind, hopefully you can enter into that conversation I mentioned earlier. When Colleague 1 says: "Duuuude, I am totally writing this awesome scholarly thing about a band, but the editor just told me I can't use lyrics in the article," your response might be something along the lines of "Well, actually, u can haz fair use, and here's why and how you can assert it."

REFERENCES

Amidon, Timothy R. 2012. "Spotlight on Intellectual Property (IP): An Interview with Members of the CCCC IP Caucus." *Kairos: A Journal of Rhetoric, Technology, and Pedagogy* 17 (2). http://kairos.technorhetoric.net/17.2/interviews/amidon/.

Critical Media Project. N.d. "Fair Use Statement." http://www.criticalmediaproject.org /about/fair-use-statement/.

Hobbs, Renee. 2010. *Copyright Clarity: How Fair Use Supports Digital Learning*. Thousand Oaks, CA: Sage.

Rife, Martine Courant. 2007. "The Fair Use Doctrine: History, Application, and Implications for (New Media) Writing Teachers." *Computers and Composition* 24 (2): 154–78.

Rife, Martine Courant, Shaun Slattery, and Dànielle N. DeVoss. 2011. *Copy(write): Intellectual Property in the Writing Classroom*. Fort Collins, CO: WAC Clearinghouse.

Stim, Rich. 2010. "Measuring Fair Use: The Four Factors." *Copyright & Fair Use Stanford University Libraries*. http://fairuse.stanford.edu/overview/fair-use/four-factors/.

Westbrook, Steve. 2009. *Composition & Copyright: Perspectives on Teaching, Text-making, and Fair Use*. Albany: SUNY University Press.

48

OPEN OR CLOSED?
Observations on Open-Access Publishers

Mike Palmquist

Open-access journals and books have been part of the publishing landscape in writing studies since the 1990s. Early open-access journals include *Kairos: A Journal of Rhetoric, Technology, and Pedagogy* (kairos .technorhetoric.net), *Enculturation* (enculturation.net), and *RhetNet* (wac.colostate.edu/rhetnet). Each of these journals began publication in 1996. The earliest open-access books published within the field appear to be Beth Baldwin's *Conversations: Computer-Mediated Dialogue, Multilogue, and Learning* and the edited collection *The Rhetorical Dimensions of Cyberspace*, which Baldwin coedited with Tim Flood. Both books appeared in *RhetNet* and are available on its site at the WAC Clearinghouse. Sustained efforts in open-access book publishing within writing studies include the WAC Clearinghouse (wac.colostate.edu), established in 1997, Computers and Composition Digital Press (ccdigitalpress.org), established in 2007, and Writing Spaces (writingspaces.org), established in 2008.

Open-access publishers make content available at no charge to readers in digital formats, including ePUB, HTML/CSS, and PDF. Some early work is also available in formats such as Sophie Reader. To support their operations, open-access publishers sometimes make books available for purchase in print format. The WAC Clearinghouse, for example, has partnered with Parlor Press and the University Press of Colorado to provide low-cost versions of books that are otherwise available without charge in digital formats. During what has now turned out to be a long transitional period since the beginning of digital publication, these print books have occasionally helped convince skeptical senior scholars that a book they are considering as part of a tenure and promotion case is "real"—or, perhaps more to the point, that the publisher is legitimate.

Authors who consider various publishing venues should be aware of several key aspects of open-access publishing, including the timeframe

DOI: 10.7330/9781607328834.c048

during which work will be available to readers, the copyright licenses under which work can be released, terminology associated with open-access publications, and the advantages and disadvantages of working with open-access publishers.

Availability of Your Work. Many authors choose to share their work through open-access journals and book publishers because they know that it is likely to be available for a longer period and to a potentially wider audience than books published by proprietary presses. Consider what is perhaps the leading journal in our field, *College Composition and Communication.* Published by the National Council of Teachers of English (NCTE), this journal is available in digital and print format to members of the Conference on College Composition and Communication (CCCC) as part of their membership dues as well as to other members of NCTE who choose to subscribe to the journal. It is also available through the database JSTOR. To preserve the value of subscribing to the journal (or, more to the point, of becoming a member of NCTE and CCCC), NCTE restricts access to the journal to subscribers for a number of years. Once that period has passed, it becomes available to patrons of libraries who subscribe to the JSTOR database.

This poses a challenge for authors who want their work to be made available to the largest possible audience. Placing work in a highly regarded journal brings visibility within the field (and confers a degree of prestige to those published in such journals). Yet nonsubscribers are less likely to have access to new scholarship. In addition, even when the work is released to a database company such as JSTOR, access is still restricted. Patrons of libraries who subscribe to the journal will eventually have access to your work; those who do not can purchase copies of the work from the database company.

In contrast, scholars whose work appears in open-access journals and book publishers know that readers will have immediate access to it. Open-access journals such as *Kairos, Enculturation,* and *Across the Disciplines,* for example, allow anyone to view their work. In 2019, *Kairos* noted on its website that it was receiving roughly 45,000 visits per month. The WAC Clearinghouse, which provides access to several journals and more than ninety scholarly books, was receiving roughly 225,000 visits per month in 2019 and, in the previous full year, had recorded more than 2.4 million downloads of work in PDF and ePUB formats.

The length of time work is available is also a key factor in deciding whether to publish in open-access venues. The arguments in favor of traditional journals and book series, such as those sponsored by professional organizations and university presses, are the longevity of these groups. In addition, many of the journal articles produced by these groups are being digitized and, at a minimum, made available in full-text databases. In contrast, open-access journals often lack the steady sources of funding available to more traditional journals—and in fact, as is the case with *Kairos* and the WAC Clearinghouse, may operate without any dedicated sources of funding whatsoever. (Unlike open-access journals in other fields, open-access journals in writing studies have largely eschewed charging publication fees to authors whose work has been accepted for publication.) The Clearinghouse, for example, operates largely on donations, modest amounts of revenue from print sales of books, and contributions of time and effort from scholars who have joined the project. As a result, entire collections of work can and have disappeared.

Yet many open-access journals and book publishers have shown impressive survival rates. *Kairos* and *Enculturation* have thrived since their founding two decades ago. *Across the Disciplines*, which resulted from the merger of *academic.writing* and *Language and Learning across the Disciplines*, can trace its roots to 1994, while the *WAC Journal* was founded in 1989. Even work published in *RhetNet*, which ceased operation in the late 1990s, continues to be available. A key advantage of these journals is the ease of access to their articles. Some are regularly indexed in databases, which point to their locations on the web. And most open-access journals in our field regularly publicize new work. Similarly, open-access books are routinely listed in WorldCat, a database that lists library holdings at most leading U.S. and international libraries.

Open-access books, while less common than open-access journals, appear to have clearer advantages over traditional books. Over the past several decades, even as the number of new books published by university presses has increased (Townsend 2003) and even as publishers in general are producing more books than ever before (Lambert 2015), the average number of printed copies of scholarly books has declined. To a large extent, this reflects a drop in book purchases by libraries, which have been faced with escalating costs for databases and journal subscriptions. As recently as the 1980s, purchases by libraries were sufficient to ensure the economic viability of most books produced by university presses. By the early 2000s, however, publishers were pointing to significant declines in those purchases, with some books being purchased by as few as twenty-five libraries nationwide (Charles Bazerman, personal communication). As Darrin Pratt, past president of the American Association of University Presses, noted in a recent conversation, the typical press run for a scholarly book has declined to about 400 copies—and it might be fewer than that.

Open-access books, in comparison, tend to circulate far more widely. The web page for the first original (as opposed to rereleased) book published by the WAC Clearinghouse, Charles Bazerman and David Russell's edited collection *Writing Selves/Writing Societies: Research from Activity Perspectives*, has been downloaded in whole or as individual chapters more than 240,000 times since its publication in 2003. A more recent book from the Clearinghouse, Asao B. Inoue's monograph *Antiracist Writing Assessment Ecologies: Teaching and Assessing Writing for a Socially Just Future*, has been downloaded more than 86,000 times since its publication in June 2015. The result has been a tendency toward higher rates of citation of open-access books. In 2008, for example, Bazerman and Russell's collection had garnered roughly seven times as many citations as an award-winning print book that had been published at the same time (Bazerman et al. 2008).

Choosing Copyright Licenses. Anyone considering an open-access journal or publisher should be familiar with copyright licenses. In most cases, open-access journals use Creative Commons licenses (creativecommons .org). These licenses allow the copyright holder to specify whether, how, and for what general purposes a document or media item can be made available, shared, reused, or remixed. Creative Commons licenses use concepts such as attribution, sharing, commercial versus noncommercial, and sharing to develop specific licenses. Each license has both a "human readable summary" and a detailed specification, including Public Domain, Attribution Alone, Attribution + Noncommercial, and so on.

Open-access publishers within the field of writing studies have varied recommendations regarding copyright, but most fall under some variant of the Creative Commons framework. *Enculturation* publishes work under the Attribution-Noncommercial-ShareAlike Creative Commons license; *Kairos* encourages authors to choose from any of the Creative Commons licenses; and the WAC Clearinghouse encourages book authors and editors to use an Attribution-Noncommercial-NoDerivatives license and journal authors to choose from any of the Creative Commons licenses.

Gold and Green, Gratis and Libre: Understanding Open-Access Terminology. Within the larger open-access community, two sets of terms have become increasingly important. *Gold* and *green* refer to who makes a document available in open-access forms. Gold open-access refers to works that appear in open-access publications, such as articles in an open-access journal. Green open-access refers to articles that appear in subscription-based journals but are subsequently made available. This often happens when authors retain copyright to a published work and then release it through a university library's repository. Green open-access is often required by government funding agencies, foundations, and colleges and universities.

Gratis and *libre* refer to terms developed by Peter Suber (2008) to distinguish two main types of open-access work. Gratis open access refers to works that an author makes available without charge but also without necessarily granting rights to remix, reuse, or create derivative works. Libre open access refers to works that are released without charge and with as few restrictions as possible on the further use of that work.

Within the open-access community, these terms have become as close to "fighting words" as you can imagine, with many favoring libre open access taking a strong stance against any restrictions on reuse of work. The argument most commonly advanced in response to the libre camp is the benefit to authors, particularly those whose evaluations are based in part on citations and journal impact factors, of ensuring that their work continues to be credited to them. Recently, for example, several books published by the WAC Clearinghouse were removed from the Open Textbook Library because they carried Creative Commons licenses that restricted reuse.

Advantages and Disadvantages of Open-Access Publishers. The primary benefit of open-access publishing, beyond increased availability of your work and potentially higher citation rates, is contributing to a movement that has the potential to lower costs for your college or university library. As more authors choose open-access publication venues, more high-quality work will be available at no or low cost.

The primary disadvantages include challenges from colleagues who place open-access publishers within a lower tier of scholarly venues. To some extent, these challenges echo the old print-digital divide, in which work published in print was considered of higher quality—even, somehow, *better* by virtue of its physical nature—than work published in digital format. For examples of this debate, see the multi-journal collaboration on the future of electronic publishing hosted by *Enculturation* (Blakesley et al. 2002). Of greater concern, some faculty members might have reservations about what they view as high acceptance rates at open-access journals. In contrast to journals such as *College Composition and*

Communication and *College English*, which accept less than 10 percent of all submissions, acceptance rates are indeed higher—often much higher. (Should you face this critique, your best option is to choose publishers with strong editorial boards, strong review processes, and a record of publishing high-quality work.)

Additional areas to be aware of range from publishers who will expect you to pay a subvention fee prior to publication, predatory publishers, and the potential of playing a larger role in the production of your document than you would with a traditional publisher. Within the field of writing studies, few journals charge subvention fees. This is a common practice in other fields, however, and it might become more common in our field. If you are asked to pay a subvention fee, seek resources from your institution. Many colleges and universities will underwrite such costs. Be aware, as well, of predatory publishers, which charge fees but fail to provide the editing and production services expected of reputable publishers.

Perhaps the greatest area of surprise for authors who choose to publish in open-access journals and books series is the expectation that they'll play at least a minor role in the production process. Be prepared to learn about technical specifications for images and various types of files. You might be asked, for example, to provide images in TIFF format with a thirty-two-bit color depth, using CMYK color definitions, at 600 dots per inch. While it's relatively easy to learn about these settings, I've found that some authors find these kinds of requests to be a significant stumbling block.

As you consider open-access publishers, keep in mind that they are likely to be managed by people like you. They'll most likely be scholars who are donating their time to a cause they believe in. Journals such as *Kairos* and *Enculturation*, as well as the journals and book series at the WAC Clearinghouse, have published high-quality work for decades. Newer journals, such as *The Journal of Working Class Studies* and *Prompt: A Journal of Academic Writing Assignments*, operate under similar assumptions about the value of the work they are doing. When you choose to work with them, you'll be joining a community of scholars whose goal is to share excellent scholarly work as widely as possible.

REFERENCES

Bazerman, Charles, David Blakesley, Mike Palmquist, and David Russell. 2008. "Open Access Book Publishing in Writing Studies: A Case Study." *First Monday* 13 (1). http://firstmonday.org/ojs/index.php/fm/article/view/2088/1920.

Blakesley, David, Doug Eyman, Byron Hawk, Mike Palmquist, and Todd Taylor, eds. 2002. Special multi-journal issue of *Enculturation, academic.writing, CCC Online, Kairos,* and the *Writing Instructor* on electronic publication. *Enculturation* (Spring). http://enculturation.net/4_1/.

Lambert, Craig. 2015. "The 'Wild West' of Academic Publishing: The Troubled Present and Promising Future of Scholarly Communication." *Harvard Magazine,* January–February. http://harvardmagazine.com/2015/01/the-wild-west-of-academic-publishing.

Suber, Peter. 2008. "Gratis and Libre Open Access." *SPARC Open Access Newsletter* 124. https://dash.harvard.edu/bitstream/handle/1/4322580/suber_oagratis.html ?sequence=1.

Townsend, Robert B. 2003. "History and the Future of Scholarly Publishing." *Perspectives* 41 (3). http://www.historians.org/Perspectives/Issues/2003/0310/0310vie3.htm.

49

TEXT/DESIGN/CODE
Advice on Developing and Producing a Scholarly Webtext

Douglas Eyman

I've been an editor at *Kairos*—one of the longest continuously publishing peer-reviewed journals in writing studies—for over twenty years, and during that time, I've developed a repertoire of advice for authors who want to embrace the challenge of creating digital scholarly works that take full advantage of the multimedia and networked affordances of the web. At *Kairos*, we call this kind of article a "webtext," both to distinguish it as not-only-print, which seems to be the common understanding of "article" but also to acknowledge that it is not, formally speaking, "hypertext." (We considered sticking with "hypertext" just to annoy the late-1990s hypertext theorists, but since some of those folks were our authors and one of our audiences, we went the Ulmerian route of replacing a perfectly good extant word with our own neologism.) Webtexts, it turns out, are a lot harder to craft than traditional print journal articles. For one thing, most of us don't have the depth of training and practice in producing multimedia that we have in print-based writing. There's also the additive nature—not only does a webtext author need to produce an argument (usually supported by alphabetic writing), but that argument needs to be elucidated and supported by both the content *and the design* of the webtext—and the text, media, design, and code all have to work together to present a coherent and usable end product.

When developing a webtext, it is important right at the outset, in the process of invention, to simultaneously draft the text, the design (including media elements such as image, audio, and video) and the code; the final work should integrate all three as equal contributors to the overall rhetorical effect of your work. It's also important to consider two critical aspects that we don't usually consciously address in the traditional article: usability and accessibility. Building with usability and accessibility as key aims from the outset will prevent time-consuming and potentially technically challenging revisions as you move toward publication. In the

DOI: 10.7330/9781607328834.c049

following three sections, I'll present some succinct advice for authors of scholarly webtexts, focusing on text, design, and code.

Text. Even though we tend to be well trained in text production, it's never a bad idea to do some preparatory work when drafting a new article or transfiguring a seminar paper or conference presentation into a publishable work. As a reviewer of both digital and print scholarly works, I've found that the biggest challenges relate to audience, context, argument, and organization. I find it helpful to draft a short specifications document that explicitly identifies the audiences I want to reach. This document also includes a brief report about the target journal, addressing questions like: How does that venue articulate its audiences and purpose? What do the editors say about the journal's goals and requirements? What media and design platforms do they support? What citation format do they want? This last piece of information may seem relatively inconsequential, but it actually helps to understand what the journal values—if they use an author-date format for in-text citations, then the timeliness and currency of the references you use are seen as important; if they use MLA style, then the authority and status of the people you choose to cite are more important.

The more you know about the journal you aim to publish in, the more likely you will be crafting a version that will resonate with reviewers for that journal (see also Duffy's chapter in this volume). I strongly advocate spending time with past issues, both to see how articles in that journal are constructed and to make sure that you don't miss any relevant research that you should include in your literature review or theoretical framing (both editors and peer reviewers notice when authors fail to do their due diligence).

When you are working on a webtext, I strongly recommend using a plain-text writing platform that will allow you to develop the text in the environment you plan to publish in; basically, don't use Microsoft Word, because its design will be the default—and you will want to develop your own sense of design.

Design. For most authors, design is the most challenging element of creating a webtext. Most of us are great with words, but don't often have to craft the design of our work (beyond the occasional opportunity to select the fonts used in our textual products). Design is an integral part of a webtext, and it must be decided upon early so that it can be woven into the work as a whole; if you simply write a text and then add design, it will be neither well integrated nor effective. The design choices you make should guide the reader through the text and should facilitate the relationships between text, image, and media that you want to foreground. The selection of media is also key: which media work best to illuminate your argument? If you need both sound and video, then video works; if you just need sound, select audio files (i.e., don't default to video if it's not the most appropriate vehicle). PDFs are notoriously inaccessible (and difficult to edit), so be certain their use is necessary and warranted if you decide to use them.

I've found that thinking in terms of visual metaphor is a productive way to start working on a design, asking what metaphor would best support your argument. If your argument is about networks or rhizomes, then a network visualization might be a good starting point. You can also use the core principles of contrast, alignment, repetition, and proximity, as well as hiding and revealing, to solidify the overall design. And, of course, spending time looking at other scholars' design choices and analyzing their effectiveness is an excellent way to build your own design sensibilities.

Design is not just visual, though—it's also important to consider the full effect of the interface (visual, auditory, kinetic) as well as the ways in which your readers will interact with the text. Navigation choices and implementation are very important elements of your text's information design: good navigation schema can enhance usability and accessibility; bad navigation can render your work unreadable. And, of course, all of your design decisions need to be supported by the underlying code.

Code. Perhaps one of the biggest editorial challenges we face is cleaning up and optimizing the HTML, CSS, and JavaScript code that serve as the infrastructure for a webtext.

Although it is beyond the scope of this brief chapter to provide detailed instructions, I can note some "best practices" that all webtext authors should engage. The main issue for coding is consistency—consistency in file-naming conventions (keep them all lowercase; don't put spaces in the name), consistency in the naming of *divs* and *spans* within the HTML code, consistency in following and using a standard (such as the recommended HTML 5). Webtext authors should be careful not to use proprietary systems (like Adobe Flash), because they are difficult to sustain. Webtexts should also be portable and archivable (thus, sites like Wix and Weebly should be avoided until or unless they are more easily exported). The coding choices made should support the design and the argument—for instance, it's not a good idea to use a fancy JavaScript if the effect isn't an integral or supportive element that furthers the main purpose of the webtext.

Adding metadata—embedded information about the webtext itself, such as the names of authors, title, date of creation, and copyright information—is part of the coding process, but the particulars of how to code metadata may be specified by the journal (much like the citation format for the text). Metadata is a critical component that improves findability and long-term sustainability.

Finally, when working on the code of a webtext, it is an excellent practice to keep in mind (just as it is while working on the design) usability and accessibility issues and to learn about and apply the code-level features (such as responsive design and accessibility standards) that support them.

A well-designed webtext can perform a scholarly argument through the interplay of text, design, and code—but each element needs to be as carefully crafted as all of the others.

50
SPEAK TO OTHERS AS YOU WOULD LIKE THEM TO SPEAK TO YOU

Craig Cotich

I want to address a fairly unusual kind of writing class, one that demands a small amount of traditional academic writing, but a significant amount of rhetorical precision: the professional editing class. As co-director of the professional editing track within the professional writing minor at UC–Santa Barbara for the last ten years, I've had the honor of working with some of the strongest writers on our campus. These students apply to the minor with impressive work experience, often including a good amount of professional and published writing to supplement the academic writing they do within their majors. Given their credentials and their GPAs, these students arrive at the professional editing classroom confident in their writing abilities. But this series of classes stretches them in totally new ways.

The vast majority of the work within these classes requires that students not only correct errors within a range of writing genres, but also provide feedback to authors about how to improve the writing. In our first major assignment within the capstone course, for example, students copyedit an academic journal article about William Shakespeare as a child. The excerpt I use was borrowed from my amazing predecessor in the minor, Leonard Tourney, and it's a good document to use because it's academic in nature but not mired in academic jargon and literary theory, which means that students from biology and psychology will have generally the same understanding as those English majors do. Without a doubt, those first assignments will be turned in completely covered in red ink, and most of those edits are rewrites of sentences and even paragraphs, with notes to the author that are blunt and direct. Although ineffective as a means of building a relationship with authors, this is a fundamental first step toward becoming a more careful, sensitive, patient editor.

I think it's crucial to imagine what students are experiencing when they read passages that they don't quite understand, that they have to

DOI: 10.7330/9781607328834.c050

slog through, or that use words or phrases or even structures they don't use in their own writing. When they experience discomfort reading someone else's writing, they naturally try to move toward their comfort zone, which means rewriting it so that it sounds like their own voices. And when I talk to them after they turn in these first assignments, they express their frustration with the author: "It was written horribly!" "I couldn't stand reading it!" "I wanted to rewrite the whole thing!"

Overall, the documents are written well; in fact, virtually all of the documents we use in class are published texts (usually excerpts). However, when I remove punctuation from some of the longer sentences or insert grammar errors, students can find the result to be quite confusing or unpleasant. For example, I've inserted errors and removed most of the punctuation from this Stephen Greenblatt sentence, from his book *Will in the World: How Shakespeare Became Shakespeare*: "A Stratford legend recorded around 1680 by the eccentric gossipy biographer John Aubrey held that Will Shakespeare apprenticed to be a butcher like his father, occasionally took a turn at slaughtering the animals" (54). Without punctuation in the right place, this sentence becomes ambiguous, and when many sentences look like this across a document, students get the impression that the writing is sloppy. Their frustration with the writing introduces a fantastic teaching moment, a time to turn the tables and ask them how they would like to see their writing come back to them in the form that they've just given to an author. At first, most of them say that they want to be told the truth about their writing, and that they would want that truth told to them directly.

However, the vast majority of writers would prefer to receive their submissions back with just five words written in caps at the top of the page: "PERFECT! DON'T CHANGE A WORD!" The writer so gifted to receive this comment, assuming that a competent editor reviewed the work, is rare. We as developmental and copy editors must frame our feedback in the context of the majority of writers, whose work is not perfect and who are sensitive about their writing. I think that no matter the content, most writers feel attached to their writing, regardless of whether they admit that. Moreover, many writers feel as though they've been personally attacked when they receive critical feedback (see Cools's chapter in this volume). I encourage copyediting students always to assume—until they have proof to the contrary—that they are dealing with a sensitive writer.

Another essential assumption is that virtually every writer will benefit from editing and editorial feedback. The trick is to convince writers of that. To qualify as a trusted editor, then, students are asked to master two goals in the professional editing classroom. The first is to learn the grammar, punctuation, and mechanical rules, in addition to stylistic principles, which takes twenty weeks of intense study. The second—equally important—goal is learning how best to communicate their advice in a way that generates two responses in the writer: "I understand the edits and comments you've made" and "I would like to work with you more in the future, because I see the great benefit of your involvement in this process."

These two responses lead me to my title and also to my piece of advice to all writers, reviewers, and editors: "Speak to others as you would like them speak to you," an adaptation of the Golden Rule. Assuming that they have mastered the grammar and punctuation rules and can speak to the principles of style, editors should repeat that advice to themselves over and over as they're giving feedback to writers, on paper and in person. When they consider their audience, the author, more attentively, they begin to change the way they think of the person behind the document. I completely understand the temptation editors, especially student editors, may feel when a document is placed in front of them. They have spent a lot of time and energy cultivating their skills, and now they get to use them. My students want to flex their copyediting muscles, and that can sometimes result in a vicious mauling of the document. Although that might demonstrate a student's raw copyediting skills, the effect on the writer receiving that edit can be disastrous, because it can damage the wonderful relationship the copyeditor *could have had* with the writer, along with tarnishing any useful or helpful feedback the copyeditor may actually have to provide the writer. Ultimately, the Golden Rule of editing feedback means that editors must look beyond immediate documents and instead think about lasting symbiotic relationships with writers.

To help facilitate these relationships, I ask students to learn and articulate a number of principles to consider when writing to authors.

- **Lead with the positive.** "This is very well researched, with credible sources to support your claims. You move between your own writing and your sources smoothly. However, . . ."
- **Provide options to writers.** "This phrase might not be very clear to the reader. Are you trying to say that the Prius has zero emissions and that it also has zero pollution? Left as is, the reader might interpret this phrase as implying that the Prius has zero emissions, but that it also adds to pollution. Perhaps try to rephrase this to enhance clarity. You could try saying instead, 'He was driving a zero-emissions and nonpolluting Prius.'"
- **Remain humble.** "When I looked up the difference between *crème* and *cream*, I found that crème is generally used for foods (like crème

brûlée), while cream is the term used for topical ointments and cosmetics. Since you are referring to a cosmetic cream, the latter spelling is more appropriate."

- **Clarify ambiguities.** "*These* is a vague word here. Are your referring to mummies or the tattoos? Please replace *these* with either *mummies* or *tattoos.*"

- **Use hedging words to soften the force of the criticism.** "Instead of *died off*, consider using something more formal to fit the tone of the rest of the piece and the serious subject matter of the sentence." In addition to *consider*, other effective words are *perhaps, may, might, could, possibly, some, many, suggest, although, potentially, only,* and so on.

All of the principles and examples above come from my students.

What I'd like to leave you with is this: the writer–editor relationship should be a partnership. Because writing is so often considered a solo activity, copyediting is an amazing way to demonstrate to students that great writing is best accomplished through teamwork, which is a lesson that students can take with them into the world after graduation. One of the beautiful things about teaching writing is how practical the principles of good writing are. Even though we work so intensely in the field of copyediting, the skill of communicating to others with care and respect is one of the best lessons novice copyeditors learn, for it can help them deepen the relationships they will have with authors, with writers, and with writing.

51
READ LIKE A WRITER,
WRITE FOR YOUR READER

Troy Hicks

One of the adages that I have heard as a student writer (from grade school to graduate school) and offered as a writing teacher goes something like this: "Read like a writer, write for your reader." On the surface, this piece of advice usually applies to someone engaged in the writing process and attempting to create an audience-centered, not writer-centered, piece of work. It suggests that—as writers who are mindful of context and purpose—we should constantly be reading the work of others through a rhetorical lens, trying to understand why they have made the particular moves within a piece of writing so we may make similar moves in our own writing.

I first formally encountered this idea of an audience-centered approach when exploring the work of Kenneth Bruffee (1984) and thinking about the ways in which we, as academics, are entering an ongoing conversation. He likens the moves we need to make in our writing to the idea of coming in late to a cocktail party, cozying up to a table and listening to the conversations that are going on, and only then trying to jump in. There are social norms that must be followed to fully engage in a conversation, especially one in which specific vocabulary must be used and certain names must be dropped. More recently, this idea has been captured quite well by Gerald Graff and Cathy Birkenstein (2014) and translated into very distinct "moves" that academic writers can make. In their popular book, *"They Say/I Say": The Moves That Matter in Academic Writing*, Graff and Birkenstein argue that by understanding and employing these particular moves, writers can then engage in a sophisticated, nuanced conversation.

Thus, the advice that I offer here takes the "Read like a writer, write for your reader" mantra and pivots it to consider the ways in which you as a writer who has submitted a manuscript for publication could go about reading the reviews you have received. Of course, no one likes

DOI: 10.7330/9781607328834.c051

the bitter sting of rejection (or even the bittersweet sting of "revisions required"), and yet at the same time I think that most reviewers offer their feedback in the spirit of genuine collegial dialogue. Sure, there are reviewers who are just plain spiteful. But for most of us who offer our time to do reviews, whether positive and negative, we write them in the same spirit that we would offer feedback to students: we want you, as academic writers, to succeed.

In the section below, then, I offer a sampling of the types of feedback that I offer colleagues whose work I have reviewed for journals, edited collections, conference presentations, grant proposals, and other submissions. My aim here is to help you "decode" the types of feedback you are getting and, more specifically, explain how you can turn that feedback into actionable revision plans. Many of the editors with whom I work tell me that my reviews are some of the best that they have read, so I think that I must be doing something right. My hope is that you can understand the ways in which I compose reviews, as well as the collegial spirit in which my comments are offered, so you can be better prepared both to create and submit a high-quality manuscript and to embrace your reviews gracefully and move toward the publication stage.

Of the many reviews that I have received on my articles, chapters, book proposals, blog posts, grant applications, and various other forms of academic writing—many of which were positive, and quite a few that were negative—the best of them are written like the advice I would offer to my students. Generous and thoughtful but nonetheless firm, these reviews are the ones that may sting a bit, yet I learn from them as well.

So when I do my work as a reviewer for various journals, editorial boards, grant/advisory boards, personnel committees, and other academic work, I typically try to offer my feedback in the most generative sense possible. Whether I feel that the writing is on target or that it needs a great deal of work, I always offer some positive suggestions as well as critiques, with specific suggestions on how to move the work forward.

In a very generic sense, then, my feedback will follow a similar form in each section. Much like Graff and Birkenstein do in their book, the sections below each offer a very brief "template" of my review advice, followed with an explanation of each. It is worth noting here that no matter what the review system might look like in terms of how comments are communicated, I typically prepare a single, coherent letter first. I find it more helpful to create a holistic response that gives the writer a full context for my comments rather than trying to break things into different parts.

I always read the article twice. First I read the abstract and conclusion and then skim the entire piece. Then I read it from top to bottom and write marginalia so I can use those comments in my review. I use an iPad app, Good Reader, which will then compress all my notes—as well as the words, sentences, and paragraphs that I have highlighted in the document—into a single, unformatted email so I can copy/paste segments of the original manuscript and my comments into the final review.

* * *

No matter what kind of review I am going to offer, positive or negative, I always begin by acknowledging the contribution. Certainly, we can understand the amount of time, energy, and intellectual effort that goes into preparing a manuscript. I feel that it is critical to let my colleague/s know that, at a very basic level, I am recognizing their attempts to influence the field. Therefore, most of my introductions will look something like this:

> Dear Colleague(s),
>
> Thank you for sharing your manuscript/proposal, <Title>, with us. As someone who is also interested in <topic 1>, <topic 2>, and/or <topic 3>, I appreciate the ways in which <your framing of the inquiry questions>, <your collection and analysis of your data>, and/or <your conclusions and implications for the field> contribute to our understanding of ——. In fact, one of the most striking moments of your manuscript/proposal was when you argued/noted that "——." I can see that you have been thinking carefully and critically about these issues, and I appreciate your perspective on ——.

In this introduction, I'm trying to establish a rapport with my colleague(s), letting them know that I honor their attempt to enter part of the academic conversation. I usually write this paragraph during the middle of my review process, after I've read a manuscript and made the initial marginal notes to myself, but before I develop a specific list of concerns as full paragraphs. The introduction then helps me get focused and provide the right kind of feedback, depending on whether I'm going to offer a positive or negative review.

If a positive review ("accept" or "accept with minor revisions"). While I want to establish rapport, I also want to be concise. The author and the editor want to know very quickly what is right—as well as what could potentially be fixed—in a manuscript. In this section, I want to make it clear so the reader can move into this second portion of the review document in the right frame of mind. Here is an example of what a second paragraph may look like, often blending in different subcategories of the review process such as significance, methodology, data analysis, and implications.

> Overall, your study/presentations/grant proposal is very strong and I particularly appreciate how you ——. Throughout the manuscript, you also ——. In short, I am recommending your manuscript for publication (or revision and resubmission), though I will document a few suggestions for revision that I hope you consider. I've broken them into separate concerns, some minor and others more significant.

Again, this sets readers up for a very specific reading of the review. If they understand that I am offering a positive assessment, my feeling is that they will read the rest of the review with an open mind and willingness to incorporate some of the advice that I am offering. I will then write about major concerns—pointing out specific page numbers and even sentences/paragraphs—in about one paragraph each. I will sometimes offer specific ideas for revision by rewriting sentences or sections of sentences. Finally, I will list minor concerns in a bulleted list, with items such as this:

> Page X: You note, "Research shows . . ." Do you have sample citations you can include here to bolster your argument?

> Page X: You note, "——." I understand your intention in saying ——, but you may want to consider . . .

> Page X: Here you offer some ideas that are, I agree, useful. However, this may be beyond the scope of your article and I wonder if . . .

At the end of the review, I will reiterate my positive reaction. For instance:

> Overall, your manuscript is strong, both methodologically and pedagogically. You point to many interesting ideas about ——. My hope is that my feedback here will help move you toward an even more complete and engaging manuscript.

If a negative review ("reject with encouragement to revise" or "reject"). Unfortunately, there are times where I need to write unfavorable reviews. As I am sure you know, there are only so many euphemisms that one can use. So I try to cut to the chase. In a second paragraph, I will use sentences like this to transition from the opening paragraph into the elements needed for revision. For instance:

> That said, and from what you can tell in my notes above, I do have some serious concerns about your manuscript. I am hopeful that you can

contribute something to the discussion of ——. Your research has potential to —— and I'm hoping that you might be able to revise with the following ideas in mind.

As in the positive reviews, I will offer a full paragraph for major concerns, and then I will create bulleted lists with comments such as:

Page X: Could you describe and elaborate on —— in more detail?

Page X: You mention ——. This is what I want to hear more about because . . .

Page X: You argue that ——. In what ways might you reconsider this in light of ——?

Finally, I will summarize the negative review by reiterating the goals that I think the writer should focus on during revision.

Please understand that I feel you have the beginnings of a strong argument about ——. My main concern here is that in order to contribute significant findings to the conversation about ——, you'll have to make a much stronger case about ——. Therefore, I am recommending that you resubmit after significant revision.

Again, my goal at the end of the review is to reiterate the idea that the author is pushing the academic conversation forward. I usually wrap up with something like this:

Thank you again for sharing your work, and pushing forward the discussion on ——. I look forward to seeing your work in print/the possibility of reading your revisions.

As Bruffee, Graff and Birkenstein, and thousands of other academics already know, joining the academic conversation is difficult yet rewarding work. The feedback that you receive from those who review your manuscripts can sometimes sting, yet it can also lead you to be more productive during the revision process. Reading like a writer, especially when reading reviews, can help you write more confidently in the future.

REFERENCES

Bruffee, K. A. 1984. "Collaborative Learning and the 'Conversation of Mankind.'" *College English* 46 (7): 635–52.

Graff, G., and C. Birkenstein. 2014. *"They Say / I Say": The Moves That Matter in Academic Writing*, 3rd ed. New York: Norton.

52

EDITING TEXTS, EDITING CAREERS

Johndan Johnson-Eilola and Stuart A. Selber

In our experiences as writers and editors, the editorial work of reviewers tends to keep writers and their texts at arm's length, a situation inviting detached criticism more than collaboration or professional development that can assist a publishing career. We encourage writers and editors to work more closely together by attending to editorial concerns at both the micro and macro levels of texts.

There's often a dramatic difference between the advice writers get from editorial reviewers, especially those for journals in our field, and the advice writers get from colleagues, collaborators, and teachers. Feedback on journal submissions tends to be almost exclusively high-level and conceptual, whereas advice from colleagues, collaborators, teachers, and friends is both high-level and low-level, conceptual and concrete. Journal feedback, in many instances, tends to be very hands-off, one-way, oblique, and artificially dispassionate, while feedback from people with more of a stake in the writer contributes an important element of engagement with actual texts. We realize there are exceptions to this pattern of involvement—in fact, you may be among the lucky ones who have received a full spectrum of advice on draft manuscripts. But the normal failure to engage with texts at both micro and macro levels, hands-off and hands-on, give-and-take, all too often limits the work of reviewers and editors more to evaluation and critique than to partnership and collaboration. Thinking of editorial relationships as partnerships or collaborative endeavors is one way to create an oscillation between conceptual and concrete feedback, both of which are crucial to the process of writing development.

As writers, most of us understand "critique" as a rich, productive, engaged term. It is a keyword in the field that has become synonymous with both invention and reflection. But we often struggle to sustain that complexity when we're giving and receiving editorial comments: marginal notes can feel like attacks (and sometimes they are); summary

DOI: 10.7330/9781607328834.c052

comments can sound like dismissals rather than invitations (and some-times they are); and notes pointing out omissions or oversights can feel like put-downs (and sometimes they are). As writers, we're invested in our work. At the same time, many editors would (and do) cringe at those characterizations. We know this because we continue to work on both sides of the writer-editor relationship. What we are offering here are simply some reminders to position ourselves and our affiliations to one another as interested in collaboration and investment, in hands-on work and shared commitment. It is an ongoing goal congruent with our theory talk about the role and practice of critique—disciplinary, peda-gogical, and otherwise.

Editors, reviewers, and writers all need to think and work in certain ways if our vision is going to become more of a reality. Editors need to mediate among the concerns of texts, writers, and reviewers, attending to the whole, both as process and object.

Reviewers need to occupy writerly spaces, collaborating on texts rather than primarily commenting on (or at) them. Writers need to position their texts as open, communal texts, not simply in the sense of active reading but as many-voiced conversations. These are all common-sense ideas, but we need to take them much more literally, concretely, than we often do today.

We've been writing together for most of our adult lives. Much of our early shared work, like that of many collaborators, emerged in the colli-sions among difficult readings, challenging teachers, and engaged peers. Our early texts contained big ideas, we told ourselves, but we labored over the words and sentences, seated next to each other in real-time, taking turns at the keyboard in small offices and crowded computer labs. What we've learned from our longtime collaboration is that edits are often fractal—with levels of detail scaling up and down depending on our viewpoint, and sometimes within a single conversation. Editing activities swoop in and out, tweaking word choices for style and consis-tency, pushing large-scale structures back and forth, pulling other voices into conversations, moving back to our own texts. Discussion edges into metadiscussion and back.

Consider an example from our edited collection *Solving Problems in Technical Communication* (2013). During the editing process, we covered even more terrain than usual, poring over details of our framing essay for the collection, developing structures for our colleagues to use in their own chapters, doing close copyedits for consistency of style across all of the chapters, for a book that became a nearly three-year endeavor. Even at the late stage captured in figure 52.1, we were dealing with

⭐ **Stuart Selber**   March 15, 2012 at 11:50 AM
  Re: update
  To: Johndan Johnson-Eilola

Just finished with our overall introduction and section intros (added my initials to the end of the file name). Dang, it's good. For #2 below, I changed "students taking their first course" to novices. Be sure to change Burnett's title to what's in the final version of our big figure ("What do technical communicators need to know about collaboration"). This is crucial so I'm going to send a note to Joann to be sure we get this right.

On Mar 13, 2012, at 2:38 PM, Johndan Johnson-Eilola wrote:

I've finished checking everything and responding to author queries on everything we authored (text and figures for the front matter, main intro, and four section intros. (I actually caught some additional typos.) There's a notes.txt file in the folder that you can ignore (it's notes to myself) aside from two things:

1. The title on Burnett et al's chapter isn't what we have in the figures or any of our intro material. What we used is parallel with the other chapters, so we need to change the chapter title page. I'm assuming there's an author query on the chapter we sent Rebecca, but we should check to see how she responded to the query when we get her chapter back.

2. Main intro, p. 14: Not sure what we mean by "students in their first course" near the bottom. Students who are taking their first course in tech comm? Maybe say "students just beginning to study technical communication" instead? (Isn't the largest part of our market going to be tech comm majors who may have already had a intro/service course first and are now taking advanced tech comm?)

I'll start working on the chapters in section 3 and 4 when all the files are in.

-j

See More from Stuart Selber

Figure 52.1. Email exchange

issues at many levels, from single words to the functions of examples we were using.

At one level, the email exchange shown in figure 52.1 is extraordinarily mundane: record keeping, to some extent, cleaning up details, straightening things up into a neat package: what do we mean by "students in their first course" near the bottom? Considering different options, we make and question connections between this simple phrase and several different audiences, even at this late stage asking ourselves who our audience is. This type of concern is among the first questions most writers address: *Who am I writing to? How do they think about themselves? And will they recognize themselves in our text?* As most of us have discovered, these first questions never go away. We get a little better at asking and answering them, stumble over them less frequently, but attention to them illustrates how editing at the micro level connects the very small to the very large: a handful of words is one of the hinges on which whole texts turn.

The three options we consider structure the relationship we take, as authors and editors, to our readers: "Students in their first course"; "Students just beginning to study technical communication"; and "Novices." Each of these juggles different concerns, not the least of which is brevity (one of us tends toward wordiness, clearly). We end on "novices," a word that signals a starting position but contains the suggestions of a later state, "professional" or "experienced communicator."

There are, in the end, no isolated texts. We've grown comfortable thinking of texts as conversations, one text pointing to or quoting from another. But those same processes exist within texts, multiple voices working within and across boundaries. By bringing to the surface the shared responsibilities for textual production, editors, reviewers, and writers can weave those conversations more fully into our discourses.

REFERENCE
Johnson-Eilola, Johndan, and Stuart A. Selber, eds. 2013. *Solving Problems in Technical Communication.* Chicago: University of Chicago Press.

53

CREATING A CONVERSATION IN THE FIELD THROUGH EDITING

Mya Poe

The value of editorial work can extend beyond editing journals and collections. Strategic editorial work through various venues can also be used to create an enduring conversation in the field.

A central goal of the editorial work that my collaborators and I have done over the last eight years has been to advance a conversation in the field of writing assessment around issues of social justice, racism, and fairness. Creating a conversation in the field through editing requires more than simply looking for gaps in the literature. Instead, creating a conversation is about tackling timely problems that the field needs to solve and then inviting other people to think with you about solutions. Creating a conversation in the field also requires working through multiple avenues—not just a special issue of a specialty journal or a single book collection. A good conversation needs multiple opportunities for people to share ideas, and lots of different kinds of people to participate in that conversation. This requires working strategically with journal editors and publishers. And most important, creating a conversation in the field means sustaining that conversation. That's where it is important to advance knowledge in each iteration; whether it be a special issue, a conference workshop, or a journal article, one must have a sense that the conversation is *going somewhere.*

Be prepared for resistance, though. There is a reason lingering problems are unsolved, ignored. On one hand, it might be that the problem challenges orthodoxy in the field. On the other hand, a problem may be lingering because the expertise to solve it hasn't been cultivated yet; the right mix of approaches hasn't yet been brought together to provide meaningful options for solving the problem. Thus, my last piece of advice for creating a conversation in the field is to look both within and beyond the field for people who share your passion for problem solving.

DOI: 10.7330/9781607328834.c053

* * *

In the 1970s and 1980s, the Cincinnati suburb of Mount Healthy was a community that looked like a civil rights ideal—an integrated community of working-class and middle-class African American and white home owners surrounded by a 2,500-acre county park. The school district included college prep courses, foreign language courses, many sports, and a well-regarded music program. It was a place where race and class integration seemed to work. Yet, growing up in Mount Healthy, I not only witnessed the various ways Mount Healthy wrestled with racism and classism, but also the ways that the educational system simply didn't reflect those tensions but ended up amplifying them through policies related to assessment and educational tracking.

In graduate school, I struggled to find a way to make sense of those lessons from Mount Healthy. Instead, the assessment literature in the 1990s hailed direct writing assessment, in which students produced a "sample [or samples] of the behavior that we seek to examine, in this case a text that the student composes" (Yancey 1999, 486)—as a fairer, more valid measure of student writing ability (see Huot 1990 for a review of direct writing assessment). Indeed, direct writing assessment was an advancement in assessment practices. In working to address the scoring inconsistencies in direct writing assessment identified by Paul Diederich, John French, and Sydell Carlton (1961), researchers like Fred Godshalk, Frances Swineford, and William Coffman (1966) had made direct writing assessment into a methodologically sound and politically reputable means of assessing student writing. But coming from a community like Mount Healthy, I just didn't see it. I saw too many cracks in topic selection, task design, and scoring. Most importantly, I saw too often how the consequences of assessment decisions perpetuated inequality. I read *Critical Race Theory* (Delgado and Stefanic 2001). I found Claude Steele's (1997) and Tukufu Zuberi's (2001) research and wrote my dissertation on racial stereotypes in placement testing. It was a qualitative study that ended up challenging the virtues of direct writing assessment.

In trying to publish my work, I discovered the perils of challenging disciplinary orthodoxy. In struggling against such orthodoxy, I looked to conversations about fairness in the educational measurement literature. Those conversations had stretched since the 1960s, advanced by special issues of journals like the *Journal of Educational Measurement*. Likewise, leaders in the field like Lee Cronbach and Samuel Messick had worked to reshape theoretical notions of validity to consider the consequences of validity—a controversial move, given that many educational measurement researchers prefer to focus on the technical details of assessment, not the social implications. In expanding my reach, I needed other people who were also willing to think through issues of structural inequality, fairness, and justice in assessment.

With good fortune, I met Norbert Elliot and Asao B. Inoue (both of whom are contributors to this volume) in 2008. We hatched a plan for an edited collection—what would become *Race and Writing Assessment*. When Asao and I embarked on *Race and Writing Assessment*, our plan was threefold: (1) invite "famous" people to author key chapters, (2) cultivate additional submissions by up-and-coming scholars, and (3) invite scholars of color who might not otherwise write about assessment to respond to the chapters. We wanted *Race and Writing Assessment* to be an enduring contribution to the field.

After rejections from two presses, we learned important editorial lessons from *Race and Writing Assessment*. We could begin to change the field if we worked strategically. We needed to invite fellow researchers into the space we were fighting to create. Over the next eight years, we sought to create a variety of editorial opportunities to further the conversation. There was a 2014 *Research in the Teaching of English* (*RTE*) special issue that came as the result of a featured session at the Conference on College Composition and Communication (CCCC), a *Journal of Writing Assessment* (*JWA*) special issue in 2016, and a *College English* special issue in 2016. The *RTE* special issue included contributions from international researchers in education. The *JWA* special issue included contributions from assessment scholars as well as rhetoric scholar Ellen Cushman on the topic of ethics. The *College English* special issue included the contributions of diverse researchers, including scholars of color, LGBTQ scholars, and a non-tenure track researcher. That *College English* special issue also yielded another collection, *Writing Assessment, Social Justice, and the Advancement of Opportunity*.

Beyond the editorial work, we kept the conversation going through workshops and talks as well as articles and chapters that we authored together or individually. What's important here is not the number of publications per se, but rather how, through editorial work, we cultivated new connections—to education scholars in the United States and abroad, to legal scholars, to graduate students, to non-tenure track researchers, and to scholars of color. We purposely limited the number of manuscripts from senior researchers in favor of cultivating newer voices from diverse perspectives. We asked measurement scholars to review our work outside of the normal peer-review process. We used each venue as an opportunity to reach in new directions, meet new people, and keep the conversation going.

The editorial work yielded other important insights about how to create and sustain a conversation. Beyond diversity of venues, among the key elements we discovered that sustained our conversation about writing assessment and equality was building in lots of time for developmental editing. If we were going to invite graduate students and early career researchers into the conversation, we would need to invest in developing first-rate manuscripts. This also meant rejecting publications when things didn't work out—but also offering to help those authors get their work published elsewhere.

Likely the most important lesson that we have learned from our editorial work is the necessity of attending, constantly, to moving the conversation somewhere. We have moved from primarily programmatic concerns at four-year colleges to questions of classroom assessment and have begun to learn from the insights of community college researchers. As a result, the conversation on writing assessment and justice is alive. That conversation could never have become as inclusive or meaningful if it weren't for the value of using editorial work to create and sustain a conversation in the field.

REFERENCES

Delgado, Richard, and Jean Stefanic. 2001. *Critical Race Theory: An Introduction.* New York: New York UP.

Diederich, Paul B., John W. French, and Sydell T. Carlton. 1961. *Factors in Judgments of Writing Quality.* Princeton, NJ: Educational Testing Service.

Godshalk, Fred I., Frances Swineford, and William E. Coffman. 1966. *The Measurement of Writing Ability.* Princeton, NJ: College Entrance Examination Board.

Huot, Brian. 1990. "The Literature of Direct Writing Assessment: Major Concerns and Prevailing Trends." *Review of Educational Research* 60 (2): 237–63.

Steele, Claude. 1997. "A Threat in the Air: How Stereotypes Shapes Intellectual Identity and Performance." *American Psychologist* 52 (6): 613–29.

Yancey, Kathleen Blake. 1999. "Looking Back as We Look Forward: Historicizing Writing Assessment." *College Composition and Communication* 50 (3): 483–503.

Zuberi, Tukufu. 2001. *Thicker than Blood: How Racial Statistics Lie.* Minneapolis: University of Minnesota Press.

SECTION 4

Getting (More and Different Types of) Feedback

*Navigating Reviewers and Understanding
Editorial Responses*

54

COMING TO TERMS WITH THE INEVITABILITY OF EPIC FAILURE; OR, ONCE MORE UNTO THE BREACH

Ryan Skinnell

In the call for this collection, the editors outlined a series of potential issues around which contributors could consider offering advice about publishing in rhetoric and composition: inventing arguments, incorporating feedback, expanding projects, and so on. The suggestions were clearly, and appropriately, directed at eliciting supportive responses. Valuable though such supportive advice is, however, some of the best advice I received about publishing in the field has a slightly more negative frame. The best advice I have gotten is about some of the more unpleasant parts of the publishing process—rejection, failure, and pain. There is positive advice that results from the negative framing, however. In what follows, I contend that *recognizing the inevitability of rejection, failure, and pain in publishing can help writers engage in the process in more productive (and less destructive) ways.*

How better to begin a negatively framed essay about failure than with a painful demonstration? In writing this essay, I revisited a number of responses I received from journal editors and blind reviewers over the past ten years. I picked out some of the more biting snippets to share here—snippets, I should note, that are more or less taken verbatim from correspondence:

> Perhaps some further reading would be helpful.

> This essay is not eligible for publication, and I don't see how it can be fixed. The experiment it reports is neither authoritative nor useful, and I don't see how the author thought it could show anything that is not clear from ordinary observation. I do not see why this author took so much trouble to do it.

> I think the author is naive.

DOI: 10.7330/9781607328834.c054

This next will sound harsh (sorry), but I would suggest that it is the author, and not [the subject of the essay], who is trafficking in class-based stereotypes.

The argument seems a bit wobbly, tending to cover a lot of ground without clearly defining its terms or making its case.

The bulk of the paper is largely derivative: a historical review that runs roughshod over complex issues and doesn't develop any meaningful support of a thesis. I strongly encourage you to read more deeply in our discipline's scholarship and history before you continue work in this area.

I selected these comments to share not because they're indicative of what editors and reviewers will say, but because I believe they are indicative of *how responses can make authors feel.* Each of these comments was part of a rejection, and the indisputable fact is, rejections are painful. Most of the comments here are actually small jabs pulled out of much longer, much nicer responses from very professional editors and reviewers. But quite honestly, I remember these comments better than any of the supportive ones.

Frankly, some of them still hurt my feelings even though they're all several years old and, I must admit, mostly right.

A reasonable conclusion to draw might be: don't submit things for review that are poorly written. I certainly could have used that advice on more than one occasion. But however reasonable a conclusion, it is probably not actionable. Rejection is part of the process. Even acceptances often bear some form of rejection—whether "This is a great article, but it needs some minor tweaks" or "The idea is solid, but the execution needs a complete rehaul."

Rejection is actually the most common outcome of publication attempts. After all, a journal's quality is often predicated on how low its acceptance rate is. In recent years, *CCC* has published less than 10 percent of submissions, *Rhetoric Society Quarterly* around 12–15 percent, and *Rhetoric Review* between 10 percent and 20 percent. Not all acceptance rates are so low, to be sure, but acceptance rates can often determine a publication's value in the eyes of a hiring or tenure committee. Book presses are commonly judged in the same way. Given these numbers, it does not take a math whiz to recognize that rejection, failure, and pain are inescapable elements of publishing. And if publishing is an element of a scholar's academic career, then rejection, failure, and pain await.

No doubt this all seems pretty bleak; but believe it or not, my goal is not to discourage people. To the contrary, the inevitability of rejection is an opportunity—or, better yet, a heuristic—for conducting the kind of honest self-assessment that publishing requires. Therefore, for the rest of this essay, I plan to offer some of the heuristic possibilities of rejection, failure, and pain.

First and foremost, not everything is worth publishing, or even attempting to publish. Sometimes it is not especially hard to determine what is or is not worthwhile. I often know, for example, when I have engaged in hard research versus when I have raised interesting questions based on a book or two I've read. Of course, it is possible (maybe even common) in academia to fall into the Dunning-Kruger effect, which is when a novice believes he is more competent in a given area of knowledge than he actually is (Kruger and Dunning 1999). But my guess is most people, given a moment of honest reflection, can judge the difference between a good/interesting idea and a demonstration of hard-earned expertise. Good or interesting ideas are starting points, and can often be sufficient for conference papers, but they are not usually publishable without lots of additional effort because publications demand that writers speak as experts.

That's the easy self-assessment. For less obvious decisions, it is necessary for a writer to ask herself some important questions: What do I hope my work will accomplish? This question comes in other forms: What's the point? So what? Who cares? Why would anyone ever be interested? If a writer-scholar can't answer these questions, or if the answer boils down to "It's really cool stuff that no one's thought about," chances are good there is still work to do. Publishing is not simply a matter of writing about something a writer find interesting (sadly). There is a reason Kenneth Burke's famous parlor conversation analogy retains its explanatory power—writers cannot find success (save the occasional lucky strike) without considering whom they are talking to, what they are talking to them about, and why.

These questions are wrapped up in others: What are the stakes of the argument? What is the writer advocating? Who is involved or implicated? How would things change if people took up the argument? Who would benefit and what might be the drawbacks? Answering these questions is hard work, sometimes harder work than the actual research. Answering them requires that a writer develop a deep understanding of her work in relation to the field's values, publication venues' requirements, and procedures for making arguments. If a writer's work engages these questions in the preparation of a manuscript, it may well be ready for submission and (hopefully) publication. But, it is necessary to realize that rejection is still a possible—even a probable—outcome. And writers must learn to accept that sometimes ideas, even good ideas, must be abandoned, restarted, eviscerated, or absorbed into other good ideas.

Being prepared for it—at least inasmuch as that is possible—helps writers recognize that the rejection is just a small part of the larger ongoing process of publishing in the field. As my dissertation advisor once told me, "If you don't have enough rejections to wallpaper your office, you're probably not submitting enough." Hyperbole notwithstanding, the reality is that publishing involves rejection, and trying to avoid the latter all but requires avoiding the former.

Of course, given the inevitability of rejection, failure, and pain, one response might be to tuck tail and run. Instead, I suggest facing it by

- learning to be prepared for rejection,
- learning the difference between critique and abuse—accept the former, forget the latter,
- learning to accept productive critique, even when it hurts,
- learning that publishing should be positive for you and for the field, and
- learning to be a better respondent—when you're called upon to read, do the things you appreciated and don't do the things you disliked.

These tips don't guarantee success, but to repeat myself, the process can be more productive (and less destructive) if writers accept and confront the rejection and use it to their advantage.

REFERENCE

Kruger, Justin, and David Dunning. 1999. "Unskilled and Unaware of It: How Difficulties in Recognizing One's Own Incompetence Lead to Inflated Self-Assessments." *Journal of Personality and Social Psychology* 77 (6): 1121–34.

55

REJECTION
It's Not the Last Step

Heather Lettner-Rust

I recently submitted a proposal to a journal soliciting a special call. This call described a focus related to a course I've taught for the last ten years. I've been theorizing about the students' work off and on but never put my thoughts to paper. Here was an opportunity, and I took it. As I draft this piece, I'm waiting to hear about my submission.

I don't recall ever discussing rejection during graduate school or early in my career. As I started a tenure-stream job, I didn't want to volunteer the subject of my rejections. It wasn't until I'd had a particularly difficult year in which I received three rejections that I reached out. I emailed a friend at another institution and a mentor I had met at a Writing Program Administrator's Conference. Their advice was enough to keep me going. Still, I'm not sure that as a field we talk about rejection enough. To get some help with this subject, I've contacted some prolific scholars in the field who have experience as editors too. This is what they said, along with some of my own experiences and advice.

So You've Received a Rejection; What's Next? If you haven't yet received a rejection notice after submitting an article or a proposal, you will. And for some amount of time, you will be disappointed, despondent, even despairing. The length of time you spend in this state is shaped in part by your environment. If you are in graduate school, in a cohort of peers who support you, or have cultivated a good relationship with your mentor or advisor for your dissertation project, others may be readily available to talk with. Search them out. The opportunity to work through this moment is there. Take it.

If you are in your first job, concerned about your publishing record and your ethos as a young scholar, it can be disorienting to now be at work on your own after having been surrounded by a cohort in graduate

DOI: 10.7330/9781607328834.c055

school. Search out that cohort or someone to connect with professionally in your institution, perhaps in another department. Peers and colleagues are typically relieved to talk about rejection; it's one experience we all have in common.

SHARE YOUR REJECTION LETTER. Maybe your peers or colleagues have already read your submission and helped you edit it. Get their advice again. Don't sit with your rejection alone. The worst you can do is sit with the rejection and do nothing. Seek the advice (and perhaps a bit of consolation) from your community. An objective pair of eyes may help you read the rejection a bit differently. The conversations generated by your sharing might help flesh out why the piece was rejected, what parts of the manuscript can be revised—which may be highlighted in the rejection—and where you might send the piece in the future. Rejection simply tells you what your next step is.

DEVELOP A NEXT STEP. When I look back at a particular rejection early in my career, there were a few key mistakes on my part. One, I submitted the piece because a special call for proposals in a leading journal was the same subject as my dissertation. *Nearly.* I had written a dissertation intending to study one thing and, as will happen, my data led to another finding. It was this finding I quickly wrote up and submitted. Not reading my situation correctly *cost me.* Was I ready to submit for a special call? And to a leading journal?

I was stung when the reviewer said my work was undertheorized. Looking back, I see now that I hadn't taken the time to sit with the findings. I needed to develop the literature review and understand whether my finding was even ready for primetime. Furthermore, a special call garners submissions with much more seasoned research. A special call was high stakes; all I was thinking about was what I *thought* I had and how topical my dissertation was.

LEARN FROM YOUR FEEDBACK. An acceptance with specific changes requested is a wonderful thing. A revise and resubmit means you're still in the game. While this is not an outright rejection, it's not an outright acceptance. You might, depending on the advice, be able to revise and resubmit right away (see Kornfield's chapter in this volume). Or it might be best to revise and resubmit at a later date.

Grant the changes if you are willing. Twice now, I've had reviewers who were split in their advice for a revise and resubmit, and yet the editor wanted to see the piece published. We worked together. I took the advice and made changes, added research, rearranged the structure. I was eager to have direct feedback from an editor, but more than that, I was working with an experienced editor, learning each time how an editor perceives the writing for the journal under his or her leadership. I am grateful for the experience.

As a reviewer, I have been directed to write advice that was helpful—as a direct address to the writer with positive constructive advice—no matter what the final decision was for the piece (see Hicks's chapter in this volume). This was not always the case. There has been a paradigm shift in the last twenty or so years, moving away from the anonymous, critical missive to more personal and detailed feedback designed to be helpful to the writer. After all, we are teachers of writing.

TRUST THE PROCESS. Researching, designing a study, analyzing findings, drafting, revising, revising again, and then submitting are all part of the process. Rejection doesn't mean stop. It means think again. There are a myriad of reasons for rejection: the methodology was flawed, the literature wasn't well represented, the piece doesn't fit the journal's audience in style or research; none of this means you stop. You decide if the flaws are fixable, and you revise. Consider another journal, ask a colleague for advice about revisions or journals, or take the piece to a conference to further share and deliberate its merit. You've lost only if you stop writing. And some people do. On the other hand, productive scholars have their fair share of rejections. Ask them.

For me, when the article based on my dissertation was rejected, I stopped writing about it. Initially, it was because of the sting. I questioned what I had spent my time researching. When I look back now, I realize I didn't have the desire to dig into past studies and figure out what I really had in the finding. At the time, I was early in the tenure stream and designing new course preparations. I couldn't carve out time to start that research, and I wasn't going to berate myself into working on a new project. A better use of my time was to draft research based on my current work. Those articles have been productive.

Today, I am waiting to hear about my current proposal. In the meantime, I have developed the proposal into a full article and will move forward with the journal I selected or another, as soon as I know what my next step is.

Acknowledgments. Thank you to Chris Anson, David Russell, Elizabeth Wardle, and Kathleen Yancey, all of whom sat for a conversation about the subject of rejection with academic submissions and as editors shared their experiences and their advice.

56

"I AM RECOMMENDING THAT THE EDITOR REJECT THIS SUBMISSION"

Patrick Sullivan

Because we seldom get to see conversations between journal editors and writers, we do not often have the opportunity to "look under the hood" as the scholarly editorial process unfolds. Consequently, this process can appear mysterious and inscrutable to those who don't routinely publish work. My experience in this regard has been rather extensive, and I am pleased to report that the conversations that unfold between editors and writers are often richly collaborative and profoundly rewarding. This has certainly been the case for me (with just a few exceptions).

As Joseph Harris has noted, though, "revising is the sort of thing that is fairly simple to describe but very hard to do well" (2017: 100). I have come to believe that writing *is* revising, and I have learned that a great deal of this work happens as editors and contributors talk together about a manuscript. This is the forge where many great books and articles are created.

I'm not sure if I'm typical or atypical of scholars in our field, but I have come to enjoy writing and revising very much. I love the different ways writing challenges me—as a scholar, as a communicator, and as a thinker. Part of this enjoyment is the feedback I receive from editors and reviewers. I actually look forward to seeing what readers will say about my latest submission or draft. I have found that the feedback I receive has almost always pointed me in important new directions—encouraging me to deepen my engagement, reread and rethink, and listen to new ideas and perspectives. This additional work I have done in response to suggestions from editors and reviewers has helped me produce stronger, better work. I am deeply thankful for it.

I want to share one experience that has become paradigmatic for me in relation to this process of publishing in rhetoric and composition. It involves an essay of mine that appeared in *Teaching English in the Two-Year College* in 2011, "'A Lifelong Aversion to Writing': What If Writing

DOI: 10.7330/9781607328834.c056

Courses Emphasized Motivation?" Readers may be surprised to learn that this essay's road toward publication began very inauspiciously, with one reviewer advising the editor to reject my essay. Here is the feedback that reviewer provided to me:

> Although I agree wholeheartedly with your argument that compositionists must attend to motivational factors in their teaching, I am recommending that the editor reject this submission. In its current form, the essay did not help me locate the contribution it was making to the field in terms of (1) the context it identifies (which could be more complicated in regard to the political implications of forces that teach students aversion to writing, the literacies students do possess in place of what's defined here as writing, and the pedagogical difficulties that could arise by situating students always as resistant writers as this essay seems to do); (2) the research (sources are listed here, but rarely engaged to the extent that it's clear where they might be missing the significance that motivation can/should play or where their contributions are being brought together into a conversation that might make need and means more discernible); or (3) the suggested "Family History" activity (which doesn't seem altogether unique and which is not contextualized in regard to the broader pedagogical ecology of classroom/institution practices that I would think necessary to challenging factors that train some students to be apathetic in the face of writing tasks).

This essay eventually ended up being published—and even received an award (the Mark Reynolds Award in 2012 for best article in *TETYC*). My experience revising this essay confirmed some of my most foundational beliefs about how to listen, how to work with editors, and how to be a writer.

The key moment in my correspondence with the editor, Jeff Sommers, and my two anonymous reviewers—and a moment that made an invaluable contribution to this essay and to my thinking about motivation and teaching writing—was the comment cited above about my use of research sources. The reviewer challenged me to dig deeper: "sources are listed here, but rarely engaged." As much as it pains and embarrasses me to admit this, the reviewer was right. I hadn't engaged the research on this subject nearly as deeply as I should have.

I had read much of Alfie Kohn's work (1993, 2000), and I had carefully studied Edward Deci's book about motivation written for general readers, *Why We Do What We Do* (Deci and Flaste 1996). But what I heard this reviewer asking me for was a more substantive, more richly detailed overview and application of this research. The reviewer appeared to be interested in this subject and clearly wanted a more serious, research-based discussion. This meant that I would have to become much more conversant with the scholarship written for specialists in this field, especially the work of Edward Deci and Richard Ryan, perhaps the two most important scholars in the field of motivation theory. This research would be written for social science professionals, and I would have to read, therefore, across disciplines, across disciplinary boundaries, and outside my comfort zone.

I did this work, but I'm not going to lie—it wasn't easy. I spent months delving deeply into this body of work. Much of its content and style was complex and daunting, but I kept at it until the topography of this science began to emerge clearly for me.

Eventually, I began to see what the research was actually saying about motivation. A turning point for me came as I was reading Deci, Koestner, and Ryan's essay "A Meta-Analytic Review of Experiments Examining the Effects of Extrinsic Rewards on Intrinsic Motivation." Originally published in *Psychological Bulletin* in 1999, this is a landmark study in motivation theory that synthesizes 128 research studies.

I spent many weekend hours that November curled up by our wood-stove with this essay, reading and rereading it, annotating it, and trying to figure out just what this research revealed. I must have read the essay five times before I finally understood it. This experience has become an important milestone for me about how readers and writers work that I now use in my writing classes.

"Sometimes," I tell students in my classes, "readings are going to be complex and challenging—and our old reading strategies aren't going to be sufficient. Reading them once might not be enough. We may need to reread them several times. We may need to focus our attention in new, more significant ways in order to get even the first glimpse of an accurate picture of a challenging reading. And as college readers, writers, and thinkers, we obviously can't give up, feel satisfied with getting 'close enough,' or take a stab at something and hope it's right. Sometimes, as readers and thinkers, we have to invest time and hard work to get it right." This is just one example of how my work as a scholar has enriched my teaching practice (Sullivan, Tinberg, and Blau 2017). As it turns out, I have continued to find this field of psychology fascinating, and I have recently begun reading Ryan and Deci's new book, *Self-Determination Theory: Basic Psychological Needs in Motivation, Development, and Wellness* (2017).

I would never have attempted any of this important additional work—or deepened my understanding of this essential and luminous human dynamic, intrinsic motivation—without (1) the great feedback I received from the anonymous field reviewer challenging me to dig deeper, and (2) the journal editor's confidence that I could engage this work effectively.

Both Ann Berthoff (1981) and Nancy Sommers (1982) have written eloquently about this kind of deep revision and thinking process, and they have urged writers at all levels of proficiency to embrace the "chaos" of real meaning making—where the footing is unsure, where courage may be required, and fortitude in terms of rereading, rethinking, and revising is often necessary. This is writing for the purpose of knowledge building, discovery, and meaning making. This is something I feel I experienced firsthand as I worked on that essay, and it was exhilarating.

The additional work I did obviously helped deepen and clarify what I knew about motivation, and it allowed me to "translate" and pass on that knowledge to my readers. During this process, I even contacted Dr. Deci via email about some of the finer points of this research. He was kind enough to respond promptly and helpfully. So I had the opportunity to correspond with a legend, another very welcome collateral benefit from this generative "chaotic" revision process.

If one remains humble, curious, open-minded, persistent, creative, engaged, and flexible—all habits of mind we recommend to *students* as essential for college in the "Framework for Success in Postsecondary Writing" document (Council of Writing Program Administrators, National Council of Teachers of English, and the National Writing Project 2011)—good things often happen. I've written a book about the generative, transformative power of listening (Sullivan 2014), and I always try to follow my own advice as I interact with editors and field reviewers. If one listens carefully, with an open heart and an open mind, good things will often follow.

REFERENCES

Berthoff, Ann. 1981. "Learning the Uses of Chaos." In *The Making of Meaning: Metaphors, Models and Maxims for Writing Teacher*, 68–72. Boston: Heinemann.

Council of Writing Program Administrators, National Council of Teachers of English, and the National Writing Project. 2011. "Framework for Success in Postsecondary Writing." http://wpacouncil.org/framework.

Deci, Edward L., and Richard Flaste. 1996. *Why We Do What We Do: Understanding Self-Motivation*. New York: Penguin.

Deci, Edward L., Richard M. Ryan, and Richard Koestner. 1999. "A Meta-Analytic Review of Experiments Examining the Effects of Extrinsic Rewards on Intrinsic Motivation." *Psychological Bulletin* 125 (6): 627–68.

Harris, Joseph. 2017. *Rewriting: How to Do Things with Texts*, 2nd ed. Logan: Utah State University Press.

Kohn, Alfie. 1993. *Punished by Rewards: The Trouble with Gold Stars, Incentive Plans, A's, Praise, and Other Bribes*. New York: Houghton Mifflin.

Kohn, Alfie. 2000. *The Case against Standardized Testing: Raising the Scores, Ruining the Schools*. Boston: Heinemann.

Ryan, Richard M., and Edward L. Deci. 2017. *Self-Determination Theory: Basic Psychological Needs in Motivation, Development, and Wellness.* New York: Guilford.

Sommers, Nancy. 1982. "Responding to Student Writing." *College Composition and Communication* 33 (2): 148–56.

Sullivan, Patrick. 2011. "'A Lifelong Aversion to Writing': What If Writing Courses Emphasized Motivation?" *Teaching English in the Two-Year College* 39 (2): 118–40.

Sullivan, Patrick. 2014. *A New Writing Classroom: Listening, Motivation, and Habits of Mind.* Logan: Utah State University Press.

Sullivan, Patrick, Howard Tinberg, and Sheridan Blau, eds. 2017. *Deep Reading: Teaching Reading in the Writing Classroom.* Urbana, IL: NCTE.

57

PESTER EDITORS POLITELY

James J. Brown Jr.

By and large, editors of academic journals are conscientious people who care about their field and about getting the best research published, but they are also incredibly busy people. They serve as editors alongside teaching courses, publishing their own work, and engaging in other institutional and national service work (for instance, serving on department, university, and national committees). On top of all of these duties, they are charged with managing the peer-review process: Take everything I've said about editors, apply it to those people charged with writing peer reviews, and then consider that an editor is responsible for trying to keep peer reviewers on a reasonable schedule so that authors get timely and useful feedback.

Academic publishing is a complex mesh (mess) of people, forces, affects, victories, and defeats. And this mesh (mess) means that things get lost, emails go unanswered or get pushed to the second page of the inbox. As an author, there are many things you can't control, but one thing you can do is send emails asking for updates. You can pester politely. If a journal says that it will be in touch in six weeks, set yourself a reminder to email in six weeks. If you send that email and don't hear back, then email again a week later. That's the pestering part.

Now comes the politely part: know that the people you're writing are swamped. If you are waiting on reader reports for your article, there's a good chance others are too. That editor is likely getting emails like yours on a fairly regular basis, and your email is sitting right next to an email from that editor's department chair about a new course proposal, which is sitting next to an email from a student who wants to talk about a disappointing paper grade. Your email should keep all of these possibilities in mind. But let's be clear: *send the email*. Pester politely. (Let's be clear about something else, too: if you've sent three emails and can't get a response, you are completely within your rights to pull the manuscript from consideration at that journal and submit it elsewhere. This email

DOI: 10.7330/9781607328834.c057

can be polite as well, but no author needs to wait around six months for a response if she or he does not want to.)

I probably sound like an apologist for delinquent editors, and perhaps I'm being too kind. Maybe the editors I'm describing aren't just busy; maybe they're just not up to the job. There are no doubt some who fit this description, but I'm guessing that most editors are victims of the same system that is frustrating authors who are trying to get things published.

* * *

On Valentine's Day 2009, I was in the midst of finishing my dissertation and getting ready to move from graduate school to my first tenure-track job. I received an email from Byron Hawk that began with this sentence: "I know you're about to embark on the hell that is assistant professorship, but I'm looking for someone to be the submissions editor or managing editor for *Enculturation*. I just can't keep up with it." The email went on to describe the position: check the website at least every couple of weeks, make sure articles are assigned to reviewers, make sure authors get feedback, guide authors through the revision process. At the time, I was confused for a couple of reasons. First, what was so hellish about the life of an assistant professor? And why was I, someone who didn't even have a PhD yet, being asked to do such an important job?

I found out that the answers to these questions are actually linked. First, let me say that I think Byron was being a bit hyperbolic with the word *hellish*, and I know for a fact that he loves the life of teaching and researching at a research university (for evidence, see Byron's chapter in this collection). But I now understand what he was getting at. I was about to enter a job that would pull me in a number of different directions. It would be made clear to me in meetings about the tenure process that I needed to publish a lot, but I also had courses to teach, committees to serve on, conferences to attend, and more. Like any academic, I would have to balance a lot of responsibilities. Having worked in a "cubicle hell" job for three years prior to grad school (one shot from the opening scene of the movie *Office Space* was literally a shot of my morning commute on I-635 in Dallas), I would not give up my job as an English professor for anything. But I really had no idea what I was signing up for when I entered academia.

This discussion of the challenges of an academic life leads to an answer to that second question: Why me? Well, I learned that it's *really difficult* to find people who want to be editors and who can do the job well. It requires a "particular set of skills" (apologies to Liam Neeson). In retrospect, I am actually a decent fit for such a position. I'm a checklist and calendar person. I'm pretty good at staying on top of things and holding myself and others to deadlines. However, one's own skills are only part of the equation. In fact, this is actually the thing that being an editor and being an academic researcher have most in common: a lot of things are out of your hands. I can be the best editor in the world, making sure I check in with reviewers, providing prompt responses to authors, and giving useful guidance along with those "revise and resubmit" messages. But I can't control a reviewer not responding to email, and I definitely can't control the reasons for those nonresponses (illness, a death in the family, anxiety, just to name a few). An author can compose the sharpest, most important article the field has seen in decades, but he or she can't control a reviewer who doesn't "get" the project and that author may not be aware of another journal where a similar piece is included in the issue that's about to go to print.

I've received plenty of those pestering emails over the years, and nearly all of them have been polite. I appreciate those kindnesses, since I know that authors are frustrated and under pressure, but I also appreciate the very fact of those emails. Those emails keep me honest and put things on my radar that might have slipped off.

Everyone—authors, editors, reviewers—needs to be pestered every once in a while.

58

FROM EDITORS WITH LOVE . . . OR MAYBE NOT SO MUCH!

Lilian W. Mina

We all want to get published and to see our names in print (I know I do), but we also need mentoring and guidance. Over the past three years, I have received loads of feedback from editors of the collections to which I've contributed. Throughout the long and complicated writing and publishing process, I've learned to navigate the murky waters of editors' feedback while building sustainable professional relationships and accumulating solid experience of the publishing process. I've learned to tread new grounds and find publication venues that nurture me as a scholar through mindful and respectful review of my work. More important, I've learned that not all editors are the same, and that editors' attitude, style, and tone of feedback matter as much as the content of their feedback.

* * *

When I was in grad school, everyone told me about the greater value of getting published in high-profile peer-reviewed journals than in edited collections. By the time I graduated, I had a peer-reviewed journal article and a book chapter in an edited collection published. The two experiences made me embrace a different perspective from that of my professors and the mentors I communicated with outside my school. As a junior scholar who needed to be socialized into the academic publishing process, I found that working closely with collection editors was enriching, inspiring, and rewarding for me. Well, at least working with the right editors is. And what exactly does this mean? Let me explain from my experience with two groups of editors and my response to each of them.

After accepting my proposal for an empirical study-based chapter, two editors of what then sounded like an interesting and suitable book collection responded to my draft. I was excited to read the feedback and to revise the chapter. But . . . my excitement faded gradually, replaced by dismay, with every feedback comment I read.

DOI: 10.7330/9781607328834.c058

While I could see some merit in the content of the feedback, I was shocked at the style and the tone the editors used in responding to my draft. The editors' style was more like first-year writing teachers commenting on the writing of students right out of high school (although I have to say I infuse more humor and respect in my feedback to my FYW students). The feedback was not only negative and dry and unnecessarily formal, it was disrespectful, redundant, and at some points disheartening and disconcerting. Yikes!

After having cooled down a little, I decided I'd brush off the negative feedback style and tone, revise the chapter, and send it back to the editors. I didn't want to waste a publishing opportunity. But that was the wrong decision because their feedback on the revised chapter was even worse! I'll spare you the unpleasant details. I communicated with two senior scholar friends and they both advised me against continuing to work with those editors. After a few days' reflection my mind was set: I emailed the editors and withdrew my chapter from their collection. I've never looked back or regretted that decision.

Fast-forward to my experience with other editors who have gone above and beyond anything I hoped for while working on an exceptionally challenging project. I won't talk about their graciousness in welcoming and answering all my questions (so many and so often, I admit) during the drafting stage, but I'll tell you about their encouraging and complimenting feedback style. The editors' four-page letter of detailed feedback was strongly positive, commending my effort and acknowledging the potential contribution of my work. Nope, the chapter wasn't perfect and it required good deal of revision, substantial in some sections. But wait, there's more inspiring stuff. One of the amazingly motivating editors offered to Skype with me to discuss their feedback and my next steps in revising the chapter. Yes, some people are just fabulous! And of course I seized the Skype opportunity, only to receive more support and positive feedback. I felt so confident, thanks to the editors' support, that I was able to revise that chapter and take it to a whole new level. I just turned in my revised chapter a few days ago and I feel so positive about it and about working with such mentoring editors.

I enjoy working with collection editors because of the open communication channels and the more personalized approach throughout the entire daunting writing and publishing process. I've learned, improved, and grown tremendously working closely with wonderful editors whose respectful feedback style struck that balance between pointing out areas for revision and improvement while boosting my self-confidence and praising my intellectual effort. I've grown to value and appreciate editors' feedback when it is collegial, respectful, stimulating, and motivating for me to get out of my academic and writing comfort zone.

Graciously mentor junior contributors to your collections and help them achieve more and aspire higher because if you do, you'll be nurturing the whole field of rhetoric and composition.

Acknowledgments. Thank you to Kathryn Comer, Ben McCorkle, and Michael Harker, whose editorial style was exemplary and taught me how to be a supportive editor without compromising the rigor of scholarship.

59

WHAT'S THE WAY FORWARD?
Some Lessons and Considerations about Revising from Feedback as a Collaborative Team, from a Collaborative Team

Bump Halbritter and Julie Lindquist

You've done it. You've written it—your masterpiece. Well, it's *finished*, at least. That article is off your desk, out for review, and out of your life. It's time to move on to wider vistas, greener pastures, and a happy hour or two.

Not so fast.

While it's true that much of your work is done, it is just as true that much of your work has likely just begun. Writing those twenty or thirty pages of pure genius was never the end that you had in mind—it was the beginning.

In what follows, we will elaborate on some lessons that we have derived from our own Sisyphean experience of moving our manuscript from draft (to draft to draft to draft to draft) to publication. Again, we will use our example not as a model of how to produce an award-winning collaboratively authored article but as a means for deriving some portable lessons that may be useful in a variety of collaborative writing situations. As in our companion piece, "What's the Way In?" (see Lindquist and Halbritter's chapter 28 in this volume), each of the lessons that follow is an articulation of something we have taken away from our work together so far—but because the particulars of our situation may be, well, particular, we pose a question for you in each case—a thing you may, in establishing or maintaining a writing relationship, want to consider for *your* case.

Lesson #1: Your manuscript is not you.

Q: WHAT IS YOUR "FOR NOW" PROJECT? OR MAYBE: HOW CAN YOU SHAPE YOUR ARTICLE TO BEST SUIT THE NEEDS, PURPOSES, AND INTERESTS OF YOUR READERS?

DOI: 10.7330/9781607328834.c059

Although it is true that you have written a masterpiece, you are about to enter into a new relationship with it. You are now embarking on a journey to discover what others make of it and to imagine how it may better accomplish its goals for readers who are not you.

Yes, we know, *manuscripts* can't have goals: people/authors have goals. Manuscripts are the means by which authors attempt to realize their goals. Fair enough. However, for our purposes here, we have come to learn that it can be useful to think of the manuscript as having its own agenda—not ours per se. Consequently, we can enter into dialogue with that partial (twenty- to thirty-page) expression of our goals as something that is not *us*. In so doing, we can ask how *it* is being misunderstood rather than how *we* are being misunderstood. That move allows us to be the facilitators of its revision rather than the targets of reviewer 2's comments, even if reviewer 2 seems to be directing her ire directly at us. Refocus feedback toward what moves the manuscript—not its authors—to address the concerns of the reviewers.

The reason for this move is not merely to create an emotional barrier between us and our reviewers (though that's not such a bad motive in and of itself). The primary reason for this displacement is to accept that, even though the manuscript is ours, it is not us. While it may seem to emerge from all that we know, it does not contain all of our knowledge. It contains and says only what it contains and says. Consequently, our editors and reviewers often help expose for us views that we cannot have of our own work: the work itself and the variety of uses that others will have for it. Our job as authors becomes to try to reconcile what our editors and/or reviewers have told us in light of what the manuscript actually says and does.

Creating some distance between the goals of any piece of writing and our larger goals that have motivated the project requires the "for now" project. That is, regardless of the collaborators themselves or the larger project that brings them together, this article—this piece of writing—represents only a piece of that work *for now*—that is, for this specific venue and potential audience at this particular time. *For now*, this is what it must do and be.

In short, your job now is to revise the piece to make it fit the needs of a specific publication and particular readership. Making effective revisions will take more than listening to and following advice; it will involve trying to determine why your editors and reviewers have been motivated to make the recommendations that they have. But first, you will, we predict, likely need to process and manage your initial emotional reactions to the feedback your article receives.

Lesson #2: Expect to be disappointed (read "angry").

Q: HOW MIGHT THE EXPERIENCE OF ANGER BE A PRODUCTIVE FIRST STEP IN REVISING FROM FEEDBACK?

Okay, so you're following lesson #1: You've distanced yourself from the manuscript. Your manuscript is not you. That said, if it were a simple matter not to take feedback personally, we wouldn't need lesson #1 in the first place.

Even after all of your work and sweat and compromises and revisions already, it's quite likely that the editor's response does not say, "Congratulations! It's perfect as is! Have a drink on us!" And, no matter how good or encouraging the news, it's likely that you'll be somewhat disappointed at the prospect of having to consider additional sources, respond to requests for additional considerations, and/or reframe portions of the manuscript—if not the entire manuscript. And depending on how you perceive the tone of such advice, your disappointment may even give way to anger. Really. For the love of all things remotely rational, how could reviewer 2 recommend *that*? And how could that gullible editor kowtow to reviewer 2's preposterous demands? That is certainly what must have happened, after all. *And why is it always reviewer 2?!?!* You know that your work is excellent. How could it not be? You both have PhDs! It's a conspiracy! It's a travesty!

Times such as these can put strain on your collaboration if you are not prepared for them—heck, even if you are. But being prepared for them helped us find the way forward when one of us (Bump) had lost hope and the other of us (Julie) saw a method for finding hope once again—actually thrice again. In short, when we got our initial reviews for what was to become "Time, Lives, and Videotape," Bump fell to pieces.

Our initial set of reviews—one in particular—hit Bump hard. After finally submitting our opus to the original journal, we bit our nails and awaited a response. Several months later, it came—along with a recommendation from the editor to revise and resubmit. Not the worst possible news, to be sure. One of the reviewers of the piece found value in its potential contribution; the other (the omnipresent and notorious reviewer 2) was not persuaded that the piece had a contribution to make, insisting that because it described a research study, it should also deliver findings. Given that our purpose was not to report the results of a completed study, but rather to describe a process of decision making in inquiry, this came as discouraging news, and we were frustrated at how thoroughly our purposes seemed to have been misread.

Julie had a good bit of experience with editors and reviews, and was pretty sure that the experience was not unprecedented or unique—or that the response of reviewer 2 was not, all things considered, indicative of the value or the ultimate success of the work. Bump, however, was less convinced that what the piece would, ultimately, find a good audience. There were many moments of talking Bump down, of recalling how the process works, of pointing out that all hope might not, in fact, be lost. Bump had good reason to be worried: as an assistant professor, he knew that much was at stake in the future of this manuscript, which, reliant as it was on the slowly developing discoveries of a long-term research project, had been so long in the making. All things considered, Julie was in a better position to be reassuring. Julie, having been down a similar path before, made a few moves that were critical to finding the way forward. We have converted these moves into three general sub-lessons:

1. IF YOU'RE BOTH ANGRY, THERE'S NO ONE TO BE NOT ANGRY. First, of course, you must feel what you're going to feel. Both of you. Julie knew that Bump needed to feel what he needed to feel first—and that she needed to do the same. She too was disappointed; however, her anger was not terminal—that is, unlike Bump, she saw that the anger could subside and give way to productive action. It was critical for us that Julie was able to transition from aggrieved author to compassionate collaborator. In that move, we were able to remember that this project began with our partnership and that we needed to take care of ourselves. The important thing here is that we did not dive headlong into revisions. Instead we entertained our initial emotional responses, and then went to work on finding purchase on the comments.

2. DO NOT ARGUE WITH YOUR REVIEWERS' COMMENTS. SEEK OPPORTUNITY IN THEM. From our initial set of reviews, we perceived that our ship was taking on water fast. Reviewer 2, of course, had landed what he or she obviously considered to be a direct hit: how could we publish on a methodology and not support it with results that made evident the success of the methodology? Our responses: "Reviewer 2 is confusing methodology for methods!" (Bump); "Eureka!" (Julie). This realization helped us transfer flood to ballast. And ultimately, it is this move that may motivate you forward from anger to encouragement and ultimately toward renewed purpose.

3. YOUR ARTICLE IS NOT YOU. Lesson #2 needs to circle right back to lesson #1. Your job is not now to defend your honor or character or career or decision to do this work. Your job is to help this manuscript do the work it needs to do. And that leads us to our next lessons.

Lesson #3: Your editor is not you.
Q: HOW WILL YOUR WORK CONTRIBUTE TO THE EDITOR'S WORK?
So now your goal is to attempt to determine what may be motivating reviewers' comments based upon the manuscript itself. In other words,

your goal is to learn something about your reviewers' needs by way of the article. For example, recognize that if the submission requirements called for a maximum of 7,500 words and your manuscript is nearly 15,000, you have to trim.

The editor may have a budget that allows her to publish 125 (actual paper) pages each issue. For each extra page she allows you, some other portion of the issue may need to be sacrificed in part or all together. You are publishing your article—that's your goal. However, the editor is publishing her issue—not your article. That's her goal. So you must learn to see your manuscript itself not as the goal but as the means for gaining access into that editor's issue. Or not. You can always decide to walk away and pursue another venue. But before you do, you need to square what you've learned about this manuscript of yours through the uses that others may or may not have for it. What was eventually published as "Time, Lives, and Videotape" was originally submitted to a different venue from the one that eventually published it. Its first version was egregiously long—as we believed it needed to be to do our work. However, before the piece would even be considered for review, we were told that we needed to cut its length—due not only to the editor's budget for pages, but to the editor's agreement with reviewers for the journal. In other words, the manuscript, not our work, would simply not fit into this journal in its original form.

Lesson #4: Your reviewer is not you.

Q: HOW ON EARTH COULD REVIEWER 2 RECOMMEND THAT?

Just as the editor has her or his needs and concerns, your reviewers have needs that you do not: for example, they may have different understandings as researchers; they may be aware of conversations that you have not considered; they (apparently!) have different understandings of the sort of feedback they are to give than the sort you imagine to be most helpful; their reviews may contradict each other and/or the advice of the editor; and/or they may be guided specifically by suggestions of the editor. Beyond all of that, you need to remember, always, that your reviewers are likely reviewing your work and writing up their comments under duress—something that will sound familiar to those of you who do or have done review work and that may not occur to you if you have not.

The review work that we have done has been added to all of the other duties of our full-time work. Your mid-career colleagues are often asked to do reviews when they are not only publishing their own related work, but have made their ways into administrative positions at their institutions and national disciplinary service positions. Editors do not uniformly guide reviewers on how to write their reviews; consequently, your reviews may share little in common in terms of organization, tone, purpose, or aboutness. In short, your reviewers are likely very busy and doing the very best they can to offer a response given the time and guidance they have received. We have found that it is good to remember this as we begin reading their responses. And remember, too, that the review does not mark the beginning of the end of the process; it marks the beginning of the middle of the process. Expect that there will be yet more work ahead.

All that said, how on earth could reviewer 2 recommend *that?* In order to jump-start the process of moving forward from your reviewers' comments, we suggest following a trajectory guided by three key concepts: inquiry, discovery, and communication. In fact, our workshop-based, peer-review-centered, first-year writing program at Michigan State University leverages these very same key concepts.

1. INQUIRY: TREAT YOUR MOST INCREDULOUS RESPONSES AS REAL QUESTIONS. As we mentioned above, reviewer 2 seemed to us to simply not get it. And so we asked, "How could reviewer 2 be so confused by what the article is claiming?" By treating this as a real question, we were able to see that *the article* could more explicitly pursue the program of articulating the value of methodological design in response to a perceived research-related problem/opportunity.

2. DISCOVERY: TRY TO DISCOVER WHAT HAS LIKELY MOTIVATED YOUR REVIEWERS' COMMENTS. Your reviewers are not you. You may find that your reviewers really nail it—that you see possibility in their comments and that they are immediately helpful and lead to productive revision. However, since reviewer 2 seems not to "get it," you can assume that reviewer 2's comments will likely feel off target. But that does *not* mean that they have no value. When this happens, don't immediately discard the comments you disagree with. Try to see what may be motivating the seemingly rogue advice.

3. COMMUNICATION: HELP IT—YOUR ARTICLE—ARTICULATE YOUR DISCOVERIES. In our case, we knew our project was *not* to deliver specific study results; consequently, there was no way we could follow reviewer 2's advice to supply them. Instead, we asked what might have been motivating reviewer 2 to make such a suggestion, and that led us to the productive move of more clearly and decisively articulating the article's mission of outlining a new methodological design. Reviewer 2 apparently thought the article was about our study. Our revisions were directed toward making certain that the article accessed the study as a model of the methodology—and not the subject of the article. We began to think of ourselves, as authors, in a more explicitly pedagogical role—we needed to educate readers who may not be inclined to buy into what we thought we had to teach, and to figure out how to scaffold that lesson effectively.

In short, your reviewers' comments are not so much *right* or *wrong* as they are *resources*. Don't expect them to detail your revisions as much as direct you *toward* your revisions.

Lesson #5: Your work may evolve to be more or less one of you than the other.

Q: What happens when your article no longer seems to include you? Imagine the following scenario: you have gone through the phases of the four lessons above only to be confronting what seems to be an insurmountable paradox. The editor, still, needs you to cut the article by 1,000 words even as you have been directed to consider more similar studies and further develop your discussion of two aspects of your study.

This has actually happened to us.

Each collaboration is different. As we've mentioned in our companion work, we think of our collaboration as a band. And, if you're going to be a band, you may as well be the Beatles. So we are Lennon and McCartney: fifty-fifty all the way. Except, of course, when we aren't. In the vast catalogue of Lennon and McCartney songs, some are primarily Lennon and others primarily McCartney. But, at least while Lennon and McCartney were Beatles, all of their songs, regardless of primary authorship, were Lennon and McCartney compositions.

In our own collaboration, each work that we have pursued has followed its own life cycle from genesis to publication. Sometimes an idea has sprung forth during a conversation we were having. Other times an editor has asked one of us to write something that we then decided to pursue collectively (these two companion chapters, for example). Sometimes one of our administrative positions has demanded that we solve a problem, and we have put our heads together to do so. We're a band, after all. But that doesn't mean that all we do and all we write and all we ultimately move forward in any given work is fifty-fifty—down the middle. We normally outline a work together and then divide writing duties—even as we have done with our two companion pieces in this collection. But ultimately, what matters most in any given thing we coauthor is not a reflection in the text of the equitable division of our labor, but the purposeful accomplishment of the goals of the given text. In short, *it* matters more than either of *us*.

And that has been critical to remember as we have been directed to prune—sometimes ruthlessly—works that we have written collaboratively. We have made the decision, at times, to cut primarily the contributions of one or the other of us. And we have retained collaborative authorship in these instances, informed by our knowledge that the longer we have worked together, the more and more difficult it has become to separate out not only who crafted what language on any given page we've written or in any given documentary project we've directed and edited, but who was the originator or primary developer of any given idea. We're a band, after all. And so we are continually returned to lesson #1: no article is us. Consequently, each is. In other words, because we do not need to appear as individuals in any given article, we may each disappear into the work that any given article does.

Now that is just us. Obviously, every collaboration cannot work this way. However, it is critical for any publishing collaboration to make decisions based upon what the articles need. And those decisions will potentially involve the spotlight moving from the collaboration as a whole—as a band—to one of the collaborators primarily or in particular. "Yesterday," like all songs from the Beatles' primary songwriters, bears the mark of the collaboration: Lennon and McCartney. However, Paul wrote it and Paul sang it. Paul stood alone on the stage with his acoustic guitar as he performed it at the Beatles' shows. So it can go with bands. And so it can go with collaborations such as ours—and likely yours. Sometimes one of you will be the lead singer, sometimes the other will. John may have sung the early hits, but Paul sang many of the later hits. And then, George wrote and sang "Something."

If you're going to be a band, you may as well be the Beatles.

Concluding (and Continuing) Thoughts. When we finally wrapped up "Time, Lives, and Videotape," we were enormously relieved—that piece had spent such a long time in development, and had had many iterations at the pre-editorial stage. Even though we had published things before, we were not quite prepared for what lay ahead. When we delivered the piece after years of invention and intervention, expansions and contractions, elaborations and prunings, we were intellectually and emotionally, well, tired. At that moment, the idea that much of the heavy lifting still lay ahead was a difficult one to face. Even though the story of that piece ended well—it not only got published, it won an award for best article—it turned out to be the case that, once the piece was submitted, much of the hard work still lay ahead. And that has continued to be the case with many of the works we have written and revised and come to know differently since.

What we hope to have done in this work is to give you and your collaborators a set of global lessons for revising from feedback that we have derived from our many years of collaborating. Much as we did in the article that has served as our primary model throughout our two companion pieces, we have offered the examples of our unique experiences not as models of how to create a similarly successful article, but as a specific source of generalizable lessons.

From our band to yours. Rock on.

REFERENCE

Halbritter, Bump, and Julie Lindquist. 2012. "Time, Lives, and Videotape: Operationalizing Discovery in Scenes of Literacy Sponsorship." *College English* 45:171–96.

60

DON'T TAKE EDITORIAL ADVICE—USE IT

Bruce Horner

I have two stories to tell. Here's the first. Many years ago, in the exuberance of a year-long sabbatical, I sent an essay to a journal without having anyone look at the work beforehand. Based on previous experience, I simply assumed that the journal editors would respond with advice and, at best, a "revise and resubmit" decision. Instead, the journal editors accepted my essay without requesting a single change, and in fact, they published it in their very next issue.

In theory, this would seem to be what everyone submitting work to journals hopes for: that the editors will recognize the beauty, brilliance, even perfection of our work, and simply express gratitude for our willingness to share it with the world. But when I received the journal's acceptance letter, this is not how I felt. For I knew that the essay, whatever its virtues, needed to be put more in conversation, while still in draft form, with the insights of others in the field. (As it happened, this was an essay for a musicology journal, not composition, but the lesson holds true regardless.) And that is what I had assumed I would get from the journal's reviewers.

What I failed to take into account was that the journal editors had an interest in provoking controversy, something that the essay I'd submitted offered in spades. And publishing the essay did provoke controversy—never mind that the essay could have sparked more thoughtful controversy had it been revised. In one sense, the journal (and I) succeeded. Since its publication, the essay has earned a respectable number of citations for throwing down a kind of gauntlet in a debate in musicology, and it even spurred a renowned musicologist whose work I'd taken to task in my essay to (hand)write me a long, irate, accusing letter. Controversy was provoked.

But had that same renowned musicologist (or a similarly inclined colleague) had the chance, instead, to respond as a reviewer to my

DOI: 10.7330/9781607328834.c060

submission and express his perspective, I might have (1) received a more thoughtful (rather than simply irate) response, and (2) found a way to anticipate and answer the objections he raised to my argument, and even learned from those objections. While in one sense I "won" the argument I had made by virtue of getting it published, it's not clear whether, in the larger scheme of things, I had advanced understanding about the concerns at issue or reached those not already disposed to agree with me. In other words, *I lost the opportunity to advance the field in the very act of winning the chance to score a publication.* Fortunately (or so it now seems in hindsight), I have almost never received an "accept as is" response to other work I've submitted, despite (I confess) harboring a lingering fantasy of having editors simply express gratitude for my willingness to share my wisdom with the world.

Here's the second story. Not so long ago, a coauthor and I received advice from the reviewer of an essay we'd submitted that the case on which we'd focused our attention—an essay by an English monolingual student writer—was, in fact, not at all appropriate for our argument. What we needed, it was argued, was a case that fit recognizably with the issue we were addressing—an "ESL" writer to illustrate translingual writing.

In one sense, this experience was the opposite of the "no advice" story. Here was an instance in which my coauthor and I were getting solid, direct advice from a presumably well-meaning reviewer who engaged our argument by pointing out that it would be better served by a different exemplary case. But we did not take the advice. We did not take it because, in fact, we believed (and still do) that translingual writing is not restricted or even primarily meant to address "ESL" writers or even L2 writers generally.

However, we did *use* the advice. We used it by inserting into our opening an explanation of why we chose to focus on the writing of an English monolingual student rather than an "L2" writer. In fact, this choice and explanation became, at least in our view, a central feature of our argument, one that distinguished it from seemingly aligned arguments on translinguality that focused primarily or only on the writing of L2 writers. So although we did not follow the advice of the reviewer, we did, in fact, use it, and benefited from the reviewer's input by seeing the need to clarify and distinguish our argument from those of others who conflated translingual writing with L2 writing.

The editor accepted our revision despite the fact that we deliberately did not follow the reviewer's recommendation. Like most editors (and journal essay and book manuscript reviewers), this editor saw the value of engaging in conversation with writers, for the writers themselves and their articles but also for the field. As initially irritating as some reviewers' responses have been (and I've received very few bad—by which I mean irresponsible, not simply negative—reviews), I've found there is almost always a good use to be made of the reviews, even when I've disagreed profoundly with the perspective the reviewer articulates. (The same is true of copyeditors' suggestions.) It's worth remembering that academic journal and book reviewers rarely get any credit or merit, let alone pay, for their work. With that in mind, we need to learn to be grateful, however difficult it may sometimes feel, for the work of reviewers, and for the usefulness of that work for ourselves as writers. At the same time, we also need to keep in mind that journal editors and reviewers have interests that may not fully align with a writer's—whether it's an interest in being topical or controversial or simply grinding a particular axe, or, as is more common, a commitment to a perspective that is simply not reconcilable with the one a writer is attempting to advance.

61

REVISE AND RESUBMIT! BUT HOW?

Sarah Kornfield

You open the email (or hard copy letter) to find . . . an invitation to revise your manuscript and resubmit it to the journal! Congratulations! Take a moment to enjoy this victory. But now as you really sit and read the review letter, the editor's comments sound skeptical that you can satisfy the reviewers, and at least one of the reviewers suggests significant changes. Suddenly, the task looks daunting. What do you do?

Much of the following advice was modeled for me (and sometimes explicitly stated) by Dr. Srividya Ramasubramanian as we responded to a revise and resubmit (R&R) on a coauthored publication early in my career (while I was still in graduate school). The rest of this advice I have compiled throughout my career as I review journal article submissions, resubmit my own manuscripts, and advise graduate students on their R&Rs. This advice can help you respond to an R&R by helping you to

1. respond promptly to an R&R invitation,
2. process reviewers' feedback, and
3. write a response letter.

First, completing the R&R is your top priority; you should resubmit it within four to six weeks. (This piece of advice comes directly from Dr. Srividya Ramasubramanian, who taught me to resubmit manuscripts promptly and featured this advice on January 6, 2015, as part of her Facebook "academic advice of the month" series.) Why? Because by responding promptly, you ensure that the essay goes back to the original reviewers (instead of getting new reviewers with new ideas). Moreover, by responding promptly, you return the manuscript while it is still fresh in reviewers' minds. Responding promptly is a courtesy to them, but it also works to your advantage because they remember your article and can therefore simply assess whether you've made the changes they recommended. If you take too long, they won't remember the details of your argument or exactly why they made the recommendations they

DOI: 10.7330/9781607328834.c061

did; this results in the reviewers having to do a brand-new full review of the essay (which will likely generate more and/or different recommendations) because they don't remember its original argument and their original recommendations.

Second, when processing reviewer feedback, you need to list the recommendations so that you can work systematically through each. Copy the review letters into a word-processing document and then use bullet points or numbering to turn their paragraphs into clearly demarcated, listed recommendations. This renders their paragraphs into distinct pieces of advice. If your reviewers haven't already distinguished between their "major" and "minor" concerns, you should do so. For example, within each reviewer's list of recommendations, have one page (or more as needed) dedicated to major concerns and then the subsequent page(s) dedicated to the minor concerns. Major concerns/recommendations typically focus on your argument, evidence, and organization. Minor concerns/recommendations typically focus on typos and writing style.

You now have a document in which you can clearly see all the advice your reviewers (and the editor) offered and you can see what needs significant attention and what are minor, easily fixed problems. A next step is to turn on the reviewing function in your word-processing software, and write comments in the margins with notes-to-self about how to address each recommendation—and if you plan not to address a recommendation, why you've chosen not to do so. For example, if the reviewer was very specific and you intend to follow the advice, I recommend writing a comment for that bullet point that simply says, "Do this!" If the reviewer makes a recommendation without mapping out a specific "to-do" plan, then write yourself a comment in which you specifically list how you plan to edit your essay in order to incorporate the reviewer's recommendation. If the reviewers' recommendations contradict each other, then you should write comments next to the contradicting bullet points that say something like "See reviewer 2's third recommendation; this contradicts!" and then continue by writing out whose advice you plan to follow and why. By completing this step, you establish a game plan for how to revise your manuscript based on the editor and reviewer recommendations.

As you revise your manuscript, each time you change something in the draft itself, write a comment in your working copy. For example, if you satisfy one of the recommendations, then edit the existing comment for that recommendation so that it clearly states (1) what changes were made, (2) why you made those changes, and (3) what pages of

Table 61.1. Side-by-side comparison of reviewer and author comments/notes

Reviewer comments	My comment/notes
On a related note, you do not really address Hoerl and Kelly's and Thoma's essays in a meaningful way. (I'm tempted to speculate that the author did not actually read the essays since there are some passages in the analysis of Hoerl and Kelly that relate well to the author's own analysis.) I'm not convinced that previous scholars' choices to focus on plot is necessarily a limitation of their scholarship. But your decision to focus on extratexts might add something to the conversations, as does your focus on depictions of older, career-driven characters. You make a solid case for the ways that pregnancy marks the feminine gender in problematic ways. What really matters is that you explicate how your analysis or conclusions expand, revise, or complicate what we currently understand about constructions of pregnancy in popular culture.	I've reviewed pages 6–7 to deal more substantively with first Hoerl and Kelly's article and then Thoma's. After better articulating their contributions, I demonstrate that my piece expands our understanding of the construction of pregnancy by analyzing the depiction of older, career-driven pregnant protagonists and the integration of the actors' pregnancies as relates to the "having it all" debate.

your manuscript were affected by those changes. For example, below is a major recommendation from a reviewer and my comment on how I satisfied that recommendation. By completing this step, you begin to draft your response letter!

Third, when you resubmit your essay, you must also submit a response letter. This response letter is typically addressed to the editor, but the reviewers will also have access to it. In your response letter, thank the editor for the opportunity to resubmit your manuscript and thank the reviewers for their effort and advice. Then you need to be absolutely clear about (1) the changes you've made to the essay, (2) how the changes fulfill the reviewers' recommendations, and (3) where in the manuscript (what pages) they can see your changes. If you rejected a recommendation, you need to be polite and authoritative as you clearly substantiate why you chose not to follow a recommendation. The idea is that the reviewer (who still remembers your article because it's only been four to six weeks) can read the response letter, turn to relevant pages in the revised manuscript, and be satisfied that you've thoroughly addressed the concerns—without having to reread the whole thing. Your response letter should use clear numbering and/or bullet pointing to list how you've addressed each recommendation or concern.

For example, below I've excerpted the part of my response letter for my article "Pregnant Discourse: 'Having it All' While Domestic and Potentially Disabled" in which I responded to the concern included above:

> Following your recommendation, I have worked to address Hoerl and Kelly's and Thoma's essays in more meaningful and substantive ways.

Specifically, the revised manuscript now articulates the important contributions these articles have made and the manuscript more accurately differentiates itself by noting key textual differences (depictions of older career-driven women and extratextual elements) and its contributions (how our culture's understanding of pregnancy informs our conceptualizations of gender norms that undergird the "having it all" debate; see pages 6–7).

As you can see, the comment I wrote to myself about how I had addressed this concern became the first draft for this segment of my response letter. After carefully proofreading both the manuscript and the response letter, you're ready to resubmit!

By following this advice, you will (1) process the review letter in an organized fashion, clearly identifying significant recommendations; (2) establish a clear game plan for how to address each recommendation; and (3) keep a clear record of how you revised your manuscript, satisfying your reviewers' concerns. Then, by drawing on this record, you will (4) develop a clear, concise, and well-organized response letter that succinctly guides your reviewers to relevant revisions as they rereview your manuscript. Finally, (5) by prioritizing this project and staying organized throughout the process, you will be able to complete your R&R within a timely (four- to six-week) fashion.

62

FROM RESISTANCE TO REVISION
Staging a Response to a "Revise and Resubmit"

Jessica Enoch

You have been waiting. Six weeks ago (maybe more), you submitted an essay to a journal in the field of rhetoric and composition, and you've been waiting—excitedly, anxiously—to receive word from the editor and reviewers. There's a lot hanging on this essay. You developed it from a graduate seminar you were deeply interested in. The piece grows out of your dissertation or book project, and it reflects the research trajectory you're investing the next good bit of your life to. The essay should (hopefully) help to get you the job you want. You need this essay for tenure.

And then the reviews come in.

You knew the editor wasn't going to say, "We love it! We're publishing it as is!" (though that would have been nice). But the editor's and reviewers' comments are collectively four single-spaced pages. And the comments are extensive: consult a different scholarly conversation, revisit your thesis, attend to logical inconsistencies, rearrange, question evidence, consider new archival possibilities, excise an entire section. Not only are the comments substantive and complex, they also seem to conflict. One reviewer says trim where another asks you to expand; one reviewer likes an argument, the other questions it. Even with this criticism, there is still a window of possibility: the editor recommends that you revise and resubmit.

What do you do? Everyone responds to reviewer suggestions differently—some in ways more productive than others. After receiving revise and resubmits from a range of journals in rhetoric and writing studies, I've had to identify a process that enables me to assess comments, revise, and finally resubmit. In this chapter, I move through possible stages of response—stages I'm familiar with through personal experience and close observation of others' processes—that hopefully model productive engagement with reviewer comments, effective revision work, and, in the end, a stronger essay submission.

DOI: 10.7330/9781607328834.c062

Stage 1: Experience your resistance, grief, anger. The initial (and natural) response to criticism may be the desire to put the essay and responses away and forget about them. You may want to table—indeed, throw out—the whole essay because the comments are too overwhelming or, to you, just wrong. Let yourself experience this stage. It's okay, at first, to respond in this way; you might need to resist, grieve, and be angry.

But the key is to not stay in this place. You must, at some point (and some point soon), return to the comments and consider them. Remember: it is a *good thing* when an editor asks you to revise and resubmit an essay. It means the piece has promise. You cannot and should not let this opportunity go without seriously considering the comments. In almost all cases, you should revise and resubmit.

Stage 2: Reread. Start fresh, at the best part of your day, whenever you're most productive, and reread *both* your essay *and* the comments. Sometimes rereading your essay enables you see that many of the revision suggestions actually make a lot of sense. In this rereading, assess and collect the reviewers' and the editor's suggestions: What *exactly* do they want you to do? Where are the major revision ideas and what are the more minor (and easily doable) revision suggestions? It is critical that you take time with these comments and understand what the reviewers and the editor are suggesting before you dive in and begin revising (Cutrufello's chapter in this volume provides a useful tool for navigating different types of comments).

In this stage, I often start a new document in which I compile and rewrite the comments, using this moment to take them in more deeply and to begin to organize which comments make sense, which ones would be easy to address, and which ones I need to take more time to think about. Sometimes, too, I color-code the specific suggestions from Reviewers 1, 2, and the editor and then mark in the margins of the essay *where* the specific revisions might happen. This visual display is often extremely helpful as I work to move forward and manage the revision process.

Stage 3: Reflect on reviewer comments and try them out. Often, reviewers offer "big-idea" revisions, ones that may change the direction of the essay. Take these comments in and experiment with them. Go for a run or a walk with them in your mind. Stare out a window or find another way to meditate on them. Then, freewrite a response to them. Try them out. When I receive reviews with "big-idea" comments, I often map out what would happen to the essay if I took up the suggestion. If I did X, then Y and Z would need to change; I'd need to get rid of A and recast B,

C, and D with this new emphasis. And then I think about what the essay would look like and do. Here's the moment when I usually realize that the reviewers exerted great effort and thoughtfulness in their responses. These are smart, intellectually generous people (who are not "out to get you"), and in responding to their comments, you will often improve the quality of your essay tremendously.

Stage 4: Reconcile conflicts and make decisions. You may find that the reviewers' comments conflict—that following one reviewer's comments will disallow you to heed the other's, or that after careful consideration and experimentation, one reviewer's revision idea just doesn't seem to work. These scenarios often emerge, and it is fine not to follow every piece of advice the reviewers and editors offer. Your objective is to improve the overall quality of the essay, and following *all* the advice might not produce the best result. Regularly, however, the editor recognizes potential conflicts and offers guidance. That is, they may acknowledge that Reviewers 1 and 2 seem to want different things, and they likely will either allow you to decide the direction to take or they might state their preference (for instance, to follow Reviewer 2's idea over Reviewer 1's). If the editor does not provide this guidance, you might write to them asking for advice about these conflicts. I've often found editors to be extremely generous with their time in negotiating reviews and offering paths for revision.

Stage 5: Decide on and carry out a revision plan. After carefully considering and even trying out revision ideas, compose a revision plan. Identify what you will do, how you will do it, and how you'll address the reviewers' and editor's comments in the process. Mapping out a timeline and workplan here would also be a good idea. Then follow the plan and revise.

Stage 6: Get a reader. Given the fact you revised your essay with a litany of reviewer concerns in mind, you want to make sure your essay still makes sense and is indeed stronger after revision. You don't want an essay that frenetically addresses reviewer comments but is no longer cohesive on its own. Get a reader, ideally someone new to the essay. Make sure the revised essay offers a strong, compelling argument that would interest the journal's audience. You should also share with your reader the revision suggestions and your revision plan, so that they can offer additional suggestions as to how you might revise and carry out your plan.

Stage 7: Resubmit. When you resubmit your essay, you'll want to compose a letter to the editor that details the revisions you made. Here's the place where you say which suggestions you've taken up and which you decided not to pursue (and why). Giving a rationale for why you didn't pursue suggestions is often important for the editor to understand the decisions you've made. In these letters, I often create bullet points that identify the revision suggestion and whether, how, and where (using page numbers) I carried it out. I start with the most significant changes that I made and then move to the revision suggestions I decided not to carry out. Using this organizational format, I show the editor first what I did and the suggestions I responded to and then move to the ones I decided not to pursue.

I hope these stages of response reflect two key points when it comes to revising and resubmitting essays for journal publication: first, even though revision is difficult and time-consuming, your essay will often greatly improve after taking up reviewers' comments, and you'll likely move your intellectual projects forward in important ways. Second, as the author, you have agency in the revision process. You decide which suggestions to take up and which to leave behind. In the end, the essay is yours.

63

PRIORITIZING REVIEWER COMMENTS FOR A "REVISE AND RESUBMIT" REQUEST

Gabriel Cutrufello

So you've received a revise and resubmit request for your manuscript. Congratulations! You are on your way to publishing your piece. Receiving a revise and resubmit can seem both encouraging (because the editor and reviewers see promise in your manuscript) and discouraging (because now you have all of this additional work to do on your manuscript). Publishing scholarship can be particularly daunting for junior faculty working at institutions with heavy teaching loads and writing program administrator (WPA) duties—a reality for many of us who are junior faculty at two-year or four-year undergraduate institutions with a teaching focus that require articles in peer-reviewed journals for tenure.

Books like Wendy Belcher's *Writing Your Journal Article in 12 Weeks* (2009) can be useful for developing a process of research and writing during summer and winter breaks but often do not address how to prioritize revision work, which may come during a busy teaching semester. It's common to receive reviewer comments during the semester, and you shouldn't wait until the next break to address them; ideally, you want to spend your breaks researching and writing a new piece. So successfully revising your manuscript often depends on prioritizing reviewer comments, selecting which ones to address as you revise, and making your reasoning clear to the journal editor. The following essay details a method for prioritizing and organizing reviewer comments for busy faculty members trying to publish for tenure.

Reviewer comments should be useful, pointed, and provide a good sense of what to specifically develop in your manuscript to make it ready for publication. The best reviewer comments do this; however, individual reviewer comments can sometimes seem contradictory, suggesting different ideas for development in the same piece. These conflicting comments may be "a good sign" because "reviewers tend to disagree

DOI: 10.7330/9781607328834.c063

when an article is strong" (Belcher 2009: 299). Some comments from reviewers can seem as if they are asking for a different paper altogether by suggesting new avenues of inquiry or examples to analyze. Most common, in my experience, are comments suggesting further development of an idea that means cutting or revising another part of the manuscript. Sit with reviewer comments, think through them, and reflect on them before you begin the work of revising your manuscript.

Once you have received reviewer comments, take time to reflect on each one. Belcher offers a helpful way to list revision plans, and you can pair my advice with her planner. For this stage of revision planning, I like to use Trello, which allows me to create lists and movable cards (with sub-lists and due dates on each card), but a pen and paper, a spreadsheet, or a plain old word-processing document will do just fine.

First, create a list of all of the comments. Don't worry about vetting them yet; just make each comment its own item. Next, create different lists, each one identifying a general area or element you have been asked to revise. There are all sorts of variations on this idea, but I like the following division: context/frame, examples/analysis, and organization. These are usually the three big areas where I have received (and given) comments for revision, but you may notice more.

To prioritize items within each list, I use a two-by-two grid, which I was introduced to at the 2016 Council for Writing Program Administrator's pre-conference workshop for new WPAs (see figure 63.1). WPAs often use it to categorize various administrative projects, but we can use it for prioritizing reviewer comments. The grid is just four boxes representing the interaction of two criteria for prioritizing comments. While mapping your comments onto the four quadrants will not give you a subtle analysis, it does give you a good place to start (Samuel 2016). For my revision work, I use the two criteria of improvement and effort. How much will a reviewer's comment improve my manuscript, and how much effort (or time) will it take to make that improvement? The basic grid is shown in figure 63.1.

Using this system, you can prioritize each item in your list by placing the item in the appropriate quadrant. Will addressing a particular comment take little effort and come with a big payoff? Put it in the "Major Improvement/Minor Effort" quadrant. Will adding a new example and summarizing more of your literature review to make room for the change satisfy a main concern of a reviewer? Put it in the "Major Improvement/Major Effort" quadrant.

This prioritization is essential. The truth of the matter is that you will not be able to address every comment each reviewer made. Your

Improvement →	Major Improvement/ Minor Effort	Major Improvement/ Major Effort
	Minor Improvement/ Minor Effort	Minor Improvement/ Major Effort
	Effort →	

Figure 63.1. Improvement/effort prioritization grid

job as a writer is to sift through the comments for the most appropriate ones—the ones that will serve best in strengthening your work. The tool above helps you to consider which comments to address so that your manuscript can be stronger, while highlighting the investment of time and effort that each revision will require. I suggest placing items in each list using the quadrant titles above in the following order: "Major Improvement/Minor Effort"; "Major Improvement/Major Effort"; "Minor Improvement/Minor Effort"; "Minor Improvement/ Major Effort." Avoid spending too much time on the comments in the last quadrants as much as possible. You could remove items that fall into "Minor Improvement/Major Effort" quadrant from your lists altogether, but you will want to articulate a clear rationale for not addressing them when drafting your resubmission letter.

Once you have a good list of actionable and doable items, you can set up your revision priorities and schedule however you prefer. Some of your items, usually of the "Major Improvement/Minor Effort" variety, can be easily accomplished whenever you have some spare time. In *Write Your Dissertation in Fifteen Minutes a Day*, Bolker (1998) suggests carrying our writing with us to take advantage of any time we have new ideas. The increasingly ubiquitous use of smartphones and shared documents in cloud-based services means that we can easily carry our writing with us anywhere and perhaps tackle some smaller revision items on the fly.

The takeaway from this last part is particularly important for those of us at teaching-intensive institutions. Given the time crunch most of us work under, an hour's worth of planning and organization can help to move projects toward final acceptance and publication, which leads to the final value of the prioritized action list—writing the resubmission letter. When resubmitting a piece, I have sometimes been asked to write a short letter explaining how I responded to the reviewers' comments. Creating the prioritized lists has helped me draft these documents because I had to reflect on each comment's relative worth to my manuscript. Coupling the above advice with a daily writing routine of fifty to sixty minutes (see also Barton's chapter in this volume) can become a powerful way to develop and publish your research in a timely fashion for tenure, especially in an institutional context in which your time as a scholar may be competing with other important areas of your work.

REFERENCES

Belcher, Wendy Laura. 2009. *Writing Your Journal Article in 12 Weeks: A Guide to Academic Publishing Success*. Los Angeles: SAGE.

Bolker, Joan. 1998. *Writing Your Dissertation in Fifteen Minutes a Day: A Guide to Starting, Revising, and Finishing Your Doctoral Thesis*. New York: Owl Books.

Samuel, Alexandra. 2016. "How to Wrap Your Head around Even the Most Complex Subjects." *JSTOR Daily*, November 1. http://daily.jstor.org/how-to-wrap-your-head-around-even-the-most-complex-subjects.

64

MANAGING REVIEWER AND EDITORIAL FEEDBACK

Rebecca E. Burnett

Feedback from reviewers and editors is often difficult to manage—sometimes mired in posturing and pontificating and sometimes using jargon and conditional language open to multiple interpretations. To complicate the process further, feedback from different reviewers is often contradictory, both in the reactions to your work and in the advice about ways to correct perceived problems.

You often have a lot of editorial advice to sort through—perhaps suggestions from two or three professional friends you've asked to read and respond and then feedback from two or three reviewers on the journal's review board. You may also have comments from the editor that may not address the entirety of the reviewer comments. Your task is to ferret out the actual recommendations so that you can decide what to add, change, or delete.

Create a spreadsheet in Excel or simulate a spreadsheet in a table using Microsoft Word (or comparable open-source word-processing application). Developing and managing a feedback spreadsheet has a number of benefits for you:

- Putting the feedback in a spreadsheet makes what may seem like an overwhelming task become manageable.
- Organizing feedback by reviewer increases the likelihood that you won't inadvertently miss a point someone makes.
- Identifying the feedback by category lets you track patterns (including contradictions) in the feedback.
- Reviewing all the feedback about a particular category lets you more easily determine your responses and make them consistent and coherent.
- Constructing the spreadsheet forces your detailed attention to the reviewers' feedback in a way that reduces the emotion often connected with the reviews themselves.

DOI: 10.7330/9781607328834.c064

- Constructing your response to the editor will be easier because you have listed all the actions you've taken, which you need to summarize for the editor in your cover letter accompanying the revised manuscript.

This is advice I offer to Brittain Postdoctoral Fellows in our Writing and Communication Program in their professional development meetings with me. They often have "accepted with revision" or "revise and resubmit" manuscripts, but they sometimes feel unsure about the best way to proceed. If you're in the same position—with feedback regarding a book chapter, journal article, or book manuscript—the following process might be helpful:

- Create a spreadsheet in which you'll organize all the editorial advice you've received, with the categories of comments on the vertical axis and the names of the reviewers on the horizontal axis. The far-right column will identify the final resolution about each category. See the axes on table 64.1 for a simulated example.
- Separate the editorial advice you've received into distinct, manageable comments, each representing one task to do. Tag each with a code that refers to the reviewer, so you don't lose track of where the info came from. This deconstruction enables you to create cells for the spreadsheet. See the cells on table 64.1 for fictionalized, simplified examples.
- Categorize the comments (for example, the table shows comments that fall into the following six categories: make intro more engaging and useful, meld results and analysis, extend literature review, use literature review, style, increase coherence). You might have only one comment in a category, or several.
- Summarize the gist of each comment and then include the full quotation from the reviewer. The table presents shortened versions of fictionalized quotations.
- Select an icon to represent that a particular reviewer's comment disagrees with another comment in the same category as a way to signal the need to resolve reviewer conflicts.

Colleagues who have adopted this approach and adapted it to their own writing/revising process report that it is easy to implement, saves time, and results in more thorough and careful revision.

Table 64.1. Sample feedback spreadsheet with six categories of reviewing comments, five reviewers, and the authorial resolution.

	Advice from journal reviewer 1	Advice from journal reviewer 2	Advice from journal reviewer 3	Advice from personal reader 1	Advice from personal reader 2	Author's resolution
Make intro more engaging and useful	"Grab the readers in the beginning."	"The author should contextualize the study."	"Let me know why I should care about reading this article."	"By the bottom of page 3, I'm starting to see where you're going. That's too late."	No comment	"I have revised the intro to include an epigraph, an opening narrative, and forecasting."
Meld results and analysis	* "Please analyze the data when you present it rather than creating a separate section."	No comment	* "I don't know why you've separated the results and your analysis."	* "Excellent presentation of results. Interesting analysis."	No comment	"I have now melded the analysis into the presentation of the results, which should help readers."
Extend literature review	* "Minimally, add Able, 2014; Boxer & Brace, 2016; and Crandall, 2017, all of whom have key arguments about the topic."	* "The author should include discipline-defining sources, such as Druid, 1987; Ellinger, 1994; and Finster, 2001."	* "Perfect lit review."	* "The lit review seems a little skimpy. Who else has contributed to this conversation?"	No comment	"I have extended lit review to include more historical and current resources."
Use literature review	* "In your analysis, help readers understand the ways your lit review informs your reasoning."	* "The author doesn't use the lit review at all after it's initially presented. Readers need connections!"	* "You've done such a good job in the lit review that readers intuitively understand its relevance."	No comment	No comment	"I have referred to specific authors in the lit review in my analysis and discussion of results."
Style	"Comply with the style: use authors' full name the first time you make a reference. Use last names thereafter."	No comment	No comment	No comment	No comment	"I have revised to comply with conventions for introducing quotations."
Increase coherence	"Connect your main points so readers can follow your line of argument."	"The analysis of the data needs to be connected to the theoretical framework."	"I want to see the theory you present in the beginning play out in the conclusion."	"Can you make the parts logically relate to each other? The headings aren't sufficient."	"I had a difficult time following the main points in your argument."	"I have increased the coherence with forecasting as well as transitional sentences and paragraphs."

* Represents conflicting interests.

65

INVESTIGATE, TARGET, IMPLEMENT, PERSEVERE
Understanding the Academic Publishing Process through Editors' Eyes

Tara Lockhart, Brenda Glascott, Justin Lewis, Holly Middleton, Juli Parrish, and Chris Warnick

Literacy in Composition Studies (*LiCS*) is a refereed, open-access online journal that, according to its mission statement, "sponsors scholarly activity at the nexus of Literacy and Composition Studies." Edited in collaborative fashion by six editors from different institutions across the United States, the journal was founded to explore the contextual and fluid notions of literacies as they impact the field and practices of composition studies.

In essence, we founded the journal to make a place for a focus on literacy we did not see adequately represented in our fields, and to challenge authors to make connections between literacy work and composition/writing studies more broadly. We chose an open-access platform to ensure that the scholarship we publish circulates as widely as possible, unfettered by paywalls and extending across both disciplinary and geographical borders. Further, we designed particular features of the journal's publishing process and certain features of the journal, such as our symposium, to encourage values and beliefs that we hold dear: engagement, dialogue, mentorship, access, and exchange.

We begin with this overview of our journal not only to contextualize the advice we'd like to offer below, but to illustrate that the way editors frame journals provides important clues into how they will read authors' submissions. For example, in the framing paragraph above (much of it simplified from our mission statement), potential authors can glean that *LiCS* is, importantly, interested in both literacy *and* composition. Because we stress that we seek work "at the nexus" of these two fields, whether or not an author has engaged both fields shapes every decision we make in terms of publishing work.

DOI: 10.7330/9781607328834.c065

Although writers and researchers at every stage of their career are often advised to "read the journal to which you hope to submit," this advice can too often seem broad, vague, or even overwhelming (despite being a good general rule). In this short essay, we offer advice from our vantage point as editors, advice that we hope enables authors to effectively investigate journals for scholarly fit, target those journals to ensure a productive reception of that work, implement writing and revision processes based on an awareness of academic publishing principles, and finally, persevere through the process to ultimately see their work in print.

Investigate. Although reading the journal to which you hope to submit is helpful to acclimate you inductively to the kinds of claims, methods, and research contained within (see Hawk's chapter in this volume), equally important is *how* you read a prospective journal. A purposefully rhetorical reading of not only past articles, but editors' introductions, calls for proposals or special issue contributions, mission statements, advice to authors, and even style guidelines can provide important information about how editors view their journal's purpose and contribution to the larger fields. Reading in a strategic, rhetorical way can help potential authors flesh out the ideology of a given journal, addressing questions like: What kinds of research does it tend to promote? What are the broader conversations or questions that seem to crop up again and again? What can you tell about the journal's audience through both its auxiliary materials (mission statement, editorial board, etc.) and a survey of the articles it has published in the last three to five years? Investigating how the journal sees its place, its work, and its audience can not only help you choose which journals to submit to, it can also help you find footing for your claims.

If you are new to academic publishing, it might be helpful to map out a handful of key journals you're considering and compare how their audiences, foci, methodologies, publishing platforms, and key inquiries tend to differ. (For instructors, this is a terrific graduate student exercise in rhetorical reading to integrate into class projects.) Once you have a sense of what journals care about, you can then identify model articles from the journal, and then rely on these model articles for ideas of how authors in this journal typically present their methods, their findings, and the like.

Ideally, the process of investigation should lead you to journals that overlap with your own commitments and research interests.

Target. With initial investigations conducted, prospective authors can target a journal that interests them and that seems a potential home for their work. As we suggested in our opening paragraphs, this type of targeting is essential: the very first question that many editors will ask (or will ask their peer reviewers to ask) is whether or not the piece you have submitted is "a fit" for the journal. As editors, we are consistently surprised by submissions that don't engage with literacy, for example (or at times even mention the term!). Understanding that the criteria of "fit" will likely impact whether your submission is even sent out for review is thus crucial for prospective authors. Journals have their own editorial vision and publication agendas; finding scholarship that "fits" is thus part of moving the work of the journal forward.

In our process, for example, two editors read a submission and confer to determine whether it should be sent out for blind peer review. The most important questions we bear in mind as we read are:

- Is the manuscript relevant to the mission and scope of the journal?
- Does the manuscript develop a clear research project or argument?

As you work to match your research with the appropriate journal, a few other suggestions about targeting journals might be helpful:

- Consider taking advantage of the platform and/or features of your chosen journal, including shorter options for engagement. Certain journals may be particularly open to or invested in multimedia submissions, archival work, interviews, or other formats, given the limits and possibilities of their publishing platform. Similarly, journals may have spaces—symposia, book reviews, responses—that offer authors a variety of formats through which they can engage.
- Consider tapping into not only scholarly conversations but larger questions and issues in the public sphere. Some journals are more interested in this move than others, but if your piece seems to be particularly relevant, timely, or accessible to nonacademic audiences, editors may be excited by the reach your work can potentially achieve. (However, if your work does not readily make such connections, there is no need to force it.)
- Identify journals known to take a mentoring approach with authors, particularly if you are a newer author or someone publishing in a new research area.
- Ask for help. As you are narrowing your argument and making hard decisions while you draft, ask those familiar with the journal to read your work or to assist you in highlighting one research direction over another.

Implement. With your journal targeted, model articles at hand, and the question of "fit" squarely in mind, you have reached the writing, revision, and implementation stage of the process. If you do not already have a piece of research in mind to work up for this journal, we can suggest three additional ways to begin building a relationship with a particular journal and its scholarly conversations.

First, look for the opportunities, mentioned above, to write shorter pieces for the journal (reviews, symposia pieces, etc.). Shorter pieces can often serve as a portal to understanding the journal and its audience more deeply, as well as to establishing a productive relationship with editors. Second, use calls for proposals or calls for papers as jump-starts to move a project forward. CFPs often offer specific theoretical frameworks, rich inquiry questions, or foci that can be helpful in conceptualizing how your research could join a conversation. Third, use special issues to foster new dimensions of your work. Because special issues aim to deep dive into one area of research, and are often edited by well-known experts in that area, special issues provide opportunities to join a community of interested, like-minded scholars.

Below we provide additional questions our editorial team uses to decide whether or not a submission should continue to move forward toward publication. Knowing what editors are reading for—and rereading your work with these questions in mind—can help you craft a manuscript with a greater chance of being well-received. Questions editors often use to evaluate submissions:

- Does the piece clearly state how the project contributes to a relevant scholarly conversation(s) in the discipline (for *LiCS*, in composition and literacy studies)?
- Does it productively *engage with* recent disciplinary research on the topic?
- Does the piece seem particularly (or potentially) innovative, important, or does it fill a gap in the research? Is there something in this manuscript that excites you?

Questions editors might use to evaluate submissions and/or offer feedback to authors:

- Does the manuscript demonstrate that the project is methodologically sound?
- Is the manuscript organized in a way that makes sense and best serves the description of the project and presentation of results?

Keeping questions like these in mind while writing, or returning to these questions as you revise, can help you foreground the rhetorical situation in your composing process. By focusing in this way, authors can make a case for how their work fits into the conversations that a particular journal has invested in. The "investigative" stage of your process may also come back into play here: you can show that you understand a journal's ideological commitments by the way you frame your arguments, synthesize evidence that will be compelling to this journal's audience, cite important research that has appeared in this journal, and suggest implications that resonate with the inquiries at the heart of a given journal's endeavors.

Persevere. Our final piece of advice centers on understanding the academic publishing process so that you can successfully prepare for the sometimes (surprisingly) lengthy process. You may have already spent several months, or even a year or more, conducting the previous steps of investigation, targeting, and implementing. As you prepare to submit your manuscript, you should expect that it will likely be another year, sometimes more, before you see your piece in print. *Each stage* of the review process—from initial editorial review to blind peer review to revise and resubmit processes to acceptance, copyediting, proofing, and layout—typically takes at least a month.

It is the very rare manuscript that is accepted without any revisions at all, so you should expect to be offered the opportunity to see your work through new eyes and to use that feedback to make your work stronger. Even as you hope to put your best foot forward through your research, recognize that any journal's editorial team has a similar desire: every publication is a reflection of a given journal's larger values, and most editors take that reflection quite seriously. Entering the publishing process with the knowledge that a journal's editors hope to help you create the best possible instantiation of your work can help you stay the course through revisions and the final stages of the process.

In addition to the manuscript itself, you should also be prepared to submit supporting documents such as an abstract, keywords, a biography, permissions (to include student work or to clear copyright-protected work), high-quality figures/images with captions, and the like. Newer authors frequently underestimate the time it can take to change an article from one style to another (MLA to APA, etc.) or to conform their manuscript to a journal's style guide. Like its mission statement, a journal's style guidelines often suggest something about its values, practices, and audiences (see LaVecchia, Morris, and Micciche's chapter in this volume). Engaging with revisions with this in mind can make the process a bit more interesting and illuminating.

Last, in terms of time management, targeting journals that have a strong reputation for timely correspondence with authors can help streamline the academic publishing process, as can choosing smaller journals or online journals with regular publication schedules. However, it is often difficult to predict how many manuscripts a journal may have in the queue in front of yours. If you are pressed for time (due to promotion or tenure procedures, for example), communicate with the editorial team respectfully about your constraints or concerns.

In closing, remembering that journal editors have chosen their work, or founded their journals, because they believe in advancing knowledge in a particular area can help productively inform an author's writing and submission decisions. Guiding a manuscript and author through the academic publishing process is hard, but interesting and rewarding, work. Authors who have taken some time with each of the four strategies mentioned above will often find the process smoother, and more enjoyable, and editors will appreciate the targeted care authors have put into their research.

66

FROM FEAR TO COLLABORATION
Working with Academic Journal/Series Editors

Steve Parks

I can't speak for others, but I was afraid of editors for much of my writing career.

Perhaps it was because as a junior faculty member at a research 1 institution, I felt the editor would have significant sway over my tenure case. Perhaps it was because I equated the knowledge demonstrated within an academic series to the actual knowledge possessed by the editor. Or perhaps I just had a harder time than most in shedding my self-image as an unpublished graduate student. At any rate, I was afraid. And this fear had an impact on how I wrote, where I sent my work, and how I responded to reviewer comments.

Now, some twenty years later, I've become an "editor"—a fact that still startles me at points. It was, in many ways, an unintentional path. It began by editing community publications, moved into editing a community partnership journal, then creating essay collections with colleagues, and ultimately expanded into co-creating a university press series. Currently, I edit NCTE's *Studies in Writing and Rhetoric* (*SWR*; one of the previous editors, Joe Harris, also has a chapter in this volume). All this work, I think, has resulted in my having a hand in close to forty book-length publications and probably even more journal articles.

So what shifted for me? What made it possible for me to imagine editors differently? It started from working with one individual, who was a member of a labor union writing group in Syracuse called the Basement Writers. The group had emerged out the national Unseen America project—a project designed to have workers record their laboring lives through photography. I was asked to help the workers write about their photos. After weeks of meeting, it became clear that these individuals' lives couldn't be reduced to just work and, more important, they wanted to use writing to speak to others about the full complexity of their working-class lives. Out of this vision, a writing group was born.

DOI: 10.7330/9781607328834.c066

One particular writer in the group was deeply committed to telling his story. By his own admission, however, writing did not come easily. He would often have only one or two sentences written for group. And when sharing, he would often apologize for his writing, accepting any suggestions from his group members—no matter if the suggestion was unrelated to what he was trying to do. And more often than not, the "suggestions" that were offered were simply words of praise—"Great work . . . keep writing." Within this mix of praise and imposed visions, he found it increasingly hard to write. He started to miss group meetings.

At some point, he approached me to talk about how the group didn't understand his goals, what he wanted to write about, or what he was trying to make the piece say. The group also didn't understand that false praise was not useful him. He knew he needed to revise. Then he reminded me of stories I had told about my own working-class father and how I wished he had written about his life. He stated he was writing for his daughter, so she would know about his life as she left home for college. Then he asked if I would read his writing outside the group. I immediately said yes.

And so our work together began. It wasn't easy. Often he had to forcefully remind me of his goals. I had to tell him when a sentence didn't meet those goals, when something better was required. Throughout, we had to find a way to trust each other, even in the midst of disagreements. It was like wrenching my mind into a new place of humble authority. It was like having to learn all over again how to understand the struggles writers face and how to help them remain committed to their goals. Slowly, however, over months, he wrote and rewrote, kept his vision central, and eventually produced a short piece published in the Basement Writers' *Working: An Anthology of Writing and Photography.* He gave the book to his daughter.

Now I'm not sure if he knew it at the time—I've told him since—but he was giving me a lesson in how to be an editor. He demanded that my role was to help him understand how to effectively present his vision to an audience. His commitment helped me learn that rather than characterize what was on the page as "great," it was more respectful to believe in his potential and give direct advice on what was working and what wasn't. That is, I learned how to encourage a writer to produce the best articulation of his unique vision. I saw that it was this attention to his goals, not kind words, that showed respect for his writing.

As important, I learned about the power differential often latent between writer and editor—the pressure on the writer to just accept a piece of advice from an editor (or writing group) to ensure publication.

As the "professor" writing to an "unpublished writer," I had to develop a way of commenting that could be read as opening opportunities, not as demands that had to be fulfilled. That is, I had to be constantly attuned to making sure I wasn't imposing a vision on his work—that the goal remained him achieving his own vision through writing.

All this led me to look back at the many reviewer comments and editor suggestions I had received prior to working with the Basement Writers. As I looked at them again, I suddenly saw the same struggle to support writers, the same goal of helping writers find their own voice within an audience that they may (or may not) fully understand. I came to see that it was my own working-class anxiety that had led me to misunderstand the words on the page. I had been consistently given an opportunity to speak but, out of fear, had heard a demand to be silent. It was only by returning to a working-class community, collaborating with worker-writers, that I could understand the ethos the editors were trying to express.

It was then that I moved from community to academic editorial work, constantly trying to keep in mind the lessons taught to me by the members of Basement Writers.

Today, if I were to offer advice to my younger self from my current vantage point, I think it might be the following:

- *Breathe*: Overcome any anxiety and commit to sending out your manuscript.
- *Remember*: Editors love interesting, new, and unusual projects. Editors enjoy actively working with writers to develop manuscripts and helping them to be published. Editors are a consistent resource and colleague to emerging writers.
- *Learn*: The best writing emerges out of a collaborative conversation.

Looking back, that is, I believe writing within such a framework would have enabled me to find my own writing voice sooner as well as allowed me to more quickly develop my own ethical compass for how I wanted to navigate the field as a scholar. That is, if I had understood the editors as attempting to support me in finding the core values of my work, encouraging my growth as a writer, I might have also understood that scholarship at its best is a communal enterprise. And I might have realized sooner that effective editors actively work to shape a collaborative ethos of inquiry that marks the best aspects of our field.

That is the lesson taught to me by a worker-writer, a lesson I have tried to enact as I continue to work with academic and community writers today.

67

RUTHLESS, FUSSY, ALERT
A Quick Guide to Copyediting

Christina M. LaVecchia, Janine Morris, and Laura R. Micciche

Because the production process—the path a manuscript follows once accepted for publication—mostly takes place outside the authors' view and asks authors to give up some degree of control over their work, it is often murky, even intimidating, for writers. Our goal, as current and former members of the *Composition Studies* (*CS*) editorial team, is to demystify copyediting to help writers best take advantage of copyeditors as a developmental resource.

Typically, copyediting is the first step in preparing a manuscript for publication, before typesetting, proofing, and publishing. For some (bigger) journals, copyediting is handled by professionals working for the journal's publisher; for other, often smaller or independent, journals like *CS*, copyediting is handled in-house by the editor, editorial assistants, and/or volunteers. As copyeditors, it is our goal to help authors find the best version of their writing. Our attention to mechanics like wording choices, series parallelism, tense consistency, comma placement, and capitalization is about helping authors to find the clearest and most polished version of what they are saying without overtaking the authors' own voices—a tricky balance. Our main method is to slow down, look at the writing, and ask ourselves, does this make sense? Such slow reading forces content to the background and situates meaning in phrases, sentences, punctuation, and word choices. This process of slow reading introduces a different orientation to the writing compared to how we might review an initial submission, bringing our main focus to the language and formatting of the text rather than the argument and its development.

Most copyediting happens in multiple passes; at *CS* each manuscript is reviewed by two copyeditors. The first pass often identifies approximately two-thirds of the significant issues that fall into categories like sentence-level, mechanical, format, and content editing. The second

DOI: 10.7330/9781607328834.c067

pass typically addresses the remaining editing issues. In real time, reading an article manuscript of twenty-five to thirty pages slowly is a four- to six-hour process for each of the two editors, with a significant portion of that time devoted to checking source accuracy as well as formatting citations.

For an illustration of what this looks like in practice, below is an excerpt of a review essay Janine wrote (2015) on Alison Bechdel's *Fun Home* and *Are You My Mother?* for a recent issue of *CS*, which Laura and Christina copyedited (see figure 67.1). Their comments showcase both the mechanical changes and larger language questions typical of copyeditors' work during this revision stage. In terms of mechanics, Laura and Christina suggested sentence-level changes to more sharply clarify meaning at the micro level; on the third line of the second paragraph, for instance, Christina directly queries Janine, suggesting she clarify that it is in Bechdel's texts specifically that she incorporates the senses. In addition, this example illustrates the collaborative nature of the editing process, as the comments invite response and dialogue—Janine is able to accept, adjust, or respond to the suggestions and queries from the copyeditors.

It's important for writers to understand that the rethinking and revising prompted by copyeditors (as illustrated in the example given in figure 67.1) are typical of the pre-publication process, especially when publishing in a one-stop shop like an independent journal (revising and copyediting stages are more distinct at larger presses and publication venues). Whatever the venue, however, we want to underscore that nearly all work evolves as a result of copyediting; to wit, we have yet to read a submission that could not be improved by copyediting.

To help writers think like copyeditors as they prepare work for final submission, we offer five pieces of advice:

1. BE A RUTHLESS SENTENCE-LEVEL EDITOR. Reread the piece *very slowly*. Isolate each sentence and watch for grammatical pitfalls that can obscure meaning at a sentence level (e.g., faulty parallelism, inconsistent use of singular or plural, shifting verb tenses, unclear pronoun references). View your sentences as a primary means by which you foreground your argument or stance, as tools for minimizing distractions from the main message you want to communicate.

2. BE FUSSY ABOUT MECHANICAL EDITING. Compare and check in-text citations to works cited to make sure spellings are consistent and all citations are present in both places. Be sure that you know the venue's style format and version currently in use. If in doubt, ask the editor or editorial assistants. Check your use of abbreviations, formatting of headers, and punctuation of numbers against the venue's house style (usually available online).

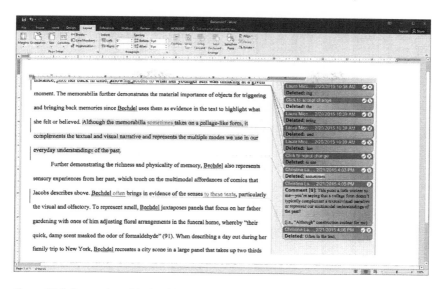

Figure 67.1. Screenshot of Janine Morris's copyedited review essay

3. BE AN ALERT FORMAT EDITOR. Review formatting consistency and read-ability throughout the document. Check cross-references, footnotes, or endnotes (depending on which the venue uses), and presentation of tables and figures. Again, save yourself time in the long run by consulting the house style.

4. DIG IN YET AGAIN TO CONTENT EDITING. We know you've probably read and reread your work many times. We assure you that you've missed something. Look closely at what seems stable in your piece: for instance, ensure the accuracy of statistical data and fair representation of source material. Question your depiction of context when working with others' ideas; remember that your readers likely don't know the material in the precise way that you do. Help them get there.

5. USE YOUR CONTACTS. Ask others to read your work with an eye toward one or two of the four kinds of editing identified here. Because the editing process is a collaborative one between editors and authors, getting early feedback on your work can prepare you for that give-and-take.

Attending to these seemingly small components on the front end can reduce stress and frustration on the back end. With a better understanding of what a copyeditor does, writers are more prepared intellectually and emotionally for publishing expectations. As well, we hope we've made clear that nearly all manuscripts require copyediting and that, in its best form, the publishing process is a collaborative give-and-take between editors and authors. Indeed, when you don't like a proposed change or feel the copyediting got something wrong, know that you can clarify your intentions, or open up a dialogue with the editorial team.

Copyeditors are allies, working together with authors toward the same goal—producing writing that will have an impact.

REFERENCE

Morris, Janine. 2015. "Multimodal Literacies and Graphic Memoir: Using Alison Bechdel in the Classroom. Review of *Are You My Mother? A Comic Drama,* by Alison Bechdel and *Fun Home: A Family Tragicomic,* by Alison Bechdel." *Composition Studies* 43 (1): 193–200.

68

AFTER THE ACCEPTANCE

Barbara E. L'Eplattenier and Lisa Mastrangelo

Our number one piece of advice to writers submitting work to a journal: work so that editors think fondly of you.[1]

Paul Silvia, author of *How to Write a Lot*, suggests that authors develop priorities in their writing to-do lists.[2] He suggests starting with pieces furthest along in the writing process. His list looks like this:

1. Review page proofs.

2. Address line edits/editors' corrections.

3. Finish projects with a deadline.

4. Revise for resubmission to a journal.

5. Do reviews (we would put this earlier, ha ha).

6. Draft new pieces.

7. Write the miscellaneous stuff—newspaper articles, letter of opinions, and so on.

Silvia has an obvious x-y axis of "amount of work" and "finished, published project" that keeps manuscripts moving to where they need to be in the process.[3] This ranking system works well, in our estimation, because it incorporates the fact that other people are also waiting for the work to be completed. And it gets the work done.

Because you don't want to be the person an editor must track down for corrected page proofs. You *really really really really* don't. Write things down, put deadlines on calendars, block in twenty minutes a day until the work is completed. Give yourself a gold star every day you do the work.[4]

In addition to following this workflow, we have a few tips for the publication process: first, become a good copyeditor (see LaVecchia, Morris, and Micciche's chapter in this volume). Any journal not associated with a publishing house (Elsevier or Taylor and Francis, for example) or a major professional organization (NCTE) usually does its

DOI: 10.7330/9781607328834.c068

own copyediting. (The cost of journal/membership is often indicative of who does the copyediting. The higher the cost, the more likely it is that there are paid copyeditors.) Journals such as *Peitho, Enculturation, Kairos, Programmatic Perspectives, Writing Center Journal*—the vast majority of journals in our discipline—do their own copyediting.

This means that you should take the journal's style guide seriously—more than likely, the editors will use the guide to do the copyediting. The more the manuscript follows the style guide, the faster it moves through the process. If the style guide says, "No automated notes" and your manuscript has automated notes in it, someone is going to have to change them. Doing this yourself means it's more likely to be correct *and* the editors will think fondly of you, because fixing things like this take an astonishing amount of time.

WPA: Writing Program Administration, for example, does all its copyediting in-house; we estimate that a single manuscript—from the moment it lands in our mailboxes to its publication—takes 40–60 hours to ready for publication; the bulk of that time, without exception, is spent in the copyediting stage. So, conservatively, a journal issue with four articles (4 × 40 hours = 160), three book reviews (3 × 10 hours = 30), and three plenary pieces (3 × 40 hours = 120) takes over 300 hours to prepare. We may seem obsessive about copyediting, but it is an essential stage in the publication of the journal. Anything you can do to decrease that time makes us like you. And honestly? We'd rather talk to you about your research and the arguments you're shaping than about copyediting.

Second, fact-check your own works cited and your citations. We've seen works cited pages that are incomplete, inaccurate (the article was published in *College English*, not *CCC*; it was published in 1967, not 1969), in multiple fonts using multiple styles (some entries in MLA 7 and MLA 8, some in APA, and some in something we don't even recognize).[5] Getting these details correct is a matter of time and attention at the micro scale, both of which can be in short supply at that stage of the game. Certainly, the first draft you send to us doesn't have to be perfect, but it should be pretty darn good. If we're at the copyediting stage, it needs to be perfect.

Finally, many of the editors in our discipline do this work for minimal compensation; most get a course release, but many do not. They too juggle their research, their classes, and their service with reading manuscripts and writing peer reviews, working with authors, and preparing manuscripts for publication. Whatever you can do as a writer to help them in the process of doing their work will make them think fondly of you.

Why do you want editors to think fondly of you? Because if they know you will get the work done and it will be good work, they'll be faster to say yes to other projects with you.

NOTES

1. Why do we think we can tell you these things? Because together, we've edited two collections (*Historical Studies in Writing Program Administration* and *Working in the Archives*), one newsletter that was rolled into a peer-reviewed journal during our tenure (*Peitho*), and one established journal (*WPA: Writing Program Administration*).

2. Silvia's work (2018) is great. We also recommend Boice 1990. King 2012 is also excellent. The content of all this work boils down to one thing, however: sit down and write and do it regularly.

   And honestly, that goes double for the peer reviews you are asked to do; early is good, fast is even better, early and fast means the editors will have to talk about not using you as a peer reviewer too much because you are awesome!

3. We've been lucky enough to work with a lot of people who are considered leaders or luminaries in our discipline. What we've noticed, almost without exception, is that these people treat all parts of the process—whether it's revising in response to comments, copyediting, or checking proofs—as, for lack of better words, part of a 9–5 job. That sounds weird, so let us explain a bit more. These people act as if their working time is finite, limited, and they budget their time and work carefully. When it is time to do the scheduled work, they do it. This results in work getting done very quickly or on schedule.

   Also, they don't seem to post on Facebook very often, but when they do, it's usually about their exciting and interesting hobbies and not about how much work they have to do. (For the record, we'd like to be more like them.)

4. No, seriously. Give yourself a gold star. A real one. Go to Office Depot or Amazon .com or wherever and buy yourself some gold star stickers and stick one in your planner on each day you write. Writing often feels like it has no end reward, or the reward is a long, long, long way off, and a gold star is a visceral way to reward yourself and flood your brain with dopamine. (Go, B. F. Skinner!)

5. Hey! We've done it ourselves, so no judgment. Well, not the one we don't recognize. We haven't done that.

REFERENCES

Boice, Robert. 1990. *Professors as Writers: A Self-Help Guide to Productive Writing.* Stillwater, OK: New Forums Press.

King, Stephen. 2012. *On Writing: A Memoir of the Craft.* London: Hodder.

Silvia, Paul. 2018. *How to Write a Lot: A Practical Guide to Productive Academic Writing.* 2nd ed. Washington, DC: APA Life Tools.

SECTION 5

Moving On

69

THE TEN-YEAR PLAN

Laurie Gries

Working on a monograph is a sustained, immersive process that often zaps your intellectual energy. Ideally, after your monograph is published, you would have time to rejuvenate—to rev up your intellectual juices, so to speak, for the next big project. But unfortunately, and especially if you are employed at an research 1 institution, time for rejuvenation is more a pipe dream than a reality. The pressure to keep publishing never fades, especially if you are still working your way toward promotion. You have to keep researching, you have to keep writing, and you have to keep proving your worth. My number one bit of advice in such situation: *First, think strategically about how you can extend your scholarly reach so that you develop a broader contribution to your discipline than a single research project. Second, come up with a ten-year plan for making that contribution come to fruition.*

Ten years may seem like a long time. But you are not a machine that works by automation, untouched by the events around you, easily fixable when broken with a few quick tinkers. Life often unfolds in ways that decelerate your productivity, and you need to allot time for the unpredictability of life. In addition, in the rare instance in which your research maintains uninterrupted momentum, chances are you will bored after ten years anyway and want to change gears. You have to be strategic, then, in how you accomplish your larger goals so that once the ten years are up, you will have gained the credibility and experience needed to head off with support on your next scholarly venture.

Thinking strategically about how to extend your scholarly reach and coming up with a ten-year plan requires that you do three things:

1. Develop personal goals as a scholar that will help you create a research identity that you can constantly work toward.

2. Design a set of interrelated projects that bleed into one another and work toward your larger, broader goal.

DOI: 10.7330/9781607328834.c069

3. Create a balanced lifestyle so that you can maintain the energy needed to pursue your scholarly goals while keeping the rest of your life on track. We all work at different paces; you have to honor your own rhythms and plan realistically to make sure you can achieve all your goals without letting other parts of your life fall apart.

MY TEN-YEAR PLAN

Personal Scholarly Goals: Become a leading voice in visual rhetoric and circulation studies. Become well respected for methodological invention and innovation and open up opportunities for others to do the same. Challenge self in ways that require risk taking, constant learning, and experimentation.

Scholarly Project Goals: Develop a monograph, an edited collection, and a digital book all related to visual rhetoric or circulation studies. Gain experience needed to acquire funding to create a software program to support iconographic tracking (iconographic tracking is a digital research method I invented to track the circulation, transformation, and consequentiality of new media images) so that others can use this method for their research with more ease and efficiency.

TIMELINE FOR INTERRELATED PROJECTS

2012–2015	Finish a monograph introducing a new methodology and research method called iconographic tracking for studying visual rhetoric. In that book, I coined the term *circulation studies* to name a field of inquiry that I saw my work contributing to and in which I noticed other visual rhetoric and other rhetoric scholars working.
2015–2017	To advance the field of circulation studies, put together a collection on circulation, rhetoric, and writing in which I solicit chapters and responses from scholars doing outstanding work with circulation in our discipline. This project will not only help solidify circulation as a threshold concept in our field but also cement circulation studies as a projective area of study in our discipline.
2016–2018	Co-produce a digital book called *Digital Visual Studies*, which brings together a number of inventive methodologies (data visualization, queer archiving, augmented reality, 3D printing, glitch studies, virtual geosemiotics, etc.) to advance studies of visual rhetoric and visual culture. Also, produce two to three single-authored articles that help establish my expertise in visual rhetoric and circulation studies
2015–2022	Solidify the research method of iconographic tracking by experimenting with data visualization strategies that can be used as part of this method. Design a software prototype called PikTrack that will make the tracking, coding, visualization, and analysis of visual data possible in one easy to use interface. Secure grants to seek funding for this project. Keep writing articles.

HOW TO BRING A TEN-YEAR PLAN TO FRUITION

Bringing a ten-year scholarly plan to fruition takes self-determination and discipline, community support, a productive environment and, not least, a good amount of luck. Ideally, this plan will unfold as you are writing your first monograph and begin to imagine who you want to be as a scholar. Self-determination and discipline are key to helping you stay focused. Having a ten-year plan enables you to articulate a coherent agenda, defend scholarly choices, and stay attuned to your own scholarly desires. It also will help you establish the support you need from your department and college, disciplinary organizations, and publishing venues. If you are lucky, as I have been, you will find a press that believes in your work and wants to support your multiple projects. Sticking with a single press may not seem advantageous in many of your colleagues' eyes. However, working with a single press over time can help you establish robust working relations that ultimately and hopefully afford flexibility, experimentation, and risk taking.

In terms of my own ten-year plan, I am still on track. I established this plan halfway through working on my first monograph and have thus far been able to finish the monograph and the edited collection in addition to several articles. I have also finished the first full draft of the digital book project, and as I continue to experiment with digital visualization techniques, I have begun to write grants seeking support for the software development of PikTrack. At this point, I have full confidence that the trilogy of book projects will unfold as I imagined. As far as the software development goes, the verdict is still out, as I have yet to secure the funding needed to begin development. But I am still trying.

I am also beginning, however, to imagine the next ten years of my scholarly career and am quite excited about putting iconographic tracking to work toward a new digital public humanities project. A ten-year cycle allows us to potentially pivot at ten years and devote our energies toward new projects that demand new kinds of learning and activities in order to stay engaged. Too often, I think, we see scholars burn out and fade away behind the curtain of tenure. The beauty of a ten-year plan is that it gives us the liberty to set off in new directions (if desired), to revitalize our energies toward new goals, and to mature in our research and writing in ways that even we cannot totally predict. A ten-year plan, of course, may not work always out the way we imagine, but at the very least, by giving ourselves the opportunity to begin anew, we are more likely to stay the distance with a passion for our research, writing, and teaching. At least that's the promise I am banking on.

70

AIMING FOR AFTER
Doing Time-Consuming Projects with a Sense of an Ending

Douglas Hesse

When you're in the throes of a time-consuming project, keep in mind two things: this isn't the last thing you'll ever write, and this project is but part of your larger life.

I've been invited to discuss recovering from time-consuming projects and finding work–life balance, so it may seem cavalier to talk about "during" rather than "after." However, unless you keep some perspective during immersive tasks (whether immersion comes from seduction or threat), eventually you'll find it difficult to recover or balance anything after them. Your life will, in fact, be to engross yourself in projects, the only real question after each finish being, "What's the next one?"

If you keep in mind that a given project isn't the last thing you'll ever write, you'll license yourself to finish the task at hand and point to the aftermath of its completion.

Take consolation that, while "good" is admirable, even crucial, "perfect" isn't necessarily—or necessary. There will be other opportunities to get things better. This is true not only at the level of obsessing about craft and expression but also at the level of ideas. At junctures in a complex project when you're buried with possibilities, sources, and beguiling potential avenues, consider shunting some of them off to the side "for future consideration." I use two strategies to do this. One is a notebook in which I scrawl ideas, readings, and notes that I preserve for the future, safely out of the manuscript mainstream. The other is a side file, usually with the unceremonious title "Junk," into which I can copy and paste stuff that threatens to consume even more of my time. Some of it even becomes the seeds of my next work.

Living like a project is but part of your life is like keeping a sourdough starter going even when you're not baking bread. Even when you're in the middle of it, I recommend keeping routines that have nothing to do with the project. Meet friends or colleagues for coffee. Participate

DOI: 10.7330/9781607328834.c070

in an interest group or avocation. (Throughout my life and career, I've sung in one or more choruses, including currently with the Colorado Symphony Chorus.) Exercise or play (I know this sounds trite), especially with others. Sure, all of these things can seem to get in the way and steal time; *I'm busy and need every waking minute, dammit!* However, when you work in perpetual "wait until I have time" mode, you tend to encounter an awkward void when you finally do, one that's hard to fill—except by another project. I'm not judging this. However, if you suspect you might bolt upright in bed when you're fifty or sixty or seventy and wonder, "Is my career my identity?" then live otherwise while you're in the middle of projects.

Finally, when you do finish a time-consuming project, don't feel guilty about coasting for a spell. After all, if you've followed my first advice and kept track of possibilities for next things, you'll eventually get to them with fresh energy.

* * *

Thirty years ago, I wrote my dissertation in six months, at significant cost to my family, social life, and personal well-being. Sure, it was finished expeditiously, and I had a job offer. The dissertation even supported publications to tenure, so I might rationalize that obsession as a good investment. I surely did then. I remember once around 2:00 a.m. campus security knocked on my office door, sent by my wife, who hadn't heard from me since I left the apartment and our two children, nineteen hours earlier. I'd like to say that once the dissertation was done, normalcy returned, life was balanced, and peace and satisfaction reigned. The truth of the matter, at least for me, was the press for tenure, marked by an endless succession of time-consuming projects—waves with the briefest, shallowest troughs. It was a period of professional success at personal cost, one repeated throughout my career, although I've since learned strategies and gained some perspectives.

Time-consuming projects fall into a two-by-two matrix, one dimension being duration, the other intensity. Long-term projects take several months, at least. They may be low-intensity, such as working on a book that doesn't have a demanded deadline, or high-intensity, such as finishing a book under a contract date. Short-term projects take a few to several weeks, as in the case of manuscripts or conference talks. As with longer ones, the presence or absence of deadlines shapes intensity, but so does the visibility or prestige of the outcome, as in the case of giving a keynote address, for instance. Obviously, the most challenging circumstances—the ones most needing "recovery"—are long-duration/high-intensity, followed by short-duration/high-intensity.

Like most of us, I've worked in both circumstances. Completing a new edition of a several-hundred-page textbook takes months of layered work. Not only is there drafting, there are strata of revising, editing, approving designs, securing permissions, and proofreading. A given week might include writing a new section of one chapter, responding to editor's suggestions on another, approving copyediting on a third, and reviewing first-pass pages (initial design and layout) on a fourth. There are five or more people involved, all on budgeted time and expense. I'm only one of them, but missing delivery dates has significant material consequences well beyond me. Such writing stints can easily demand every waking moment not otherwise preempted by teaching, meeting, eating, and similar unassailable claims on one's time. I'm myopic, obsessive, antisocial, and cranky in those conditions, though not nearly as much as I used to be because I've learned not to let the project totalize life.

Long-term intensity gets matched when I'm writing a significant (at least in my own mind) shorter thing, like a keynote talk. I'm a slow writer—or rather, I'm a fast writer who generates lots of ideas and possibilities that cost huge amounts of revision time, walking drafts back to something that fits the time or space allotted. On November 17, 2016, I delivered the NCTE president's address, something allotted a strict thirty minutes, with a full version to be published in *Research in the Teaching of English* (delivery deadline December 15) and an abstracted version (750 words, due the same day) to be published in the *Council Chronicle.* Because I knew a couple thousand people would hear the talk and that it would be visibly preserved in NCTE annals (although whether anyone other than future nervous presidents would read it was another thing), I began fussing the second week in October. By three weeks out, everything else in my life was set to lowest maintenance. After the convention, I took off a week at Thanksgiving, then ramped up to revise the final piece (delivered forty-eight hours late). And then for a month, I read. I wrote postcards and friendly emails, put together a book of photographs about my grandmother along with pages from her diary, sang some concerts, took hikes in the mountains, and fiddled (and only fiddled) with some ideas I'd shunted off to a notebook. Only after several weeks had passed did I feel the urgent desire to start a new project. I was confident the feeling would come, and the ideas would follow.

When I share my advice with graduate students or younger/newer colleagues, I know they can't quite hear or believe it in the same way I can. I write, after all, in the last quarter of my career, not in the first, and I well remember the pressures, both material and psychological, to establish myself in the profession, in a career whose end I could scarcely discern. There would always be time for "the other stuff" of life. Getting older reminds me otherwise. But even many years ago, I began paying attention to colleagues who seemed to have happy lives—happier than mine, which I thought was at least okay. These were people who made time to play cards or see movies or eat lunch with colleagues (not alone at their desks) or go to talks or receptions and have a drink afterwards. Some were less productive than I, some more, but they seemed—at least from afar—to be better balanced. About the same time, I realized that the marginal rate of return, to borrow from the economists, on spending more time on a project beyond a certain point didn't necessarily yield higher quality or more productivity.

Spending eight hours a day writing instead of six didn't mean 33 percent more—and better—words. Now, I still talk a better game than I play, but the cycle of freneticism followed by anxious torpor is mostly broken.

71

PUBLISHING IS A BEGINNING

Joyce Carter

Even though it feels like a definitive ending, getting an academic work published is really only the beginning. With your work out in the open, now comes promoting, tracking, answering questions, and looking for follow-on opportunities and collaborations.

I like to think of intellectual work as being akin to product development. Market research is akin to a literature review. Product development (which these days employs iterative or agile design) is akin to the acts of writing, revising, rethinking, and rewriting. Production is akin to publication.

So, to continue the metaphor, why stop your work with academic publication? You've just put months or years of work into unleashing this product into the world. Your study, article, chapter, or book moves away from the realm of development and into the realm of utility. In other words, it does something. It gets reviewed. It gets cited. It is used in undergraduate and graduate classes. It generates queries from scholars who want to work with you. It may even generate revenue for you (if it's a textbook or a learning module). You want to account for all of that activity for at least three reasons.

First, most of us work within systems that require annual reports and evaluations, either on the tenure track or as non-tenure-track faculty and either in education or in the private sector. For your annual reviews, as well as your longer-range tenure and promotion cases, *track your citations, inclusions in anthologies, reviews, and uses in classes*—it's evidence of the utility of your hard work. The instant your work is published, add it to your resume or CV and whatever online identity or professional system you use (e.g., LinkedIn, Academia.edu). The same goes for any time you find a citation or reference to your work. Immediately copy the URL or get a copy of the work, archive it where you can find it again ("My Tenure Materials," for example), and add a note to your online tracking system (Vitae, Digital Measures, or something homegrown).

DOI: 10.7330/9781607328834.c071

If you don't want to put citations and positive letters in a formal track-ing system, create your own. I keep folders for "Nice Things People Say about Me," "Citations of My Work," and "Classes That Use My Work." Even if you're not sure how you're going to use them, make sure you have plenty of offprints and copies of your book, as well as a clean PDF (rather than page proofs, if you can get one). You may be submitting hard copies of this work to awards and evaluation committees for years, and you're not going to get all of your materials back from all of those award committees.

Second, new intellectual products don't immediately set the world on fire. People may not know about your work, and if you don't have a pub-lisher or other promoter, you may need to do a lot of this work yourself. *Promote and defend your work.* You can do this actively by nominating your-self and applying for awards, writing your supervisors and colleagues with the news, and by humblebragging about your work on social media. You can also take steps to enlist others to promote your work by submit-ting it to journals to be reviewed, and working with forums to facilitate scholarly exchange.

Third, *track your work's utility or influence and note which parts hold most promise for deeper inquiry.* In the commercial world, you would track demographics and locations where your product is doing well, and this same curiosity and analysis applies to intellectual work. If, for example, the marketplace of ideas uses (via citations, course usage, and reviews) one particular part of your work, take note.

You undoubtedly kept all the leftovers from your drafting, and this market perspective can help you mine that leftover writing and research for follow-up work. When you take note of a review, a course inclusion, or a citation, in addition to storing it and accounting for it (per above), read through these materials carefully and see if you can assign scores or values to parts of your work. I have digital folders for each of my pieces of work, and these folders contain drafts that led up to completion, the work itself, and then a subfolder for follow-ups such as what I'm describ-ing. Those items are highlighted—and correlated, if possible, to my work. You could also do this in an annotated version of your work that contains notes, quotes, and hyperlinks to these other materials.

* * *

Some of what I've written for you is derivative of my work in finance and entrepreneurship, where tracking effort and gauging market success is vital. One does not engage in product development just for the joy of making the product, but rather to sell that product to generate revenue. In user experience courses in our field, we talk about iterative design, the process whereby we make a little, test a little, learn a little, and then make the next version. It's one of the key rationales for formative and frequent usability testing. Writing studies argues for the same thing at a micro level in our orientations toward process and revision. Well, the same perspective holds—in products, writing, or scholarship—at the macro level. When the product is finished, assuming your firm is more or less successful, you are likely to learn from the marketplace and perhaps make adjustments for a follow-up product. To do this, you have to pay attention to what customers and reviewers say, track that information, and identify feasible opportunities that may guide you in this product revision.

I also was trained as a computer programmer, and I learned from my very first programming classes that the inspiration in the code—whether it be the right algorithm, an elegant piece of code, or a call to a subroutine—was only partly useful. To create fully useful code, good programmers write copious comments, explaining why this particular variable behaves this way, what to expect from a call to a subroutine, or how their thought processes worked. You may be writing for a future version of yourself, that is, when you return to the program to debug something or to begin revisions. You may be writing this for another programmer to take up after you've left the project. I've always thought of intellectual products in much the same way—I try to document the thoughts and evaluations of myself and others so that a future version of me will have a leg up in approaching either revision or a derivative intellectual work.

As for documenting your successes and possible revisions in real-time, I cannot recall who mentored me about this, but I'd like to thank whoever it was for such a wonderful suggestion: if you wait until you have to write a report for someone else, you're like the guy who brings a shoe-box filled with receipts to the tax office to begin trying to reconstruct a particular tax period. Far better to account for, document, and reflect on the journey and impact of your intellectual work as soon as you discover it than to file shards of evidence away thoughtlessly, with the idea that you can always come back to them. It's never that neat.

72

YOUR BOOK HAS ARRIVED!
Now What?

Kim Hensley Owens

The moment you've been anticipating for years has arrived: your book—the tangible evidence of thousands of hours of research, writing, conversations, revision, and editing—has come in the mail. What do you do? If you're me, you immediately run up the stairs to shout the news to your spouse, but in your haste, you trip, managing to hurt your foot in one of those unspecified ways that ice *mostly* fixes in the moment, but that continues to provide occasional unpleasant reminder-twinges for months. My first bit of advice, then, is simple: do not run to tell anyone the exciting news of the publication of your book. Walk. Walk slowly and in the dignified manner that befits the author of a new book, and you will be spared the embarrassment and physical pain that might accompany running to share this news.

Ideally, the day your book arrives will be a day on which you were already working on a new project, because books take so unbelievably long to come out. But perhaps, as happened to me, your book might arrive after you've just moved your entire family across the country to start a new job, and maybe you're not actually getting much writing done on that new project yet, because each time you start, you're pulled away to unpack a box, find a doctor, enroll a child in a summer camp, or answer questions you don't yet know the answers to in your new position. Maybe you think, "I wrote a book. Isn't that enough for a while?" Or maybe you think, "This is the first time in years I can honestly say I'm not working on my book. And I don't have anything under review right now. *OMG, what am I doing?*" Or maybe you think, "I put it all in the book. I can't write anything smart again. I can't devote that much time to anything ever again. I just can't." I thought all those things. (Or maybe you're unlike everyone I know and when your book arrives you're already four chapters into drafting another book, in which case you will

DOI: 10.7330/9781607328834.c072

not be reading this book of advice because you've already got it together in ways the rest of us can only imagine.)

My advice actually pertains to long before the book is out. Consider those interview questions you prepped for when you were going on the market—questions about where you saw your research going and what you thought you'd be working on in five years. At the time those questions seemed quasi-ridiculous, your answers probably carefully thought out, but also at least half made up. How can you possibly know what will be interesting to you in five years, where your thinking will be, or where new information will lead you? But at the same time, if you're not thinking a few years ahead, perpetually seeking new answers to new questions, reading around trying to find those answers or refine those questions, you're not really doing the "scholar" part of scholarship.

Of course your answers and interests will change, will evolve, over time. The project I said in those initial interviews would be my second book became instead a coauthored one-off article—my interest in that topic completely waned. And most of the articles or book chapters I wrote while also working on my book couldn't have been anticipated, couldn't have existed without the kairotic moments from which they emerged. Likewise, the project I'm working on now, which I'm not ready to name as a book in progress, but which is at least a loose collection of ideas and manuscripts in various stages (two of which are under review as I write this), concerns issues I couldn't have fathomed back when I was on the market, and emerges as much from who I was before I even went to graduate school as it does from what I learned in grad school or as a scholar since. My advice, then, is always to be considering what it is you want to know, and what it is you want to say (and usually back and forth and back and forth)—getting to research, writing, and publication from there takes time management and resolve. This might mean starting a big new project sparked by your previous one. Or now might be the time to shift your focus—perhaps you've been writing for years about what you've thought the field wanted to hear, and now you'd like to transition to what you think it *needs* to hear. Maybe you've had a pet passion outside academia that hasn't had a clear relationship to your scholarship up to now: this is a time to explore making that connection. Read work in new fields (and outside academic work). Go to different conferences. Change your routines so your thinking can be refreshed and you can make new articulations.

I also recommend, in preparing for the post-book-publication moment, that you say yes to a few things you're not yet actually ready to do. Propose to a conference with a half-baked new idea in hopes that you'll be forced to write it more fully. Agree to give a campus talk on a project that doesn't exist yet when you say yes. Apply for local grants. Apply for national grants. You won't get them all. You might not get any, but you'll have written something that requires you to imagine the research and plan the project, and that's a critical stage to reach, because once you've done that work, you'll want (and possibly need) to come back to it, to finish it. You'll want to learn more and share what you've learned with others.

As you're proposing projects that aren't yet ready, I'd also recommend sending out manuscripts that aren't quite ready, too—first to your friends and colleagues who will give you a kind, critical read, but then, once you've revised but before you know it's perfect, send it out to editors. Blind reviewers can certainly be cruel or sometimes seem to deliberately misunderstand an argument, but they can also often see the strengths and weaknesses in a piece that you couldn't have found even with months more of on-your-own revision. They can always see things you simply can't. Learn to send out the projects when they're "good enough," without trying to make them perfect.

Thus far my advice for life after book publication seems to be all about the moments before the book actually comes out, or the literal moment when it does, but that's the point. While the moments after the book comes out can feature a blend of emotions—excitement, vindication, disappointment (success so often leads to a letdown), a sense of starting over with "nothing" because blank pages look really different from hundreds of pages of drafted words—in many ways the book (or tenure, for that matter) changes nothing. The work is the work. Writing is writing. Publishing is publishing. Rejection is still more common than acceptance. (Nearly everyone I know has experienced a spate of ego-crushing rejections after publishing a book and/or attaining tenure— I've found it slightly less ego-crushing to know how common that is.) Getting back to publishing is a matter of getting back on the horse you've probably never really gotten off in the first place—the cycle of reading, researching, thinking, proposing, drafting, getting feedback, revising, submitting (and sometimes re-revising, resubmitting, etc.). The publication merry-go-round is there, going around and around, waiting for you to jump back on.

73

PURSUE MEANINGFUL PROJECTS
Learn to Keep Learning

Ellen Cushman

So you're officially done with a major time-consuming project. Congratulations! Bask in the glow of this accomplishment. Share the work. Listen carefully to questions or critiques. Imagine. Above all, learn to keep learning.

* * *

It seems like my entire professional career has been made up of time-consuming projects, ranging from eighteen months to six years. In the shortest term, I've run or contributed to quite a few projects or committees that delivered curricular or programmatic innovations, grant findings, and online materials. Three articles I've written that received the deepest and most thorough reviews went through several rounds of rewriting, and edits took over eighteen months. Edited collections that I've contributed chapters to or have coedited, such as *Literacies: A Critical Sourcebook* (first and second editions), have typically taken two to three years to complete. Coediting a major research journal, like *Research in the Teaching of English*, has demanded a five-year term.

But the largest, most time-consuming projects have been two single–authored books based on several years of research. These books required two to three years of collecting data in communities and archives; months of discussing drafts and ideas at talks and conferences; more months drafting chapters; time spent circulating the prospectus and securing a publisher; more time rewriting and revising the chapters; and months of final production. All told, both of my books, *The Struggle and the Tools: Oral and Literate Strategies in an Inner City Community* (1998) and *The Cherokee Syllabary: Writing the Peoples' Perseverance* (2012), took six years each to complete.

Along the way, I benefited from wonderful colleagues, a good number included in this collection, who modeled their processes for me. Some I would simply observe and listen to as they delivered talks and

DOI: 10.7330/9781607328834.c073

keynotes, paying particular attention to their methods and methodologies. Others I asked for help or they aided me directly in their roles as editors, reviewers, and mentors who were my senior colleagues—Joe Harris, Peter Smagorinsky, Deb Brandt, Mike Rose, Juan Guerra, Cheryl Geisler, Jaqueline Jones Royster, and Victor Villanueva. They offered the long view on how to keep learning after a single time-consuming project was completed.

Other peer mentors included colleagues who provided just-in-time advice, support, and a listening ear while I was working through a project. These colleagues, of course, were midstream in their own time-consuming projects; I like to think we helped each other tackle a hurdle or interpret comments or find an efficient way to manage a workload.

The next generation of up-and-coming colleagues offer fresh perspectives on the field, pressing questions, or, with their own nascent projects, help me see my work in a different light or model an innovative method to help answer a question.

Then there are students at every level: their questions help me to translate my research and to think of other audiences or readings or connections to recent trends.

In short, the advice I'm offering here is really gathered across generations of generous colleagues and students who help me do deeper thinking and continue to ask questions about my work after a project has been delivered.

They've helped me understand the lifelong learning that must necessarily go into developing fresh lines of inquiry and new impetuses for work after time-consuming projects are completed. My advice, then, is an aggregate of guidance, suggestions, questions, nudges, comments, insights, reviews, and conversations gathered from generations of mentors, colleagues, reviewers, and students. I've given this advice to colleagues at various stages of their careers when they've just completed a project and are basking in the quiet glow of the accomplishment. Maybe they've achieved a career-making milestone, such as submitting a dissertation or a research-intensive manuscript, or they've published a monograph or edited collection. Or maybe they're at the end of a predetermined leadership role not tied to a research project and they want advice on how to recharge. Or they've completed an end-of-semester or other research project and are thinking of going to graduate school, pursuing a new career, getting a job, or asking for a promotion. Whatever the case, the completion of a time-consuming project is a milestone that marks both the end—and the beginning—of another deep commitment of time and energy.

That's why the end of a project is so important in a professional life. When a large project closes, it's tempting to relax into the achievement, to check that box off your to-do list, to become absorbed in the maddening mundanity of day-to-day duties, and to not think beyond the next coffee break, end of the day, or upcoming pay period.

The end of project is also a time when one has typically moved from being a novice to a more experienced professional. It's also often a time when you might receive invitations to work on projects that may or may not be important and valuable to you, your institution, or your workplace.

The end of a project is precisely the time to ask yourself, trusted mentors, boss, and those closest to you: Where am I now? Where do I want to be in three to five years? What questions remain—questions that I perhaps could not pursue in a previous project, or that arose out of my last project? Asking these questions can lead you to projects in a coherent way, so that by the end of a decade, the projects you've worked on add up to a cohesive professional identity and lead to work that's meaningful to you, your institution, and your workplace.

* * *

When a time-consuming project is completed, take three steps to ensure that this ending is also a beginning:

SHARE: Distribute the work widely, get feedback and reviews, and listen. What questions has this project raised? How has it been received? What questions still remain? What unintended implications or impact has it had on what audiences? Answers to these questions can help you see new areas to contribute to in your next projects, or help you think through lingering problems that may still remain and beg for more work. Circulating the work not only helps others give you credit for a job well done, it also helps others learn from your mistakes. Reviews can be challenging, flattering, or more about the reviewer than the work. Regardless, they're important reflections on what went well and what can be done differently in the future. It's that second part that helps you see the beginning from the end.

REFLECT: What did I learn from doing this project? What mistakes did I make? What makes me passionate about this type of work? For whom am I doing this work? Is this work still meaningful to me? Remembering why you do this work keeps you finding intrinsic motivation to begin another project. If a project was a flop or went sideways, then that too is an important moment of growth. It will help you do better work next time. Failure is not only acceptable, it's necessary for learning. Success is nice while it lasts, but success without personal meaningfulness will always be hollow.

IMAGINE: Take the time you need to imagine yourself in the future. What would future you want you to be doing? Where would you be doing this? With whom? This means not only identifying lingering questions or finding fresh questions to drive your next projects, but also continuing to read, listen, research, and absorb what you need to begin to answer those questions. It also means making sure you're picturing yourself and your work a few years out. Imagination, Einstein reminds us, is greater than knowledge.

What you may find at the end of this taking-stock moment is that the process of learning from your life's work is cyclic and ongoing. The cycle begins with the remaining questions, moves into the incubation of terrific ideas, develops with methods and processes particular to the project, comes to fruition with your deliverable, and begins again. As one project ends, another emerges—making possible a lifetime of learning around work that should always be meaningful to you and those who sponsor and/or receive this work. Learning to keep learning around meaningful projects is key to making the most of the end of a project.

74

DON'T DO ANYTHING YOU CAN'T WRITE ABOUT

Jeffrey T. Grabill

One of the best pieces of advice ever given to me is "Write about everything you do; don't do anything you can't write about." This advice is a useful framework for understanding how to retain one's research and publication work while moving into different administrative institutional positions.

I need to begin with a caveat: there are some administrative roles that make forms of scholarly work nearly impossible, such as being the chair of a large academic department (I barely maintained a publication program under those circumstances), and other administrative roles that fundamentally change one's identity—which is how I have experienced moving into an associate provost's role. Admittedly, much depends on how one approaches the role of a department chair; my comments here assume a 100 percent focus on that chairship, including the strategic direction of the unit, the effective management of a large-scale and diversely populated organization, and a commitment to student experience and to faculty development. With the change in identity comes a major shift in what it means to write about one's work (more on this below).

With that big caveat out of the way, it seems to me that there are two fundamental ways to address the question of how to retain research and publication activity while moving into different institutional positions. One concerns *management* and the other *identity*.

The management question involves boring things but, like many boring things, management turns out to be important. Changed institutional positions, particularly administrative positions, make demands on time that require serious attention. As my close colleagues know, I'm convinced that many faculty misallocate their time, such as spending too much time on teaching (the issue here is inefficiency, not commitment to being an excellent teacher) and persistent mismanagement of time

DOI: 10.7330/9781607328834.c074

focused on the work of the institution (what we often call "service"). Each is much more common than inefficiencies in research, but those exist as well. Ironically, an administrative role can often make a faculty member more efficient (if it doesn't kill him first) because it demands efficiency.

Let's start there, with the old adage that administrative and service work expands to fit all containers. There is real danger in administrative appointments even for those who are less than 100 percent focused on the position, of course, but those in full-time administrative appointments who have a desire (or who face an expectation, whether implied or explicit) to publish must employ excellent management skills. There are people (perhaps contributors to this book) who are better at personal management than I am. Still, a couple of suggestions: I am a big believer in establishing time patterns over the course of a week and allocating significant blocks of time devoted to categories of work—blocks for meetings, blocks for teaching (and prep), and blocks for research and writing. Blocks work very well in a context in which many people commit to the same blocks. This is not the case in most universities, I realize. But it's worth a conversation with close colleagues and collaborators in particular to see if shared time patterns are possible. Regardless, an individual can block time, and I'd encourage that (see Barton's chapter in this volume).

Then there is the issue of "meetings." Meetings must be managed to create time and space for research and writing. Here again, there is lots of advice available to the curious about managing effective meetings. Like much of that advice, I'd recommend consistent use of agendas, a clear understanding of the purposes of meetings (to report? to discuss? if so, what, precisely, and why?), limiting all meetings to thirty minutes, and starting and ending on time. The default that a sixty-minute meeting must always take sixty minutes seems crazy to me, and it is a good indicator of time misallocation. All that I have written here assumes that we must have meetings at all; we should resist that as an assumption. The most productive work cultures have very few meetings. People can be in the same space to work together, yes, but that is a very different thing than "the meeting" as it is commonly understood.

That was my brief take on management, and while it may seem a bit mundane and obvious, my point is simply that the only way research and writing will continue during a change in institutional role is to get control of one's time. Failure to do that will result in lots of frustration, poor productivity, and unhappiness.

Beyond management, the bigger issue is that which I've called "identity." One of the best pieces of advice given to me by Pat Sullivan, my dissertation advisor, was "Write about everything you do; don't do anything you can't write about." This advice has served me well, although it helps to be in a discipline in which it is possible to write about teaching and administrative work in addition to writing about one's research. As a consequence, I have always written about my work as those efforts have crossed the missions of the universities where I have been appointed. Pat's advice, however, is also about how one identifies as a professional academic. That identity is fundamentally about understanding the work of higher education as intellectual work that comes in many forms.

As academics, we write about our intellectual work. We write about the work of teaching, about directing programs when that is the case (e.g., an internship program, a first-year writing program), and about administrative efforts. This only works if there are forums and audiences for publication, which in the big tent of rhetoric and composition there are (a feature that shouldn't be taken for granted). But this also only works if labor outside of research and scholarship is understood as intellectual work and one identifies with this labor as an intellectual, especially with regard to administration.

With regard to teaching, for example, this means a number of things. It means, first of all, taking an inquiry stance and sense of wonder into the work of teaching, which should result in a set of questions that frame and drive teaching. For me, they have long been questions about student learning: how learning differs from performance, what learning looks like in writing, and how best to facilitate learning. But as an intellectual stance, this approach carries over to other issues associated with "teaching," such as curriculum development (e.g., what are the best sequences of experiences that lead to the learning we'd like to see?), mentoring of early career teachers, professional development of colleagues, and so on. All of this is intellectual work for a professional academic. Teaching, then, can easily become a category of research and writing activity if one's career moves in a direction where it is a larger part of the whole.

The same can be true for administrative work, though this is much less clear and often more challenging to execute. Here again, much depends on how one identifies with the work of administration: Is it intellectual work? Or is it "stuff that gets in the way" of real intellectual work? If the latter, then writing about administration might be impossible. If the former, then administrative work can help sustain publication activity during a change in institutional role if one also brings genuine questions and a sense of wonder to the work.

Becoming a department chair provides a number of opportunities, including questions about the effectiveness, outcomes, and experiences of programs, along with questions about how best to help one's colleagues develop into happier and more productive faculty. There are forums in rhetoric and composition interested in scholarship about these issues, and some of these questions will result in work that will be of interest to other administrators as well.

Let me close with one dynamic that deserves attention, and that is the fact that movement into different institutional positions can entail a major shift in identity that is quite disruptive. The move into the provost's office has taken me out of the disciplinary context that I carried into every other change in my career. One of the uncertainties for me concerns the forums where people who share my role also share their work. They exist, and I am finding them, but this takes time. Still, even with this shift in identity for me, Pat's basic advice still stands: the work I've been asked to do is intellectual work that demands an inquiry stance. The questions I have will shape specific inquiries that will not only determine how I conduct myself as an intellectual with an administrative role but also how I will write about the work. Writing about one's work across the mission of a university is possible given a productive stance toward the nature of what it means to be an intellectual.

75

CONVERSATIONAL PUBLICATIONS

Jeff Rice

In this chapter, I focus on two important parts of post-editorial work. The first involves turning a successful essay or chapter publication into more publications; the second offers advice for generating work that follows a book publication. This advice focuses on a basic premise: publications do not need to end but rather can lead into other publications.

While academic writers may view their work as singular moments of output (a conference paper, a published essay, a published book), more often it is the case that academic writing belongs within a larger network of ideas and writings that are not limited to an initial publication. Understanding the publication process as a series of singular ideas without connection to one another can be a mistake. This position characterizes publications as a "one-shot deal" in which one merely sends out unconnected ideas to different journals or presses in the hopes of landing an acceptance. An alternate position—and this point holds true for many tenure and promotion as well as hiring committees—stresses that publications can be understood as larger trajectories of thought, interconnected ideas that build on one another. In this chapter, I support the second position: a publication should be viewed as a part of an overall thought process or network of ideas.

I begin with the question of publishing an essay, noting how one published essay can generate other publications. A prominent example of this process can be found in the cultural studies/theorist Fredric Jameson's work on pastiche. Jameson published a series of essays on pastiche, beginning with "Periodizing the '60s," which appeared in a 1984 issue of *Social Text*, and extending to "Postmodernism and Consumer Society" in Hal Foster's volume *The Anti-Aesthetic*. These publications—and their focus on the 1960s and pastiche—led to Jameson's canonical critique of *American Graffiti* in his celebrated *Postmodernism; or, The Logic of Late Capitalism*. Each of these publications works off a single theoretical premise—the question of pastiche as it relates to critical thought. Yet

DOI: 10.7330/9781607328834.c075

the publications are not the same. While one can identify similar ideas or patterns in all of these published pieces, if one were to read from the first to last publication, one would discover a writer working through complex ideas. Each publication builds on previously circulated ideas, adding to and revising what preceded it.

In addition to the Jameson example, I offer an example from my own work and how I have followed a similar trajectory regarding essay/chapter publications. The exigence for my trajectory was the theoretical concept of the technical image. When I first began working with Vilém Flusser's concept of the technical image, I approached the idea via a discussion of the Occupy movement and the viral John Pike pepper-spraying image ("Occupying the Digital Humanities"). In this first essay, I worked through what I felt were the reasons an image can convey meaning not actually located in the image itself. My interest in this idea, though, did not stop with a discussion of Occupy; I identified other examples in which I believed the technical image generated meaning based on associations and accumulated references. I continued with this concept via food issues and anger at horse-consumption status updates on Facebook ("They Eat Horses Don't They") and an exploration of online outrage often created by headlines and not content ("Digital Outragicity"). These three publications allowed me not to repeat an idea, but rather to work though overall theoretical issues. Eventually, my *Philosophy and Rhetoric* essay "Circulated Epideictic: The Technical Image and Digital Consensus" refocused my previous work but also extended it into a more complete theoretical explanation and included two additional case studies: the resignation of Tim Wolfe as president of the University of Missouri and the false repeated claim that Israel had opened dams to flood Gaza. My arrival at this final essay could have been achieved only via my previous work. With each publication, I used my writing to navigate a complex idea, not to treat each moment as a finished work. With each publication, I learned more about the issue that interested me and was able to convey that new knowledge in further work.

I understand my three published monographs similarly, although their content differs. Each book extends a similar question: what is the rhetoric of digital work? While no one text could answer such a question, I have found myself working out that idea via a discussion of disparate issues: composition studies history (*The Rhetoric of Cool*), network theory (*Digital Detroit*), and social media (*Craft Obsession*). Each book is different from the last, but all three constitute a conversation regarding the rhetoric of digital work. I don't understand my publications as distinct entities, but rather as continued trajectories building on my previous work. Together, these publications attempt to create a conversation.

My emphasis here is on the notion of conversation. We enter into conversations with other writers and ideas when we publish (citation, argument, building on and contributing to previous writings), but at some point, we build a conversation among our own writings. One problem writers often face is that they treat their own writings as a set of distinct, unconnected work. Writings over time and space, however, can allow the writer the opportunity to grow and explore complicated concepts or to further one's thinking as it changes and develops.

One does not have to, of course, continue a series of ideas from book to book or article to article. There is no obligation to do so. The framing of one's overall work as a conversation, however, is worth consideration as one moves to the next project. When we think about post-editorial work, we can shift focus from completion (i.e., what's next?) to the continuation of thought. In this sense, the objective is network, not closure. Networks are open; they expand and contract with connections and interactions. They do not close. I have seen many graduate students as well as colleagues struggle to move from course work to exams to writing a dissertation to publishing work because they have treated each step as a separate and unconnected process (i.e., not allowing course work or exams to inform the writing of the dissertation, for instance, or being stumped over what to write about when one project concludes). The same holds true with publishing in general. Publishing involves the creation of a network of ideas—with those whose voices one writes with and with one's own voice. This network generates a larger conversation. One's work, overall, is a conversation. There is good reason to keep that conversation going.

76

IT'S NEVER DONE
Rethinking Post-Publication

Donna LeCourt

Be willing to reconsider old arguments as possibilities for new publications. Don't assume any piece of writing can say it all or is completely final. Use the time away from writing to rethink possibilities.

* * *

There were many things it took me a long time to learn about publishing early in my career, but one of the most important lessons came much later. Only recently did I begin considering post-production as part of the writing process. For most of the work I've published, frankly, I was happy to see the ending and wouldn't even read the published version lest I catch a typo or (even more scary) a flaw in my logic. Once it was in circulation, revision wasn't possible so I didn't want to look. It was in print, done, for me never to return to. Hopefully it would live in citations in someone else's writing. Occasionally, of course, I would cull from old pieces—a definition here, an example there—so I didn't have to reinvent the wheel, but even then the writing was done. I was only mining gems I didn't need to recut and polish. It never occurred to me to see the knowledge I created in my publications, rather than the writing itself, as open to continual revision.

There were a lot of reasons for not considering my *ideas* as open to revision. To do so made it too difficult to publish. One of the things I feared most the first few times I sent out my work for publication was that it would be "wrong" and that others would see all its problems. I would finally be revealed as the imposter I knew I was. This fear, as well as a desire for perfection, would lead to me questioning all my premises again and again until I felt I could say little that was definite. Unless I could get it "right" beyond a shadow of a doubt, I shouldn't send my work out for others to consider publishing. That voice had to be silenced for me to send anything out for publication.

DOI: 10.7330/9781607328834.c076

As a result, I let publication eventually determine the value of a piece of scholarship. I deferred my sense of "worthwhile" to an external valuation mechanism, silencing my own critical sense about my work after publication. To be fair, if I didn't silence that voice—what some will recognize as a specifically classed and gendered voice that fears she is never good enough unless an institution deems her so—my work would never see the light of day. But silencing that voice also meant rejecting or ignoring my past work in many ways. Once it was completed, I didn't want to see it so I wouldn't second-guess it. (Case in point: I just had to look up the title of the article I discuss below. I started reading the first paragraph and stopped. I already saw things I wanted to change.) When my thinking inevitably progressed beyond that piece, I would launch a new project, presuming others would understand by the dates that I had moved on. I never directly or explicitly confronted what I saw as a flawed argument from the past.

What I've learned, though, is that a piece is never truly finished. The ability to resee one's own positions in light of new data, theories, teaching experiences, and other things not accounted for in the original argument is not a failure, but rather an opportunity. It's an opportunity to build on one's own work. It's an opportunity to fill in gaps and, yes, "correct" aspects a writer comes to see differently. But most important, it's also an opportunity to demonstrate to readers the power of such re-vision for making knowledge, for engaging in the kind of recursive discourse we say we value, and for acknowledging factors that may have limited one's vision in the first piece. No one ever told me this. But it is something I should have learned by watching my mentor Andrea Lunsford, as she has done this many times, particularly with her enduring essay on audience with Lisa Ede, which they have "rewritten" twice (Ede and Lunsford 1984; Lunsford and Ede 1996, 2009).

The first time I learned this was with my *College English* article "Performing Working-Class Identity in Composition" (2006). This essay began as my response to a position by Sharon O'Dair. In coming to understand why O'Dair's essay made me so angry (typically my best impetus to begin writing), I honed in on a premise she needed to build her argument about providing working-class universities for working-class students: the oppositions composition scholarship set up between working-class and academic discourse. In realizing that this premise is what made her untenable conclusion possible, however, I also had to acknowledge that I had helped create that premise in various works, from my own narrative of working-class experiences to my book *Identity Matters: Schooling the Student Subject in Academic Discourse* (2004). I couldn't argue against O'Dair, as I was beginning to do in a draft, without arguing against myself—or, more accurately, without admitting my complicity in helping to create O'Dair's argument. As a result, much of the "Performing" essay involves a rereading of student narratives from *Identity Matters*. I bring the same data into the argument, confess to my original misreading, and discuss how I reread the narratives and why.

Rethinking, reusing, recasting: all are acceptable modes toward publication. But they are particularly useful, I found, as a "post-book" moment. Rarely have I ever felt like I said all I had to say when finishing a book. More likely, I had reached exhaustion and just needed the damn thing done. Unexpectedly, it's the longer projects I find need the most rethinking once one has the distance, space, and rest required to reconsider what one has produced. I had never before considered rewriting my argument or admitting to "missing something" in an analysis to be the prompt for a new publication, but now I do. To assume that one's engagement with an idea has finished when a work is published, I finally realize, is both hubris and a way of looking at knowledge that theoretically I find suspect. Rather than a weakness, such moves are a form of feminist action against reified views of knowledge that would ossify it and silence the role the writer plays as interested interpreter. I hadn't realized I was engaging in perpetuating a view of academic knowledge by my own practices until my ire was raised. Now, such reenvisioning is something that always stays open as a possibility.

REFERENCES

Ede, Lisa, and Andrea Lunsford. 1984. "Audience Addressed/Audience Invoked: The Role of Audience in Composition." *College Composition and Communication* 35 (2): 155–71.

LeCourt, Donna. 2004. *Identity Matters: Schooling the Student Body in Academic Discourse.* Albany: State University of New York Press.

LeCourt, Donna. 2006. "Performing Working-Class Identity in Composition: Toward a Pedagogy of Textual Practice." *College English* 69 (1): 30–51.

Lunsford, Andrea, and Lisa Ede. 1996. "Representing Audience: 'Successful' Discourse and Disciplinary Critique." *College Composition and Communication* 47 (2): 167–79.

Lunsford Andrea A., and Lisa Ede. 2009. "Among the Audience: Audience in an Age of New Literacies." In *Engaging Audience*, edited by M. Elizabeth Weiser, Brian M. Fehler, and Angela M. Gonzalez, 42–69. Urbana, IL: National Council of Teachers of English.

O'Dair, Sharon. 2003. "Class Work: Site of Egalitarian Activism or Site of Embourgeoisement?" *College English* 65 (6): 593–606.

77

AFTER THE END

Sid Dobrin

Before, the book ended. As did the article. That is, writing the book ended; writing the article ended. As the writing ended with the review, the meditation, the interview, the response essay, and all else that academics wrote. And, despite our disciplinary heralding of the process, it was the product that signified the end of the writing, its publication the signal of completion. The End.

When the book ended, we concluded it was time to begin again with a new writing: a new book project, a new article, a new publication. One after the next, we embraced the end of each artifact we fabricated, rejoicing in its completion, in its end; anxious about what we would do next; obligated to start again after each end. An academic's imperative to begin and end repeatedly. Not ending suggested failure: the end of each product validated through publication, entombed in the archive, and memorialized in curriculum vitae. Rosters of works laid to rest. Our body-of-work count assessed in job searches and tenure and promotion files. The more we finished, the greater our stock. The more we finished, the more we were expected to finish next. Quality and quantity both emphasized.

For the academic writer, each end implied a success, an independent act of completion contributing to a larger corpus of work, but ultimately a singular accomplishment, a professional whole. Even if we told ourselves that one project was an extension of another, that our books ended only because we had a deadline and had to "let them go," the truth is that such work was always required to end. And when we finished each work, the product became the asset of the field. Its distribution the responsibility of the publishing house or journal; its content fed to the body of the discipline. We washed our hands of it, not returning to it in any way other than perhaps nostalgically. We hoped a journal would take notice and publish a review, but when the review writer reached the end, the book ended again. We hoped to see traces of it in citation, but

DOI: 10.7330/9781607328834.c077

we did not wait for its reappearance. We had moved on to the next and the next, accumulating as many curtain calls as we could over the course of a career. We had little or no control in directing the work beyond its completion, except, on occasion, suggesting to a publisher to whom they might send notice of the publication. For us, the work had reached its end; what breath it had left was dependent upon what others chose to do with it. We had finished writing.

And, then, the digital age changed everything, the cliché tells us. The end was no longer the end. Completion of book or article or review signified not the end, but aroused what must come next. Now, we need our work to live beyond the end; we need it to circulate, to be recognized, to be made known to the field in ways quite different than before.

After the end, we must now take a new kind of responsibility for our work. An awkward responsibility in that we are uncomfortable generally with self-promotion—a peculiar drawback for a population eager for recognition of our work. However, now, the book or article does not end. We announce our success of completion, feigning humility with tags of "self-serving, I know, but I just finished this thing" on social media, providing links, directing friends, colleagues, and readers to the work. We post excerpts or articles to Academia.edu. We take on the role of promoter to ensure that our work is not finished, but circulating. In an age of network and velocity, we need our work not to end, but to propagate.

In the past, publishing the work was, generally, enough. The line on our vitae giving us credit for completion. Works in progress and works forthcoming held relatively less value than works on shelf, works no longer progressing, works that have come and, in some cases, gone. Ultimately, little else mattered than that the writing was complete (other than perhaps our individual personal satisfaction). We would get credit. Checkpoint passed. Progress saved. Level complete.

But our assessment models have changed. The vitae line carries only so much capital. Data gathering mechanisms like Academic Analytics account not only for what we have published, how much we have published, or how frequently we have published, but by whom works have been published and how often those publications are cited by others in the field and in the media.[1] Individuals and departments are measured not merely for production quantity, but for how frequently individual works are referenced and how widely they circulate. Academic Analytics' "Faculty Counts" provide numerical data about a person's productivity using comparative data sets in five areas of publishing: books, articles, grants, awards, and citations. Our value is no longer measured in terms of quantity and quality, but in velocity and circulation—spiders and bots crawling all over our bodies of work accounting for our proclivity. The more promiscuous the work, the better. Citations accumulated and reported on one's social media pages identify numbers of followers, friends, or likes.

Academics—because we do not operate independent of the culture at large—have entered a period of necessary self-promotion because we have entered a time when big data tools measure the velocity of our intellectual reach. Comparative data matrices (like those employed by Academic Analytics) conclude value in scholarship by comparing a faculty member's publishing productivity numbers to those of other faculty both in and out of field, in and out of one's institution. Such models strive to ask not merely how many pieces we publish, but where we are publishing them and how the quantification of our scholarship compares with that of our peers. Academic Analytics asks whether we are publishing in the "right" journals, whether we are writing about the "right" topics, and whether our peers are citing our work. Some digital publications now identify numbers of readers who have accessed the article or book, as though number of views conveys a particular caliber of work.

Will My Writing Go Viral? As more institutions begin to rely on such data-driven assessment tools, we become more dependent upon our ability to ensure that our writing reaches as broad an audience as possible. This will require that each of us develop strategies for using digital media and social media to promote our own work among colleagues. University presses and academic journals are underfunded and are not in the position to take up this additional promotional task as part of the publishing initiative (despite their own benefit from potential increased sales). This must fall to each of us.

The cornerstone to this collection: advice. Before the book ends, plan your promotional campaign; when the book ends, promote, circulate. And, most important, always cite this chapter.

NOTE

1.   Academic Analytics currently houses data about more than 270,000 faculty members and is used by more than 385 colleges and universities for developing strategic plans and for benchmarking.

INDEX